James Hain Friswell

Modern Men of Letters

Honestly Criticised

James Hain Friswell

Modern Men of Letters
Honestly Criticised

ISBN/EAN: 9783744710626

Printed in Europe, USA, Canada, Australia, Japan

Cover: Foto ©Thomas Meinert / pixelio.de

More available books at **www.hansebooks.com**

MODERN MEN OF LETTERS

HONESTLY CRITICISED.

BY

J. HAIN FRISWELL,

AUTHOR OF "ESSAYS ON ENGLISH WRITERS,"
&c., &c.

London:

HODDER AND STOUGHTON,

27, PATERNOSTER ROW.

MDCCCLXX.

UNWIN BROTHERS, PRINTERS, BUCKLERSBURY, LONDON.

To His Excellency

M. SYLVAIN VAN DE WEYER,

MINISTRE D'ETAT,

ENVOYÉ EXTRAORDINAIRE ET MINISTRE PLÉNIPOTENTIARE,

IN ADMIRATION OF HIS GENIUS AS A WRITER

HIS SKILL AND HONESTY AS A DIPLOMATIST

AND IN GRATITUDE FOR HIS FRIENDSHIP

This Volume is Dedicated.

PREFACE.

❧

THE ordinary mode of criticising the results of a scholar's hard and long-continued work is, *as we are well aware*, to test it here and there by means of the index, and to show off the critic's second-hand learning at the expense of the literary subject which he is dissecting, pointing out a weak point here and an unsound spot there; but such a mode of treatment would be entirely beside the mark *in the present case*."

The above sentence from a review in the *Athenæum* of May 21st, will be a sufficient explanation of, and excuse for, the words on the title-page, "honestly criticised." The italics are not those of the journal, but added here to mark the openness of confession, and, at the same time, the curious reservation in favour of Mr. Cox's work on the "Myths of the Aryan Nations," as if in any case so perfunctory and essentially dishonest a method could be excused.

But there is even a worse "mode of treatment" with some critics, which is to fall into, or even to commit, blunders and errors, and to attribute them to the more correct author. Those who have suffered from such a treatment, have learnt the value of such criticism, and the causes which make the ordinary book-notice valueless. As a rule, if an author be good and strong, he will succeed, and the more antagonism he meets with, the better. The only thing valuable in this life is Truth, and although at present we may be overborne with a multiplicity and superabundance of error, although we are quite aware that Truth can effectually be stamped down and hidden for years, still the more ardent and constant grows our belief in the ultimate triumph of that which is earnest and right. A bad book may have a wide-spread influence and may succeed for a time, but, as a rule, that influence is contemptible and its reign is exceedingly short; goodness and wisdom win the day, they only are permanent and endure.

Another great fault in the criticism of the present day is its *cliquism*. If the author of a book be unknown, if he veil his name for a time, he may chance to meet with a valuable, because an unbiassed, review of his work. So well is this known, that we could count on our fingers ten of the best authors of the day who have written anonymously for the express purpose of eliciting from the Press a true value of their work; and as these gentlemen— among whom we may count Mr. Disraeli and Lord Lytton—have more than once resorted to this method, we presume that it has been successful. The simple suggestion, often most erroneous, that Mr. A has been very successful, and that his works bring him much money, is sufficient to make the envious and unsuccessful irritated and inimical. Not that critics have no generosity, they have often exhibited much, but that in the poorly-paid and poorly-prized profession to which they belong, the trials of which are so acute, and the nature of those engaged in it so sensitive, some seem to feel the success of a fellow or a contemporary whom they hardly recognised, as a personal insult. There is also a Celtic and Bohemian delight in following the practice of that humorous Irishman who, wanting to fight with somebody, walked out of the tent or booth, and felt outside its canvas for the hardest, roundest, and biggest head of those who leant against its sides, gave it a crack with his shillelah,

and then waited for its owner to come and defend
himself. Many a peaceful author, thus refreshing
himself after his labour, has been cruelly assaulted
in this way, and the pain resulting from such a
wound is acute—for it is but human nature that a
man who has written a wise or clever book should
desire the guerdon of praise. That, we know from
the purest and best penman who ever lived, "is
the last infirmity of noble minds." Let us add,
that if the wielder of the shillelah belongs to a
clique, he spares the heads of his friends, out of a
prophetic feeling that they in their turn will spare
his.

"To-morrow," says Disraeli in "Lothair," "the
critics will be upon us. Who are the critics? they
who have been unsuccessful in literature and art;"
to which we would add, not always *un*successful.
One of the greatest dangers of an author arises from
the successful, the genial, and the friendly critic,
who *will* applaud his mistakes, quote his platitudes
for beauties, patronise him in a way as open as it
is oily, and who, while he reveals his bias, shows
nothing else in three columns of grammatical commonplace. Such writing as this deprived a certain
paper of its *selling* value. There was a time when

a review in —— would sell an edition of a novel. "If you can promise me a review *there*," said a well-known publisher to a well-known lady writer, "I can raise the copy money by £150 or £200!" But he would not do so now. As the *Economist* wisely notes in other matters, the Press, especially the London Press, is losing its influence; the cause is, that much of it is losing its truth. A paper known to be skilful and honest is as influential as heretofore. We have no reason surely to regret the loss of an influence which is essentially immoral; we may be certain that the Press will regain that influence when it deserves it, and that the really influential portion does, even at present, both hold and deserve it.

Lastly, criticism which, as is too often the "mode,"—to use the word of the *Athenæum*,—lays on the praise, or the contrary objurgation, in huge layers, simple without being pure, is unworthy of the name. To judge fairly, you must at least be a judge. "It is an easy task to praise or blame, the hard task and the virtue to do both." This sentence has been borne in mind throughout this book, and has never been absent from the writer's mind. Where blame has been freely expressed, reason has

been given for it.   We are getting weary of false
friendships and falser animosities in literature ; it
is time to call a spade a spade.   As the great
Dryden—for the touch is his, though found in Sir
William Soame's translation from " Boileau," which
he altered and amended—said :

>   " In our scribbling times
> No fool can want a sot to praise his rhymes:
> The flattest work has ever in the Court
> Met with some zealous ass for its support:
> And in all times a forward scribbling fop
> Has found some greater fool to cry him up."

And the present Laureate has left it on record that
reviewers are " indolent," and that "raffs are rife
in prose and rhyme."   The best way to discourage
the terrible waste of paper and print at present
going on, is for competent critics to speak out
firmly and fully, with an honesty which will secure
attention, with a judgment that will carry conviction, with a severity which is more kind in reality
than ungrudging praise, and with a decision which
must arise from all three.   How far the writer has
been able to follow his own rule, he leaves to the
most kind, yet severe, the most unbiassed and most
competent of all critics, the PUBLIC, to say.

September, 1870.

A CAVEAT,

WHICH THE AUTHOR EARNESTLY REQUESTS THE
READER TO LOOK OVER, AND NOT TO OVERLOOK.

" We see that Mr. Friswell has in the press a volume entitled
' Modern Men of Letters honestly Criticised.' We confess we
are not a little anxious to see the book. If it be what it
professes to be, the author must be a more fearless man than
most literary men are. If his criticism be unfavourable—and
surely it cannot all be flattering—he will find he had better have
put his head into a hornets' nest. Let him beware of the little
clique of brethren of the Society for Mutual Admiration. If
he refuses them the due to which they fancy they are entitled,
it will go hard with him."

THIS paragraph, from the *Literary World* of
September 2nd, will prove to the reader that some
alteration is needed in the present mode of criticism,
if the fears expressed by the honest and able sheet
whence I quote it, have any foundation. It is to
be sincerely hoped that they have not. Surely the
English critics, from whom personally I have received so much kind consideration, are too manly
to be biassed by pique or spite. The paragraph

is cited, however, because it affords the writer an opportunity to explain the nature of his book, and to apologise for its shortcomings.

The reader will perceive that the sketches are bibliographical and biographical as well as critical; too many authors are debated to allow of the reviews to be exhaustive, or to be other than they are—an introduction to the study of modern writers. The reader will also please to note that although the writer has the honour to be known to almost all the subjects of these pen-and-ink sketches, the personal notes are such only as could be made from the public appearance, or from the photographic portraits of the authors; and that while earnest opinions are strongly expressed, it is trusted that such expression never oversteps the bounds of good breeding, nay, even of good nature.

CONTENTS.

xiv CONTENTS.

CHARLES DICKENS.

MR. CHARLES DICKENS.

THE great humorous novelist whose life stands first in our volume is but lately dead. What follows was written while he was alive, but on careful revision the writer finds nothing to alter. He was not one of those who flattered Dickens while living, nor is he one who would alter his opinion when dead. What is written was and is felt, and the late author knew how dangerous and fallible, how hurtful to a living author is criticism which is injudicious in its praise and unthoughtful even in its fault-finding. A French writer, if we believe the newspapers, relates that Dickens said to him that " he had been spoilt by over-much kindness," or words to that effect; "this," said the gentleman, "was not true; but he felt it, and if he felt it, it *was* true." For a young author looks

B

for kindly guidance and a wise supervision.   He
seldom finds either.   The ordinary critic

"Wonders with a foolish face of praise"

at his brilliant passages, praises him too often
for his faults, checks him when he should be
encouraged, and nurses a folly till it becomes a vice.
" Don't mind the critics," said Thackeray to me, " I
never read what is written of me ; I am tired of
seeing my name in print."   With these few words
written without *arrière pensée*, let us proceed to our
subject.   The paragraph which follows I quote :—

" Charles John Hougham Dickens (the two intermediate
names being never used by him) was born on the 7th of
February, 1812, at Portsmouth, his father being Mr. John
Dickens, once a clerk in the Pay Department of the Navy,
but who, at the close of the war, retired on his pension, and
came to London as a newspaper reporter.   After being
educated at Chatham, Charles Dickens was articled to a
solicitor in Bedford Row, and reminiscences of his office life
are to be found in the clerkly doings at Messrs. Dodson and
Fogg's, and through the pages of " Copperfield " and " Bleak
House."   But he did not take kindly to the law, and, having
acquired the mysteries of shorthand, soon obtained employment
as a reporter.   His first engagements were on the *True Sun*
and the *Mirror of Parliament*, but he soon joined the staff of
the *Morning Chronicle*.   The late Earl of Derby, then Lord
Stanley, had on some important occasion made a grand speech
in the House of Commons.   This speech, of immense length,
it was found necessary to compress ; but so admirably had its
pith and marrow been given in the *Morning Chronicle*, that
Lord Stanley sent to the office requesting that the gentleman
who had reported it would wait upon him at his residence in

Carlton House-terrace, that he might then and there take down the speech in its entirety from his lordship's lips, Lord Stanley being desirous of having a perfect transcript of it. The reporter was Charles Dickens. He attended, took down the speech, and received Lord Stanley's compliments on his work. Many years after, Mr. Dickens, dining for the first time with a friend in Carlton House Terrace, found the aspect of the dining-room strangely familiar to him, and on making inquiries discovered that the house had previously belonged to Lord Derby, and that that was the very room in which he had taken down Lord Stanley's speech.

"It is a mistake to suppose that Mr. Dickens's earliest writings appeared in the *Morning Chronicle* under the editorship of Mr. Black. Mr. Dickens first became connected with the *Morning Chronicle* as a reporter in the gallery of the House of Commons. This was in 1835-36, but Mr. Dickens had been previously engaged, while in his nineteenth year, as a reporter for a publication entitled the *Mirror of Parliament*, in which capacity he occupied the very highest rank among the eighty or ninety reporters for the press then in Parliament."

It was a natural leap from reporting to "sketching," as the term then was, and a Mr. White, in his "Mornings at Bow Street," had made such sketches possible and popular. In 1835 Captain Holland conducted the *Old Monthly Magazine,* and in these pages sketches of a humorous character, signed "Boz," first appeared. Almost simultaneously with these was written a comic opera, entitled "Village Coquettes," the verses of which survived for some time, being sung at various concerts by Braham. When a gentleman who, writing to a paper, signs himself "J. G.," took the editorship of the *Old*

Monthly, Captain Holland, excellent editor! had forgotten the name of his contributor, although "J. G." had marked the verve and worth of the "Sketches." With some trouble it was found, and Dickens, when written to, offered to furnish matter at eight guineas a sheet of sixteen pages ; in six months from that date, so rapid was his rise, he could have commanded one hundred guineas. Thus Dickens commenced literary life. How easily he succeeded he has told us in a speech he made at a literary dinner. "I began to tread this life when very young, without money, without influence, without companions, introducer, or adviser," and he adds, " I met with no dragons in the path," to which one may add, "No, but with many friends."

These "Sketches" were reprinted in 1836 and 1837 respectively, and published by Mr. Macrone, of Regent Street, illustrated by George Cruikshank, whose name was relied on to sell them rather than that of the author. The papers and illustrations are worthy of each other; both are exaggerations, rather than caricatures, the exaggeration being but a veil through which the truth was easily seen. Each character is drawn *ad vivum,* and our fathers thought them very vulgar if very funny, but there is now and then a touch of real genius ; the sketch of Monmouth Street is not only fanciful, but at the same time true and pathetic. Their value as true pieces of art may be seen in their present popularity in Mr. Bellew's Readings, and at "Penny Readings." They are not above the calibre of the lower middle-class, and suit persons easily amused by pantomimic action. Some of them are far too free for strait-laced people of the present day, and the "Blooms-bury Christening" has been objected to by more than one clergyman as profane. In a volume of Dickens's life, hastily got up, it is asserted that Dickens formed his style upon Mr. Pierce Egan's "Tom and Jerry; or, Life in London." He did no such thing; he has named one of his sons Henry Fielding and Smollett, and the influence of those writers on Dickens, no less than on Thackeray, is distinctly traceable on every line of his works.

The success of Dickens in the good old days when publishers really now and then suggested works to authors, had the effect of inducing Messrs. Chapman and Hall to propose that he should write certain *libretti*, to plates of a comic character, and of the sporting-life class, furnished by a very clever humorous artist, Mr. Robert Seymour. There is no doubt that all that Dickens was expected to do was to write up to these plates, and the accounts given by himself and Mrs. Seymour, widow of the artist, naturally vary. The idea floating in the mind of the publishers was, that they would put before the public in Dickens's own words, "a monthly something to be the vehicle for certain plates to be executed by Mr. Seymour." This is distinct enough, the inferior position was assigned to the literary artist. Here are Dickens's words : —

"I was a young man of two or three-and-twenty, when Messrs. Chapman and Hall, attracted by some pieces I was at that time writing in the *Morning Chronicle* newspaper, or had just written in the *Old Monthly Magazine* (of which one series had lately been collected and published in two volumes, illustrated by Mr. George Cruikshank), waited upon me to propose a something that should be published in shilling numbers— then only known to me, or, I believe, to anybody else, by a dim recollection of certain interminable novels in that form, which used to be carried about the country by pedlars ; and over some of which I remember to have shed innumerable tears before I had served my apprenticeship to life. When I opened my door in Furnival's Inn to the partner who represented the firm, I recognised in him the person from whose hands I had bought, two or three years previously, and whom I had never seen before or since, my first copy of the magazine in which my first effusion—a paper in the 'Sketches,' called 'Mr. Minns and his Cousin'—dropped stealthily one evening at twilight, with fear and trembling, into a dark letter-box, in a dark office, up a dark court in Fleet-street—appeared in all the glory of print ; on which occasion I walked down to Westminster Hall, and turned into it for half an hour, because my eyes were so dimmed with joy and pride, that they could not bear the street, and were not fit to be seen there. I told my visitor of the coincidence, which we both hailed as a good omen, and so fell to business. The idea propounded to me was, that the monthly something should be a vehicle for certain plates to be executed by Mr. Seymour ; and there was a notion, either on the part of that admirable humorous artist, or of my visitor, that a 'Nimrod Club,' the members of which were to go out shooting, fishing, and so forth, and getting themselves into difficulties through their want of dexterity, would be the best means of introducing these. I objected, on consideration, that, although born and partly bred in the country, I was no great sportsman, except in regard of all kinds of locomotion ; that the idea was not novel, and had been already much used ; that it would be infinitely better for the plates to arise naturally out of the text ; and that I would like to take my own way, with a freer range of English scenes and people, and was afraid I should ultimately do so in any case, whatever course I might prescribe to myself at starting. My views being deferred to, I thought of Mr. Pickwick, and wrote the first number, from the proof-sheets of which Mr. Seymour made his drawing of the club, and his happy portrait of its founder—the latter on Mr. Edward Chapman's description of the dress and bearing of a real personage whom he had often seen. I connected Mr. Pickwick with a club, because of the original suggestion, and I put in Mr. Winkle expressly for the use of Mr. Seymour. We started with a number of twenty-four pages instead of thirty-two, and four illustrations in lieu of a couple. Mr. Seymour's sudden and lamented death before the second number was published, brought about a quick decision upon a point already in agitation ; the number became one of thirty-two pages, with only two illustrations, and remained so to the end. 'Boz,' my signature in the *Morning Chronicle* and in the *Old Monthly Magazine*, appended to the monthly cover of this book, and retained long afterwards, was the nickname of a pet child, a younger brother, whom I had dubbed Moses, in honour of the Vicar of Wakefield, which, being facetiously pronounced through the nose, became Boses, and, being shortened, became Boz. Boz was a very familiar household word to me long before I was an author, and so I came to adopt it."

This account has been questioned, and Mr. Dickens has told us that "Mr. Seymour never originated an incident, a phrase, nor a word in the book; that Mr. Seymour died when only twenty-four pages of the book were published; that he (Dickens) only saw Seymour once in his life, the night before his death, and that then he offered no suggestion whatever."

In effect, the artist, overburdened with work, in a fit of derangement, committed suicide; and, very luckily for Dickens, Mr. Hablot Browne, a young artist who, by a drawing of John Gilpin, had won an academy medal, was called in to do his work. He threw himself with ardour into the task. Mr. Dickens named himself " Boz," H. K. Browne called himself " Phiz; " the character of the work was altered, *two* illustrations were given instead of four, and thirty-two pages of letter press instead of twenty-four. For some time the work was not very successful, but at last it hit the public, and the success was immense. The publishers presented the author with some silver punch-ladles, which, like apostles' spoons, bore the chief characters in little gilt and modelled figures on the handles, and gave him a very handsome addition to the *honorarium ;* it is said that the firm made £20,000 by the volume !

By most people " Pickwick" is accepted as Dickens's *Magnum Opus.* It certainly is a typical one, but while the whole book is farcical in the extreme, while character degenerates to caricature, and fun to pantomimic romp and " rally," there are now and then touches of very clever shrewd observation, most admirable sketches of character—Sergeant Buzfuz and the trial scene are evidently quite true

to nature, and pathos of the genial easy and ordinary kind in which the author delighted. But as
a novel of nature and of plot and character compared
to Fielding, " Pickwick" is very small. Who ever
met with man, woman, or child, who could sit down
by a winter fire and tell the " plot" of " Pickwick ?"
Had it come out as a whole book, it would have
failed to find readers, it would, like Hudibras, have
palled on the taste; it is too full of incident, scene
succeeds scene, and adventure, adventure. The
novel is crowded with persons, and each person is—
how different from real life and Mr. Trollope—not
cut to pattern, but a character. There is the fat,
bland, benevolent, silly, vulgar tradesman, Mr.
Pickwick, a man with a good heart and a soft head,
with his unequalled servant, Mr. Sam Weller, who
one of the editors of the *Spectator* says, is superior to
Falstaff. There are the volatile Jingle, the cheat,
and the rascal, and his servant Job, the canting
hypocrite, drawn as pendants to the honest master
and man; old Mr. Weller and the mother-in-law,
the man in the Fleet, the lawyers Dodson and Fogg,
Stiggins, the dissenting minister, with his proclivity
to pine-apple rum; Bob Sawyer and Ben Allen, Mrs.
Leo Hunter and her party, Potts and Slurk, the rival
newspaper editors of Eatanswill; Mrs. Potts, the fat
boy, and the pretty housemaid; all these sketches
dwell on the memory; the people lived then; do they

live now? do we meet them? That question truly answered will determine Dickens's value as a true artist, as one who drew from nature.

When "Pickwick" was finished, the author rested for some months, and then brought out "Nicholas Nickleby." As in "Pickwick" he had made a violent attack on the Fleet Prison and imprisonment for debt, so in "Nicholas Nickleby" Dickens determined to tilt at some of the social evils which will always beset us. Going down to Yorkshire to study the cheap schools of that county, horrid places at which there was carried on an advanced species of baby-farming* combined with education, and pretending to have the child of a widow to put to school, he met with the original John Browdie, and it is more than suspected with the original Squeers. The first said to him, "Well, misther, we've been very plaisant together, and I'll speak my mind tivvee. Doan't let weedur send ur little boy to yan o'our schoolmeasters, while there's a harse to hoold in a' Lunnun, and a gootther to lie asleep in." Mr. Squeers said many precious sentences, and sat for his portrait. This picture of Squeers in "Nickleby" was so true and natural that

---

* What a terribly grim satire there is in the German word for baby-farming, "angel-making." Alas! what will be the after punishment of those who thus people heaven by the slow martyrdom of those whose "angels" always behold the face of God!

many of the schoolmasters identified themselves with it ; and one individual who happened to have but one eye, and who, therefore, resembled Squeers physically as well as mentally, threatened the author with an action at law.

Mr. Crummles and his company show that the author had an intimate acquaintance with provincial theatrical life behind the scenes—there is indeed a legend that he acted at Rochester theatre ; whilst Mrs. Nickleby is as true a picture of a genial, blundering, tiresome, affectionate, egotistical, silly, garrulous, middle-aged lady, as is Mrs. Primrose in the "Vicar of Wakefield." Mr. Mantalini, with his gross overdoses of affectionate humbug, and continual "demmit," is just what one would expect a good-looking, unprincipled man-milliner to be—but he does not do for too close consideration. Tim Linkinwater, Miss La Creevy, Sir Mulberry Hawk, and Lord Frederick Verisopht ; Mrs. Wititterley, and the Kenwigses, including Mr. Lillyvick, besides many minor characters just sketched in, such as the young proprietor of the hair-dresser's shop, can scarcely be exceeded in their truth to nature. Ralph Nickleby, the uncle, has been objected to as too theatrically scowling and malevolent, and too calculatingly wicked. The other usurer, Gride, is a more common-place personage—simply a miser. Bray and his daughter, again, weakly melodramatic,

but beneath the veil of exaggeration there is something of the reality of life. Newman Noggs is an
eccentric creature, one of whom it is just possible to
meet in a lifetime, and the like of the Brothers
Cheeryble must be rare birds indeed. No sensible
critic will accept such straw-stuffed figures, such
benevolent theatrical dolls as truth, or anything near
it. With an obstinacy which continually manifested
itself, Mr. Dickens vehemently asserted that they
existed, "and that their liberal charity, their single-
ness of heart, their noble nature, and their unbounded
benevolence, are no creations of the author's brain."
Happy, indeed, must be the poor who come within
the orbit of their influence ! Nicholas himself is the
portrait of a generous, somewhat common-place, and
natural young man ; and Kate is a very pretty girl—
a fit sister to such a brother. There is little attempt
at high-flown or sensational writing, and the interest
is, to use a stereotyped phrase with critics, well
kept up.

In spite of Dickens's assertion that he had no friend
or companion to help him when he commenced
literature, we must own that his success, his talent,
and his genial manner soon brought him many. Mr.
John Forster, of the *Examiner*, and biographer of
Oliver Goldsmith, devoted many patient hours to
the correction of all his proof-sheets; Mr. W. H. Wills,
the sub-editor of *All the Year Round*, was ready

to aid him as a faithful henchman, and to these were added Mr. Mark Lemon, Sir E. L. Bulwer, and even the trenchant Jeffery, of the *Edinburgh Review*. Indeed, the lonely and unaided young author seems to have been peculiarly happy in the number and the influential character of his friends, and it is to the mutual honour of these gentlemen that nothing but death has divided them, and that they who were his companions and admirers in his youth, were as ardent and warm as ever till death divided them.

It began to be whispered about this time that Dickens was well acquainted with low life, as if an author, or as he himself uses the word, an artist could paint only from well-dressed lay figures and did not delight, in the very depths of his artistic nature, in light and shadows. Mr. Dickens next endeavoured the delineation of low life, and in "Oliver Twist," first published in *Bentley's Miscellany*, of which he became editor, revealed some of the darknesses of London life, and instituted a class of literature from which we have never since then been free. This story, illustrated with a vigour and a genius equal to that of the text, by George Cruikshank, is one of the best Dickens has ever written. Never were the precincts of Field Lane, which stood opposite the terminus of the Metropolitan Railway in Victoria Street, and one side of which remains, more beneficially explored. Never were workhouses more cleverly dealt with; the heaviest blow ever given to "Bumbledom"—the name dates from the book—was therein dealt. The portraits of Fagin, Charley Bates, and the Artful Dodger, are works of art. Nor are Bill Sykes and Nancy to be forgotten; the murder of Nancy, the flight and death of Sykes, and the trial of Fagin, are masterpieces of earnest descriptive writing, and show the true intuition of genius. When Dickens read, or rather acted, the murder scene, the intensity of his acting filled his hearers with horror; the scene itself had evidently been studied for days and nights by the author, who always dwelt on his own creations. One or two characters are mere sketches. Monks is a gloomy scoundrel; and Rose Maylie, a milk-and-water damsel of the real Dickensian ideal: but amidst vice, depravity, cunning, theft, and murder, the author treads firmly and cleanly, and teaches us that best of lessons—to pity the guilty while we hate the guilt, and especially to

" Look upon the poor with gentle eye,
    For in their figures often angels desire an alms."

He had often experienced the force of his writings; he tells us that the Fleet Prison exposed in " Pickwick" is no more, and that Yorkshire schools are better. Mr. Laing, a coarse magistrate, portrayed in a like manner in this book, felt the power of the novelist, and was glad to resign.

The conclusion of "Oliver" was better carried out

than that of "Nickleby;" but the latter had been spoiled by a dramatist, now alive, who dramatised the story before it was finished. The author resented this pilfering with one or two hard blows. The dramatist suggested that it was "fame" to an author to be so dramatised. "So," said Dickens, "Richard Turpin, Tom King, and Jerry Abershaw have handed down to fame those upon whom they committed their most impudent robberies."

At the conclusion of "Oliver Twist" Dickens resigned *Bentley* to Harrison Ainsworth, with a humorous preface, about the old and new coachman, and, after the plan of Addison's *Spectator*, commenced a weekly issue, "Master Humphrey's Clock." Of this we will say little; the plan failed, the correspondents' letters were given up, and a prose epic of the "Old Curiosity Shop" soon alone remained. Poor old Weller, Sam, and Pickwick, were resuscitated, and were soon again laid in their graves. The comic portion of this book is excellent. Swiveller himself is beyond praise ; so are the Marchioness, Quilp, the old Schoolmaster, and Sampson Brass. But there is a serious side even finer. The poetry of little Nell's life, her beautiful devotion to her grandfather, her childlike wisdom, sharpened to an unnatural extent, are touching in the extreme. The poetry of her death is still finer, and the very prose, if but divided into lines, will, as Mr. Horne pointed out in the "New Spirit of the Age," form that kind of gracefully irregular blank verse which Shelley and Southey have used. The following is from the description of little Nell's funeral, without the alteration of a word :—

> "When Death strikes down the innocent and young
> From every fragile form, from which he lets
>   The parting spirit free,
>   A hundred virtues rise,
> In shape of Mercy, Charity, and Love,
>   To walk the world and bless it.
>   Of every tear
> That sorrowing nature sheds on such green graves,
> Some good is born, some gentle nature comes."

In "Barnaby Rudge," his next tale, Mr. Dickens opened up fresh ground, and commenced an historical tale of the Lord George Gordon Riots. The story is vigorous and full of beauty. The description of the riots far surpasses, in our opinion, the celebrated scenes of the "Porteous" mob, by Sir Walter Scott, to which it has been likened. The characters are replete with truth, with hardly one exception. Barnaby himself—poor mad Barnaby—with his raven, is a finished picture; the raven comparable to nothing in literature so much as to a certain immortal dog, possessed by one Lance, drawn by Master William Shakespeare. The rough character of Hugh, Mr. Dennis the hangman, old Varden, the charming Dolly, and Emma Haredale—not to mention the wondrously real Miggs, with Mrs. Varden reading her Protestant tracts—form an admirable group. The character of Lord George is faithfully preserved, but another historical personage is hardly treated with justice; this is Lord Chesterfield, who is attempted under the name of Sir Edward Chester; but Dickens's sketch shows no appreciation of Chesterfield's true character. In fact, "Barnaby Rudge" is at the very head of that rare class of fiction—the good "historical novel."

After the conclusion of "Barnaby," Mr. Dickens set sail to America, now about a quarter of a century ago, and produced from his voyage "American Notes," dedicating his book "to those friends in America who had left his judgment free, and, who, loving their country, can bear the truth when it is told good-humouredly and in a kind spirit." The book was met with a storm of disapprobation. False and exaggerated, were light terms to be applied to it by the Americans, but Dickens stuck to his colours, and, republishing it after eight years, had nothing to alter; "prejudiced," he says, "I have never been, save in favour of the United States." Lord Jeffery wrote a very kind letter about it, said that the account of the prisons was as poetical and powerful as had ever been written, and congratulated him on selling 3,000 copies in one week, and in putting £1,000 into his pocket.

C

In 1843 the voyage to America was again turned to account, by a new tale, " Martin Chuzzlewit," in some respects his best. The hero, a selfish fellow enough till taught and softened in the tale, is the best drawn of his heroes, and admirably contrasted with Tom Pinch; Pecksniff's name has become a synonym for falseness and humbug, and Jonas Chuzzlewit, Montague Tigg, Todgers, Bailey, Tapley, and others, are all admirably drawn characters. As in all his works, the great author, whose creative power seems unbounded, had an aim. Hospital nurses were bad enough, and a shrewd death-blow was given to them by the immortal portrait of Mrs. Sairey Gamp, the origin of Mrs. Brown and numbers of fatuous imitations. The scenes in America have been acknowledged by Americans to be as true as those sketches of England with which we are so familiar. Elijah Pogram and his defiance, and his reference to his country, whose " bright home is in the settin' sun," is immortal. We have not space to linger over the book. It was in 1843 that Dickens struck new ground in his Christmas books, of which it is difficult to speak without praiseful exaggeration. And truly, perhaps, the most wholly beautiful production of Dickens' is his " Christmas Carol." If ever any individual story warmed a Christmas hearth, that was the one; if ever solitary self was converted by a book, and made to be merry and childlike at that season "when its blessed Founder was himself a child," he surely was by that. "We are all charmed with your Carol," wrote Lord Jeffery to its author, "chiefly, I think, for the genuine goodness which breathes all through it, and is the true inspiring angel by which its genius has been awakened. . . . . You should be happy yourself, for to be sure, you have done more good, and not only fastened more kindly feelings, but prompted more positive acts of benevolence by this little publication, than can be traced to all the pulpits and confessionals since Christmas, 1842." Perhaps not that; but the story filled many old hearts with the vigorous youth of charity, and thrilled young souls with a sympathetic love of man, that drew them nearer to God.

There are four more Christmas books, "The Chimes" and "The Cricket on the Hearth," almost equal to the Carol; while "The Battle of Life" and "The Haunted Man" show a certain falling off, although those parts which relate to the Tetterby family were most touchingly written. Let us now pass over "Dealings with the Firm of Dombey and Son," as less satisfactory than most of his works, and proceed at once to "David Copperfield," the most finished and natural of his works; it is more than good. The boyhood of the hero; the scene in church; the death of his mother; the story of

Peggotty.   Poor little Em'ly; that touching love, so true, so perfect, and so delicate and pure, which the rough old fisherman has for his lost niece, cannot be surpassed.   The mellow strength and matured vigour of style, the modest ingenuousness of Copperfield's relation of his progress in literature, supposed truthfully to portray Dickens's own career; the child-wife, her death, and David's final love for Agnes—all rush upon our memory, and put forward their claims to be admired.   The original characters are all good, and the family of Micawber form a group as original as was ever drawn by Mr. Dickens. The dark and weird character of Rosa Dartle, and the revolting one of Uriah Heep, are the only painful ones in the book.   But they are full of fine touches of nature, which also illumine the dark drawing of the Murdstones.   After this Dickens gave us "Little Dorritt" in 1857, and a most excellent story—an historical novel, well considered, and worked out with abundant force—in 1859, "A Tale of Two Cities" (we have omitted "Hard Times" of 1854); and "Great Expectations," published in three volumes in 1861, a tale admirable in all respects, which had adorned the pages of Mr. Dickens's serial.

In 1851-3 he had written a "Child's History of England," as in 1846 he had given us "Pictures from Italy," and in 1860 had gathered up from *Household*

Words a number of sketches called the "Uncommercial Traveller," which are worthy of the author—which, perhaps, is too much to say of the second book mentioned; and lastly, in 1865-6 he issued his most recent work, in numbers, "Our Mutual Friend," a work full of original and eccentric characters, and studded with charming bits of pathos and of description; but, although the author never had a larger sale, the work did not obtain that hold of the public which his others have.

In spite of, and in addition to, the immense amount of work above recorded, Dickens, whose literary activity was enormous, and who seems to have been impelled always to make a closer and more familiar acquaintance with his public, established, on the 21st of January, 1846, the *Daily News*, his name being advertised as "head of the literary department." Young papers have to make readers; and, as a rule, newspaper buyers do not rate at a high value successful novelists. We need not wonder, therefore, that the *Daily News*, though now existing, and honourably known for its independence, is not so successful as it deserves to be, from the courage and vigour with which it has advocated true Liberal principles.*

---

* In 1846 appeared the first number of the *Daily News*, with Charles Dickens as its editor. His duties were uncongenial to him, and it cannot be denied that his management was unsuccessful. In his "History of Journalism," Mr. Frederick Knight Hunt, who

Mr. Dickens, though aided by Mr. Wills and by John Forster, soon ceased to have any connection with this paper, and in 1850 established a weekly periodical, taking the proud line—for a hero or a periodical—"Familiar in their mouths as household words." Connected with this was a monthly narrative, which, as containing news, involved the proprietors with heavy expenses as to stamp duty—now happily removed. The judgment was given in favour of Dickens, and the first step towards a free press thus taken. In 1851, Dickens and Lytton brought forth a project, the Guild of Literature and Art, also abortive, although it has had a certain existence, and certain almshouses, which no author will inhabit, are built on Lord Lytton's estate, near Stevenage. Lytton wrote a comedy, "Not so Bad as we Seem;" and Dickens, Jerrold, John Forster, Mark Lemon, Topham the artist, Charles Knight, and others, were the actors. To back up this comedy, Mr. Dickens

---

well knew all the circumstances. says, " Mistakes were no doubt made, and large expenses incurred, but the errors were corrected, and the losses gallantly borne." Mr. Dickens soon gave up the editorial chair ; but the "Pictures from Italy" were originally published as letters from his pen in the columns of the *Daily News*. In the preface to the " Pictures from Italy," he avows that, " Bent on correcting a brief mistake I made not long ago in disturbing the old relations between myself and my readers, and departing for a moment from my old pursuits," he was about joyfully to revert to his former style of serial publications.

and Mark Lemon produced a weak farce, called
" Mrs. Nightingale's Diary." We have noted that
our vivacious author has also written an opera, very
prettily and gracefully, and here insert a poem—
a graceful and sweet apologue, probably the best
verses ever written by him—reminding one of the
manner of Hood :

"A WORD IN SEASON.

" They have a superstition in the East
    That ALLAH written on a piece of paper
Is better unction than can come of priest,
    Of rolling incense, and of lighted taper ;
Holding that any scrap which bears that name,
    In any characters, its front imprest on,
Shall help the finder through the purging flame,
    And give his toasted feet a place to rest on.

" Accordingly they make a mighty fuss,
    With every wretched tract and fierce oration,
And hoard the leaves ; for they are not, like us,
    A highly-civilised and thinking nation ;
And always stooping in the miry ways
    To look for matter of this earthly leaven,
They seldom, in their dust-exploring days,
    Have any leisure to look up to Heaven.

" So I have known a country on the earth,
    Where darkness sat upon the living waters,
And brutal ignorance, and toil, and dearth,
    Were the hard portion of its sons and daughters ;
And yet, where they who should have ope'd the door
    Of charity and light for all men's finding,
Squabbled for words upon the altar floor,
    And rent the Book, in struggles for the binding.

"The gentlest man among these pious Turks,
    God's living image ruthlessly defaces ;
Their best High Churchman, with no faith in works,
    Bowstrings the virtues in the market-places.
The Christian pariah, whom both sects curse,
    (They curse all other men and curse each other),
Walks through the world not very much the worse,
    Does all the good he can, and loves his brother."

Following up our history, we may note that, owing to certain circumstances, having their origin in a domestic estrangement, which Mr. Dickens himself made public in 1858, and to which, nor to his married life, we have here neither space nor inclination further to allude, our author seceded from *Household Words*, and established, in conjunction with Mr. Wills, *All the Year Round*—a similar journal, in which he did excellent work, by which he aided many young authors, and through which he for many a Christmas charmed our hearts with tender and rare stories, and with such sweet and quaint creations as few but he could give ; let us instance that touching, wholly good and human Dr. Marigold, who deserves to stand side by side with the best character its gifted author ever drew.

When Mr. Douglas Jerrold died, it was found advisable for the benefit of his family to raise a fund by subscriptions from the public, and on the evening of Jerrold's funeral, sitting at the Garrick Club, two or three friends, of whom, says our authority, I was one, drew up a programme of a series of entertainments which was at once taken round to the newspapers. From the success of this arose his determination, which it seems to us was always very prevalent with him, of coming before the public and reading his own works. This he did on the 29th of April, 1858, at the New St. Martin's Hall, now converted into the Queen's Theatre, and the following speech was given by him at the opening :—

"Ladies and Gentlemen—It may perhaps be known to you that, for a few years past, I have been accustomed occasionally to read some of my shorter books to various audiences, in aid of a variety of good objects, and at some charge to myself, both in time and money. It having at length become impossible in any reason to comply with these always-accumulating demands, I have had definitely to choose between now and then reading on my own account, as one of my recognised occupations, or not reading at all. I have had little or no difficulty in deciding on the former course. The reasons that have led me to it—besides the consideration that it necessitates no departure whatever from the chosen pursuits of my life—are threefold : firstly, I have satisfied myself that it can involve no possible compromise of the credit and independence of literature ; secondly, I have long held the opinion, and have long acted on the opinion, that in these times whatever brings a public man and his public, face to face, on terms of mutual confidence and respect, is a good thing ; thirdly, I have had a pretty large experience of the interest my hearers are so generous as to take in these occasions, and of the delight they give to me, as a tried means of strengthening those relations—I may almost say of personal friendship—which it is my great privilege and pride, as it is my great responsibility, to hold with a multitude of persons who will never hear my voice nor see my face.

Thus it is that I come, quite naturally, to be among you at this
time ; and thus it is that I proceed to read this little book, quite
as composedly as I might proceed to write it, or to publish
it, in any other way."

In America and in England Dickens continued
these readings for twelve years, and the greed of
enterprising *entrepreneurs*, who were glad enough
to take a huge share of the money the great author
earned, sometimes taxed him beyond his strength.
He was very glad, however, to be before the public ;
he had the memory, the ways, the love of public
life, of an actor, and surely no author in the world
ever had such a full appreciation of his own works.
When many authors and artists gave Dickens a
farewell dinner previously to his second journey to
America, in answering for literature he spoke only
of himself, he quoted himself three times, and ended
with " the words of Tiny Tim, 'God bless you all.' "
Why those words should be assigned only to Tiny
Tim, when heaven knows they are too often, too
lightly, and too easily in all men's mouths, we
don't know. Another author Dickens quoted was
Bulwer.   He seems to have thought that the " Lady
of Lyons " was rare poetry, and in the course of
his published speeches it will be seen that he uses
three or four times the rhodomontade about—

"Those twin goalers of the daring heart,
Low birth and iron fortune——"

After being advised by his medical men to leave off

his readings, he returned to them again, and on the 15th of March, 1870, gave his farewell reading at St. James' Hall, being the "Christmas Carol" and the "Trial from Pickwick." He told the audience, with some emotion, when he ended, that his readings had given him much pleasure; that in presenting his own cherished ideas for the recognition of the public, he had experienced an amount of artistic delight and instruction which was given to few men; that in this task he had been "the faithful servant of the public, always imbued with a sense of duty to them (it), always striving to do his best, and being uniformly cheered by the readiest response, the most generous sympathy, the most stimulating support." He then concluded with an excellent advertisement of his new book—and this was also characteristic of the keen man of business —in the following words:—"Ladies and gentlemen —In but two short weeks from this time I hope that you may enter in your own homes on a new series of readings, at which my assistance will be indispensable, but from these garish lights I vanish now for evermore, with a heartfelt, grateful, respectful, and affectionate farewell." As a speech-maker perhaps no one surpassed Dickens, he always said the right thing in the right place, and said it very happily. Whether at the Academy or Lord Mayor's dinner, at the Newsvendors' or Poor Clerks' Pension

Society, Dickens made the best speech, better than
Gladstone or Bright, or any brilliant legal luminary.
Perhaps nothing could surpass in its tender happiness
the last speech he made at the Royal Academy in
reference to his friend Maclise, who had just died.
Within a few short months the "effects" of both
these men of genius were brought to the hammer,
and the relic-hunters gave more for a stuffed bird
of Charles Dickens (£120 for the raven, and a very
ugly specimen, too!) than for a noble picture or
sketch by Maclise! After concluding his readings
Dickens commenced "The Mystery of Edwin
Drood," not a good title, descriptive of Cliosterham,
Rochester, nor did the book promise to be very good.
In it he described, of course, something new. He had
been taken by Mr. Parkinson to the East End, and
he saw some Chinese coolies and other poor wretches
smoking opium! He describes this from his own
point of view, others say it is a very false one.
People smoke their opium out of pipes made of
penny ink bottles;* enough to kill a company of
soldiers! Sir John Bowring remonstrated, and sent
him a sketch of a real pipe, its size and capacity;
but Dickens replied, being as characteristically sure
that he was right, as ever "Tom Macaulay" was in

---

* An opium-pipe made by the Chinese will hold opium about
half a pea in size, and of this very little is pure.

Sydney Smith's anecdote, "that he had seen what he painted." So, also, when Mr. Lewes proved that spontaneous combustion did not exist, Dickens was sure he was right, and did not hesitate to describe a human body disappearing in smoke, and leaving nothing but a little viscous residuum like the smoke of burnt brown paper behind !

On June 9th, twenty-four hours after an attack of apoplexy, Dickens, who had been working all day at "Edwin Drood," died at his house, Gadshill Place, Higham, by Rochester, of apoplexy, an effusion of blood on the brain. He had not only been hard at work on the day when he fell, but had written three letters, which have been published, to one of which we shall refer. He died through overwork, which in his case was needless, through living always freely, and adding to the labour of his brain often an excessive labour of his body in walking and exercise.

Men of genius always die young, even when they live beyond the usual period of life, as did Fontenelle and Voltaire, Landor and Rogers; or if they die when just past middle age, as did Shakespeare, falling from us when he was but fifty-two, and had but recently written the most freshly creative and the youngest in spirit of his dramas, the " Tempest "—or Charles Dickens, who passed away at fifty-eight. The reason is, that their creations are always fresh and new, and

linger with us and people our brains, recalling our own
loved and cherished youth long after we are old.   No
one has exercised this power—which is common also
to actors, who enjoy for a very long period a kind of
factitious youth—more widely than Charles Dickens.
What with the immense circulation of his books, the
innumerable editions in England, America, Germany,
France, Russia, Spain, Italy, Denmark, Sweden, and
other countries; what with their cheap and almost
universal reproduction—without copyright—in the
United States; the popular readings given by the
author, in which he so well embodied his own
creations, and their dramatisation by other authors—
no man was ever in his lifetime so popular, or entered
familiarly into so many houses and spoke to so many
hearts.   He had a great privilege, a very great privilege indeed, granted him by Almighty God, that of
being born of the English-speaking race,—a race
which covers and owns three-fifths of the globe, and
whose language will in a very short time, perhaps, be
the *lingua franca*, or free tongue, of half the globe.
He had the privilege of speaking the tongue which
Shakespeare had rendered musical, and which Milton,
Bacon, and Locke had made classical and concise.
He was, moreover, of that great country which, with
all its shortcomings, reverences the Bible more than
any other of its gifts, and which, by subscription and
otherwise, has, in a few years, circulated upwards of

thirty millions of copies of the Word of God within its own shores, to say nothing of the numbers it has scattered abroad. And it was also the privilege of this great author to be well read in this Book,—so well read, indeed, that in a leading magazine there was lately an article which dealt exclusively with his knowledge of the Bible, and his use of its images.

Let us add to these gifts of his that great one of a tender heart, coupled with a quick and vivid apprehension, and a most joyous, lively spirit. We will not here dispute with Shelley the assertion, that

" Most wretched men
Are cradled into poetry by wrong,—
They learn in suffering what they teach in song."

We can instance Fielding, Shakespeare, and Charles Dickens, as essentially poets in tenderness and creative power,—as men who had the truest enjoyment of life, and in the midst of all their merriment the tenderest feeling for the woes of others. No man saw a thing so quickly and so comically as Dickens; and what he saw, he described as faithfully. Such are the innumerable happy touches of habit which give so life-like a character to his creations. Witness Mrs. Gamp, while watching her patients, rubbing her nose along the warm brass bar of the nursery fender,—a trick which he must have seen; Montagu Tigg, diving behind his stock to pull up his collar in a dignified way, and fetching up a string; the style in which the clerks disport themselves at the Circumlocution Office; the mysterious ways of the Punch-and-Judy men, Codlin and Short; and in that clever tale of his, "Barnaby Rudge," the obtuse old innkeeper, John Willett, who, not being quite able to realise how his son has lost an arm, goes quietly to his top-coat, which is hanging up, and feels along the sleeve, as if he might find it there! These, and a hundred other touches, are as true as the more subtle renderings of a photograph, and are such as could never be described unless seen. But not one of them is described ill-naturedly. Dickens was very often exaggerative and pantomimic. He saw things in so very comical a light, that we, of soberer brains and less extensive experience, were quite behind him in perceptiveness. But the humour was the humour of a pantomime, full of fun which delights children, and hurts nobody. The man of science whose eye Mr. Sam Weller blackens, and the beadle whom he thrashes so soundly that he declares he has spoilt him, and that the parish must find another, are, we may be sure, not very much hurt, and will come round again. He is never wantonly cruel; he never is in a rage with any of his characters, except the mean and the base. He visits Fagin and Bill Sykes with extreme punishment, but dismisses Bumble and Noah Claypole to a mean livelihood, and to infinite contempt. He is always honest, always for the rights of labour,—for the good sound workman's having his fair wage, and being happily rewarded. He is never a snob. Dickens, in all his works, never made it a question whether a man should marry on three hundred a-year, or not marry at all, but live, like a grub in a nut, a selfish bachelor. His ideal workman marries on about fifty pounds, or, at most, a hundred pounds a-year, and has a tidy neat little wife, and two or three healthy young children round his knees.

And at the same time we must remember that he did not flatter the working-man, but told him of his faults as well as his virtues. With Dickens, the most industrious of authors, whose too early death there is little doubt was caused by over-exertion, honest industry was the only way for the working-man to be honest and independent; and with it he became, as he deserved to be, a hero in Dickens's eyes. How many pleasant houses has our departed friend peopled with the humble and lowly, from Trotty Veck's poor dwelling to that of the railway official, who never can get the dust out of his hair, and who does not particularly care for tracts! And all this he did at some risk, and showed that indeed he followed Massinger's golden rule, " to look upon the poor with gentle eyes," at some trouble to himself. He arose at a time when the novels of England were both vicious and snobbish, when one set of writers was producing the Satanic school of litera-

D

ture, and another, like those poor things whom we name to forget, the Countess of Blessington and Lady Charlotte Bury, was cultivating what was appropriately called the silver-fork school. An acute reviewer, speaking of the large sums obtained for her novels by the Countess—a very cruel, bad woman, by the way—tells us that " Lady Blessington never took her pen in hand to write a story that she did not immediately proceed to describe, in terms calculated to raise a blush on a modest girl's cheek, intrigues that would shock the morality of a green-room, and the delicacy of a kitchen." This is quite true, and too many lady novelists are doing the same thing now. But when Dickens arose with all his fun—and he was very fond of fun—about babies and monthly nurses, he never wrote an improper word, or penned a sentence that could give rise to an improper thought. His was a manly way of treating things ; a manly, open, sunshiny style ; he made no prurient secrets ; he did not profess to be above or beyond Nature, nor to be feverishly full of heat, nor frigidly full of an unnatural sanctity. He abounded in honest, healthy good tone, like an upright English gentleman ; he described a sweep with all his soot about him, or a miller with his white jacket and dusty hair, face, and hands ; but these honest workmen brought no contagion with them ; they did not come from the fever court, nor were they reeking with the foul oaths of the casual ward.

Another great merit of Charles Dickens is, that he does not look down upon people. The men and women he describes are various, and some of them placed in such degraded positions that one might almost sicken at them. Yet the great author just passed away had an almost Shakesperian faculty of making his readers look upon the bright side of his rogues. Mr. Montagu Tigg is a swindler and a cheat; Mr. Chevy Slime is all that his name indicates; Mr. Mantalini lives upon the earnings of the woman he robs and cheats; and yet, while to the initiated in life this baseness is apparent, all that the innocent reader sees is a most amusing character, without any of the " flimsy nastiness," again to quote our reviewer, so apparent in the works of the silver-fork school. Surrounding these persons are others who are common-place good people,—tradesmen, clerks, and shopmen; and at these, especially at such of them as belong to the middle classes, Theodore Hook, Lady Blessington, and the silver-fork school, who were in the saddle when Dickens was a young man and was forming his style, were in the habit of sneering; their novels were made up almost entirely of abusive descriptions of the " shopo-cracy," vulgar people who dropped their H's, talked ungrammatically, were always fond of pushing into society superior to themselves, and who, with the bad morals of the aristocracy united the worst taste and the slipshod and miserable grammar of the tradesman. Charles Dickens never stooped to this. If he laughs in his juvenile sketches at the "Tuggses at Ramsgate," and a few others, it is to be remarked that he often makes his young men of business his heroes, cares nothing about a gentleman, who is a gentleman and nothing else, elevates his merchants into an atmosphere of generosity and benevolence, and finds a dozen better things to laugh at than the old, worn-out conventional, and farcical resort of making a man say, "'Ow do you do? 'Ave some happles." All this showed great taste and courage on the part of a young author; but Dickens had formed himself upon the very best model of manly English a man can have—upon Henry Fielding. Let the reader, as a proof of this, take the first few pages of "Nicholas Nickleby," and then some of those marvellously acute essays at the commencement of each book of "Tom Jones." The first, he will see, is an inspiration from the other.

But Dickens was distinguished from Fielding by greater invention; such fertility had he, that no one, except perhaps Lope de Vega with Shakespeare, has equalled or surpassed him in this respect. He has invented or portrayed, all accurately, if more or less in caricature, a thousand persons who people our brain, and of whom we talk familiarly. There are Mrs. Nickleby, Mrs. Gamp, Pickwick, Sam Weller,

Mr. Pecksniff, the Chuzzlewits, Inspector Buckle, Old Weller, the Shepherd, Bumble, and a hundred others whom the reader may supply. The French translator of his works has happily hit off this peculiarity. He says, " *C'est un panorama mouvant de toutes les classes de la Société Anglaise; * * une vaste composition où mille personnages se meuvent et posent devant le lecteur.*" And in all these crowds there are persons whom we at once recognise, persons drawn and described with wonderful accuracy; and not only persons, but animals and birds. Now and then he has made a dash at describing a pony, and his carrier's dog elicited the strongest praise from Landseer; while the raven belonging to Barnaby Rudge is known to everybody. Landscapes, houses, rooms, the very clothes of men, were so portrayed by this master, that we seem to have them before us.

Perhaps few authors—and we all receive many letters—were so plagued with correspondence as Dickens. We have spoken of his use of Bible images. He was essentially of a faithful, reverent nature; but now and then his fun forgot itself, and he made use of an image that men more strict have set aside as holy. Upon any of these occasions a dozen angry letters assailed the writer, and it is pleasant to record the answer to one such. In " Edwin Drood," chap. x. p. 68, he made a slip of comicality referring to " the highly popular lamb, who (instead of which) has so long and unresistingly been led to the slaughter "—the Saviour's image of Himself; and somebody wrote to call his attention to it. The last letter but one that he ever wrote was this, penned on the very day of his seizure:—" It would be quite inconceivable to me—but for your letter—that any reasonable reader could possibly attach a Scriptural reference to a passage in a book of mine reproducing a much-abused social figure of speech, impressed into all sorts of service, on all sorts of inappropriate occasions, without the faintest connection of it with its original source. I am truly shocked to find that any reader can make the mistake. I have always striven in my writings to express veneration for the life and lessons of our Saviour; because I feel it, and because I re-wrote that history for my children,—every one of whom knew it from having it repeated to them long before they could read, and almost as soon as they could speak. But I have never made proclamation of this from the house-tops.—Faithfully yours, CHARLES DICKENS," closed the paper.

The letter is very valuable, as indicative not only of the author's faith,—and this is strongly reiterated in his will,—but also of his peculiar " colour blindness," his determination to see things only in one way, and that way the one he wished to use them in; who could use a quotation, including an image essentially a symbol of the Saviour, "without the faintest connection of it with its original source;" but Dickens had not the scholar's brain amidst all his gifts. Nor had he the gift of drawing any noble gentle woman,—his women are at best but dolls,—or any fine, true-hearted gentleman. A Colonel New- come, for instance, or an Uncle Toby, are miles beyond his reach. As Costard says of his opponent, he may be "a marvellous good man and a very good bowler, but as for Alisander, you see how it is a little o'er-pasted." One of Thackeray's men, or Charles Reade's women, are worthy a cart-load of Dickens's middle-class dolls. His pathos is—pathetic! Don't smile; he intended it to be so, and it is, but it wants true art so much that you always see the artist; you swallow the confectionery, but you think of the cook; otherwise it is very well suited for his readers, and not a very high class of them. As in one of his sensational murders, you watch the clouds gathering before the storm begins, so you see the tenderness and tears vigorously shaken up before they affect the reader in the next page.

But, after all, Dickens worked well and loyally; he was a very great author, and he knew it as well as the public, which is always ready to cheer and help a brave man, and which paid back his work not only with money, of which he had enough and to spare, but in a hearty love and appreciation

which it is given to few men to know. "I am
satisfied," he said, "with my countrymen and their
approval, but not with the reward of my country."
Just before he died Her Majesty went to look at him;
but Prevost Paradol, in half of Dickens's literary life,
and with a tithe of his genius, was an intimate with
his Monarch, and an ambassador to a great power.
We desire even less than Dickens desired,—men of
letters to be diplomatists ; but certainly we do want
a Court that is not quite Eastern, and thoroughly un-
English in its reserve, and in its recognition of
literature.   It is said that Dickens was offered to
be made a Baronet, and afterwards a Privy Coun-
cillor, and that he refused both honours ; but the
evidence that this was true has not yet come out.

Dickens's public was not that which Milton wished
for, " fit, though few ;" but it stretched from sea to
sea, and upon the sea in out-going and in-coming
English ships,—vessels leaving or reaching that home
which his pen had made dearer to them.   " God
bless you, Dickens," wrote Hood, even then near
his own death, " God bless you for that sweet story
of yours, the ' Christmas Carol.'   It will preach
a wider and a kindlier lesson than a thousand
sermons."   This is true, the wider lesson, no doubt,
but let us remember that his was the great lesson
taught, thank God, in all our pulpits—the lesson of
peace and good-will to all mankind.

I will say nothing about Dickens's will, concerning which I have heard his friends say bitter things; that is not a literary work within a critic's province. It contained a comical kick at our undertakers, who are *not* so barbarous after all as such gentry in other countries; and it declared dogmatically that to wear any outward sign of mourning was a " disgusting barbarism," or something of that sort. It opened up the question of domestic relations best left closed, and Dickens well knew that the will would be publicly and widely read ; but it contained a manly and humble declaration of his faith in Christ, through whose meritorious sacrifice he looked for salvation. That this faith should have survived the loose fast-talkers and shallow-thinkers, with which every public man is surrounded, is a happy fact, especially as we have heard the great author claimed as a Unitarian by one party, as a Freethinker by another.

They buried him in the Abbey, and the nation was pleased. No man was so widely mourned; he had been with us from our boyhood, and was so much our own that we all felt that we had lost a dear friend. Foreign nations, even frozen Russia and sunny Italy, mourned with us, and set him before us at his true value. We know now what a kindly genius we have lost.

So let him rest with that glad hope of pardoning

love and healing faith. It is a great thought for a widely-read author, and one which must often have occurred to Dickens, that in all the many moments and the flying hours which make up Time, in that portion of Eternity which is allotted to us, and which we little beings call life, that not one moment passes but some, young or old, joyous or sorrowful head is bent down over his books, drinking in his words, loving what he pictures as heroic, hating what he has portrayed as base, and building even its moral tone, although insensibly to itself, and its future life upon his words. It must have been a consoling thought in that sharp agony of the seizure which preceded his death, when the whole wide landscape of his past life was lit up by the lightning flash of conscience, that told him he had not left one line which could corrupt, nor planted with intention one seed which could turn to poison.*

---

* The chief portion of this paper appeared in the *London Review*, November 16th, 1867.

I subjoin two letters, one from an English, another from an American paper, which will exhibit (being each curious in its way) the different estimates placed upon the author. Mr. Dodge's paper is extracted as a specimen of what appeared in the American press.

SHAKESPEARE AND DICKENS.

[To the Editor of the "Spectator."]

" Sir,—In your admirable ' Topics of the Day,' in which there is always so much to agree with, I find a note (June 11) which astounds me. In the greatest gift of genius—humour—you place Dickens beyond Shakespeare. ' He is the only English writer of whom it can be truly said that in any one line in which Shakespeare *was not only great, but at his greatest*, this other was greater than he. But as a humourist we think this is true of Dickens.' You then cite Mrs. Gamp and Juliet's nurse as parallels ; they seem to me to be quite distinct ; one is a mere hireling by the job, the other an adherent of the family, a woman of some position, a duenna of an humble sort. But take Mrs. Quickly, Gossip Quickly, and Mrs. Gamp, and then say which is the greater, broader, more natural character ? Or, take Sam Weller, and compare him with Shakespeare's greatest, Sir John Falstaff ? Why, in fifty years the fun of the one may be past and forgotten, a sealed language, an *argot* which only contemporaries could understand ; while certainly Falstaff will be as alive in fifty centuries as he is now. Shakespeare works *ab intra*, and paints human nature ; Dickens *ab extra*, and gives us particulars and classes. Has Dickens any one character to compare in *truth*, not with Falstaff, but with either Nym, Pistol, Pompey in ' Measure for Measure.' Maria, Sir Toby Belch,—not to fly at more subtle characters and higher game, Touchstone and the

Fools in 'Lear' and 'Twelfth Night?' And with all reverence for the great author just dead, whom I knew both in books and in the flesh, has he drawn any characters at all superior, or even equal, to Partridge, Parson Adams, Uncle Toby, Corporal Trim, Strap,—not to go abroad, and call up Sancho Panza?

"Comparisons are perhaps at this time more odious than even in the proverb, but Dickens when alive complained that he had been spoiled by his critics ; and his worst enemy, if he had any, could not injure him more than by a false elevation.—I am, Sir, &c.,   J. HAIN FRISWELL."

[Mr. Friswell does not understand our criticism. We do not believe, as we have elsewhere maintained, that Dickens ever drew a *real* character. Mrs. Gamp is—in a very true sense,—though it sounds paradoxical, but we have explained our meaning elsewhere, his highest idealism. Shakespeare hardly ever created a character that was not real in its whole basis. But *as a feat of humour*, we do seriously hold that Mrs. Gamp stands above Shakespeare's greatest efforts in the same direction, —even, and no doubt that is an enormous 'even,'—even Sir John Falstaff. Whether or not Mrs. Gamp may be unintelligible to posterity seems to us entirely irrelevant. *We* can understand her, and can also understand Shakespeare's highest feats of humour, and are therefore perfectly competent to compare the relative successes of the two.—ED. *Spectator*, 18th June, 1870.]

"At Gad's Hill Mr. Dickens's habits became more confirmed. He drank more often. His liquors were of the choicest kind. Wines of the rarest vintage were stored in his cellars Highly spiced beverages came to be liked, and he was vain of his skill in compounding them. The 'cider-cup of Gad's Hill'—a drink composed of cider, limes, brandy, pine-apple, toasted-apples, lemon peel, and sugar,—became famous as a speciality of the place. A friend of mine who spent a day and night at Gad's

Hill last year, a gentleman to whom Dickens felt under great personal obligations, and for whom he may therefore have emphasised his hospitality, describes the visit as a continued bibulous festivity from noon till midnight. There was the cider-cup on arriving at half-past twelve p.m , sports in the open air till two, when came brandy and water—a long walk through the fields till six, when curaçoa with other *liqueurs* were served—dress, dinner from seven till ten, with every variety of wines—coffee and cigars, and then pure spirits, or various compounds of spirits, until bedtime. If any one infers from what I have written that Charles Dickens was an intemperate man, in the usual acceptation of the word, whether in this country or in England, he mistakes my meaning. Dickens was never drunk. His intellect was never obfuscated by excess. But he ' enjoyed life.' He lived indeed too fast. This he himself felt, and hence his long walks of from six to ten miles a day, to counteract the effects of indulgence. For the last twelve months of his life he had been increasing in stoutness. He noticed this, and fearing what it portended, increased his hours of exercise. It would have been better had he begun at the other end."

[Letter from Mr. Dodge, who had been introduced to Dickens at the Exhibition of 1851, and who appears to have been familiar with him.]

MR. MARK LEMON.

MR. MARK LEMON.

I N the old and, indeed, in the new order
of nobility, we used to call, and do call,
the person whose name was admitted to
the *Libro D'oro* by the name of his chief victory.
Thus, we have Lord Dudley of Agincourt, Baron
(then Viscount) Nelson of the Nile, Lord St. Vincent,
not to mention the heroes who fought at Sobraon
and relieved Lucknow, and our latest military
addition, Lord Napier of Magdala. As for our latest
literary addition to the peerage, it was to have been
—if the premier, Mr. Gladstone, could have had his
way—Baron Grote of Greece—for surely that history,
luminous and full of learning as it is, is worth a
victory—or should we call him Viscount Grote of
Plato, or of Socrates and his Companions? Those
are true books and worth recording, and, in giving
Mr. Mark Lemon his title, it is worth while remembering his chief or his life work. He is Mark Lemon
of *Punch*, the kindly editor who has held the whip
for more than a quarter of a century; the wise

manager who has quarrelled with no man, and has
put down each of his contributors at his true value ;
the friend of Jerrold, Thackeray, and Leech : the
agent, as it were, by whom whatever money those
gentlemen earned was paid them ; a man of business
as well as a man of letters, and equally honourable
as both ; a man who was always employed in going
about doing good, and of whom the most mordant cad
of a *littérateur*—and we have one or two of the genus
cad in our ranks, not more—can say no word, no
honest word that reflects anything against him ; nay,
this very person is obliged to wind up with, " After
all he was a good fellow, jolly old Mark ! "

A plague upon Time that he takes advantage of
us !   " There are only two honest men in the world,"
says Falstaff, " and one of them grows old."   More
than sixty years, summers and springs mostly, have
fallen upon Mr. Mark Lemon's head, and have turned
the black hair to an iron grey, have lined and seamed
the face, but they have not dimmed the kindly out-
look of the eyes, and have but softened and made
sweeter the playful smile that hovers round the
mouth.   And the face is a remarkable one in its way
—it has such a look of power and good-nature
mingled.   You may see it, in company with a very
ample form, dashing up Regent Street in the centre
of a Hansom cab, which Mark Lemon fills out with
an admirable sufficiency ; you may see it surmount-

ing a fancy costume at a reading at St. James's
Hall; or you may see it coming from the *Illustrated
News* Office, or looking from a photograph of a burly
farmer-like man in Spooner's shop in the Strand;
but wherever you see it you will find kindliness,
force, good humour, concentration, and manliness.
And never more of that kindly manliness which has
distinguished him was ever seen than when, at the
funerals of his two friends Thackeray and Leech, we
saw the upturned eyes streaming with tears, great
heavy tears that came "napping" down the pale
cheeks, and again and again gathered and fell from
the saddened eyes.

Whether Mark Lemon, as we shrewdly suspect,
be of that ancient race which gave kings to Judæa
and prophets to the world, it boots not to enquire.
He was born in the year 1809, near Oxford Street,
London, and a pretty boy, with curly hair, something like young Disraeli, used to be seen, nigh sixty
years since, in a lady's carriage, when Wimpole
Street *was* the seat of aristocracy, and Cavendish
Square in its glory. From carriages and such like
our hero must have fallen to evil fortunes and days,
for there is a rumour that Mr. Lemon once purveyed
other refreshments than those mental kickshaws
which he gives us every week. He made his earliest
attempts, too, at stage plays, was jolly both off and
on the stage, and lived the life of a literary Bohemian

at the time Mr. Gilbert Abbott a'Beckett, a briefless young barrister, wrote for *Figaro*, and rubbed his stuff gown into holes by waiting in and outside the courts in Westminster Hall in hopes of a brief.

This *Figaro*—" Figaro here, Figaro there," and of course " everywhere "—was a rabid Radical publication; but Radicalism had a cause then, and, heaven knows, the Tories wanted shaving. Robert Seymour was an artist who drew and managed to live; his sketches were hardly then known; and John Leech and Kenny Meadows (whom people took for a *comic* artist!) were drawing on the gallery of comicalities in *Bell's Life*. Mr. Mark Lemon, Mr. Blanchard, Henry Mayhew, Horace Mayhew, Maginn, Albert Smith, E. L. Blanchard, and Douglas Jerrold met one day at the shop of Joseph Last, in Wellington Street, after various preliminary struggles, and did resolve upon imitating a certain French periodical, the *Charivari*—which, indeed, might itself have been imitated from our *Figaro* or *Black Dwarf*. For the *Black Dwarf* had been put in prison, and *Figaro* had died. The Englishmen might have been original, but they were not. Look, for instance, at Mr. Alfred Thomson and the *Period* —that indecent imitation of *Le Journal Amusant* and *Le Petit Journal*. Why should the conductors of the *Period*, with which is combined the *Echoes*, thus drag the name and fame of English letters in the

dirt, after a French fashion? If they must prosti-
tute themselves to the vice of the age, why not in
an original way?

Why they were so stupid as to call *Punch*—
perhaps the very best name ever suggested for a
comic paper—by the second title of the *English
Charivari*, which it is not, and never was, always
puzzled the present writer, even when, as a boy,
he bought its first number. Some of its writers
had been over to Boulogne, and Thackeray—who
was not there at the commencement, and came on
afterwards, a swell from *Frazer's Magazine*, and a
college-man—had lived in Paris; but *Messieurs les
abonnés* who took *Punch* in, knew about as much
about the *Charivari* as they did about Sanskrit.
The *Charivari* was epigrammatic, caustic, savage,
full of wit, often indecent, and strongly political.
Punch, too, had its wit, tried to be epigrammatic,
was full of sound, honest English humour, not
heartily political, but thoroughly social, and was
never improper nor indecent, but always cleanly
and manly. The very varnish on *Punch's* nose
glistened with a holy dew of cleanliness; the
very second cut which John Leech did was a
satire on those unfortunate foreigners, those loungers
of Regent Street and the Colonnade of the Quadrant
(since taken down), those " Foreign Affairs," which
Leech, from the bottom of his entirely English

heart, most thoroughly despised. Besides this, the *Charivari* was often in opposition to the reigning powers, and was actually always disloyal. *Punch* was, has been, and is, always loyal; loyal in a true, good, and wise sense, as an English gentleman might be. We are not exaggerating the fact when we say that to the wise loyalty of *Punch*, its writers, and its artists, the reigning Sovereign owes much, very much, of the best and heartiest popularity she has. We believe that Mr. Lemon has never touched one penny of public money, but we are sure that the good he has done, the value of the honest service he has rendered, has been simply incalculable.

For a nation must laugh, and there is all the difference whether it laughs like a satyr, or like those bitter fish-women did in France at blood and slaughter, or like we have laughed under *Punch's* auspices for many years. The proprietors of the paper were wise enough to find out that their editor was a good one, and we, who have served under many, and have commanded heavy vessels ourselves, here declare that a good editor is just the one thing needful for the success of a publication. You can get plenty of good writers, if you know where to pick them out; you can select your artists, and you can contrast your goods so as to show each other off; or you can call fools into a circle and spoil the lot! *Pauca pallabris;* let the world slide. "*Sessa!*"

quoth Christopher Sly; how many publishers have, with the help of editors, poured their money down gutters!

Mr. Mark Lemon did not succeed to the editorship of *Punch* till Henry Mayhew had retired, and Mr. Joseph Last, the publisher, had sold his share, and the shares of the literary gentlemen, too, we believe, to Messrs. Bradbury and Evans, who have since then published our veteran contemporary with such signal prosperity and such success. Not only was our friend editor, calling to his aid Jerrold, Thackeray, Tom Taylor, Percival Leigh, Burnand, and a host of others, and helping artists, poor old Newman, Kenny Meadows, Phiz, Bennett, M'Connell (neither of them learned), as well as Charles Keene and Du Maurier (who are learned in art),—but he was a song and a dramatic author. He has produced upwards of seventy pieces, farces and else. Where are they now? One or two of them still keep the stage, but modern dramatic literature—even such great poems as "Formosa" and "Billy Taylor"—soon drop into the grave. Mr. Lemon, as an author *pur et simple*, is not very great. He has written "largely," as the ordinary writer has it, in *Household Words* and the *Illustrated London News*, and what he has done has been done with a workman-like finish and neatness. He has written, and honestly, in the *Daily News;* has furnished the music-sellers with some capital songs;

has given pleasure to our little ones in some fairy tales of very sufficient workmanship, the "Enchanted Doll" and "Legends of Number Nip;" and when there was a run upon Christmas books, did not the industrious Mark Lemon come forward with a Christmas hamper stuffed full of good things? He has written also in *Cruikshank's Magazine* and in A. Beckett's *Almanac for the Month;* and lately—years fly by rather quickly—he let us have two novels, "Wait for the End" and "Loved at Last." Finally, he did a bold but somewhat careless piece of work in editing "The Jest Book" for Macmillan. This should have been the very best book in the language. It is not so good as we might have expected.

When Dickens was at Devonshire House—"surrounded with rank and beauty," say the liners, and for once within the memory of living man, there was a duke who took notice of pressmen, and saw that literature is a living force, not to be despised and utterly neglected—there were certain plays got up, and admirably acted, by the *Punch* staff, John Forster, and others; and amongst these actors, if Dickens was the best, Mark Lemon was the second. He has since turned this schooling to account by giving dress "recitals" of Falstaff with admirable effect.

Reading this over, and leaving the subject of our sketch alone sole monarch of *Punch*, we find we have said nothing against him. Let us save ourselves with a *caveat*. Therefore *cave, caveto!* we have never taken one penny of Mr. Mark Lemon's money, and only know him slightly and by repute, and indeed do charge him with making *Punch* successful, and, therefore, breeding a crowd of stupid imitators, who have made wit (?) vulgar, detestable, often indecent and common—in fact, to quote our wisest of witty men, frightfully " corrupting." We find, too, that we have not quoted any of our author's writings. Therefore, oh reader, remembering the sweet and gentle nature of the man, take down any volume of *Punch*, and selecting, not the long articles, but the admirably fitted in padding (for the last thirty years), pick out the sweetest, neatest, and the most pointed paragraphs and epigrams, and put them down with a clear conscience to its editor, Mark Lemon.*

---

* Alas ! since this was written, Mr. Mark Lemon died, June, 1870, but we have not found it necessary to alter a word of our judgment, nor the tenses of the verbs.

VICTOR HUGO.

VICTOR HUGO.

THE Kings of the realms of Mind, those un-
crowned monarchs who enter into our secret
thoughts, and rule us from their graves,
are very often opposed to the Kings of the World.

When the world has accepted a family for many
years, and there is a species of loyalty engendered in
the poet's mind, he will symbolise the monarch in
every virtue. She will be Una; she will be the "Fair
virgin throned by the West;" she will make bubble
upon the poet's lips honied adulation so sweet, so
exaggerated, that we poor moderns stare and gape at
the subserviency of a noble mind. But the greatness
of a monarch must be identical with that of the country before a Spenser can allegorise, or a Shakespeare
can flatter. When the interests of the country and
the spirit of patriotism are separated from the King
of Men, then the poet, without a moment's hesitation,
casts his lot with his country. The Court poets of
Charles I. were pretty singers, and there are noble
verses of Lovelace that deserve to stand side by side

with those of Milton. But we are speaking of the supreme mind. There was no question, there could be no question, which side Milton would take.

> "There can be made
> No sacrifice to God more acceptable
> Than an unjust and wicked king."

Thus he translates from Seneca; and through life, in evil or good report, he casts his lot in with the Commonwealth. So there could be no question in this case of Cæsarism on which side Victor Hugo, the supreme French mind of this century, would be when a vast shadow grew between Liberty and France, and, absorbing the strength of many mediocrities, and leaning on the fears of the Bureaucracy, Louis Napoleon rolled back the progress of French liberty, and constituted himself the Autocrat of France. Let us add, that to us—although the crime of the 2nd of December cannot and should not be forgotten—Louis Napoleon has falsified many fears, and has made a better and even a nobler ruler than one could have supposed from the crooked ways in which he crept to the throne.* But what an Englishman may forgive, a true Frenchman never can condone. Napoleon has his day—not even now so great as Victor Hugo on his little rocky asylum—and Hugo will have his: one will be Hugo the Great, the other Napoleon the Little.

---

* Written before the Franco-German war, and the utter collapse of Personal Government.

This great French writer, who is so facile a master of so many subjects of his art that he puzzles us in which to name him greatest, and who is so daring that he dazzles and frightens weak critics into a yesty hatred of his name, was born in a stormy time. His mother, a proscribed Vendéan, wandered while yet a girl in the Bocage of La Vendée. Married to a Republican colonel, this sainted and excellent mother followed her husband as a soldier of Napoleon; and the child Victor, born in the struggles of war, "began," as he said, " to traverse Europe before he began to tread the way of life:"

> "Avec nos camps vainqueurs, dans l'Europe asservie,
> J'errai, je parcoure la terre avant la vie,
> Et tout enfant encore, les vieillards recueillis
> M'ecoutaient racontant d'une bouche ravie
> Mes jours si peu nombreux et déjà si remplis."

It is curious that an opera, a work of genius, is in some way connected with Hugo before he was born. His father, General Hugo, was ordered by Joseph Buonaparte, King of Naples, to reduce the notorious brigand Fra Diavolo ! Which he, of course, successfully did.

Of all nonsense written as biographies, and there is much, perhaps that little one by Eugène de Mirecourt on Victor Hugo is the greatest. This gushing gentleman, who assures us in an airy way "that we speak of the mother of Hugo as we do of the mother

of the Gracchi and the mother of Saint Louis," shall
tell us, in his way, of the early years of Victor Hugo;
but we will get snatches in bits from him, as too much
effusion and French sentiment will not be good for
English digestions.   When he was sixteen—he was
born on the 26th of February, 1802—Hugo wrote
"Bug Jargal," but he does not seem to have published
it until after" Hans of Iceland,"which, says Mirecourt,
"frightened the youth of all of us;" and he tells us
that it was a Blue Beard story carried to the sublime,
and a "statue bigger than nature, and carved in
granite," which does not convey much to us.   Soon
after the publication of "Hans of Iceland,"which made
him, says Mirecourt traditionally, hundreds of *enemies*,
whereas we believe that a good book makes *friends*,
Victor married Mademoiselle Fouchet at the beginning of 1823.   The poet was twenty, the bride fifteen.
"If they were rich," says gushing Mirecourt, "it was
in love, in youth, and in hope;" and he quotes two
or three beautiful verses addressed by Hugo to his
wife, remarkably neat, wonderfully epigrammatic,
and especially French :

"C'est toi dont le regard éclaire ma nuit sombre,
    Toi dont l'image luit sur mon sommeil joyeux !
    C'est toi qui tiens ma main quand je marche dans l'ombre,
    Et les rayons du ciel me viennent de tes yeux."

We are afraid that the savour of these verses will
escape in a translation :

"Mon Dieu! mettez la paix et la joie auprès d'elle,
  Ne troublez pas ses jours, ils sont à vous, Seigneur!
  Vous devez la bénir, car son âme fidèle
  Demande à la vertu le secret du bonheur!"

Very pretty; a young fellow of twenty courageously
marrying a girl of fifteen, and writing like that to her,
is a spectacle to gods and men in these melted-butter
days—especially a spectacle to Miss Becker, Emily
Faithful, and the shrieking sisterhood. Poor little
Madame Hugo—how they would have patronised and
pitied her, riveting her chains of slavery at that early
age! And Hugo, whom Swinburne so loves, marrying and become *père de famille* when the Græco-
Gallic-Scotch poet was murmuring with satyr-like lips
the Hymn to Hermaphroditus;—does not, by the way
an unhealthy insubordination of women produce unhealthy and erotic poetry? All the best women the
world has ever heard of, from the blessed Virgin
downwards, were only too meekly ready to be sub-
ordinated. For of woman truly is the proverb wise,
" she stoops to conquer."

Victor Hugo had, with his father's consent, committed himself to a literary career; and in his studies
he had been so successful that his pieces had been
crowned, and he would have won more prizes but for
his youth. The restoration of the Royal family filled
his father with despair, his mother with joy, and thus
separated the parents. Loving his mother above all,

F

as Frenchmen somehow will do, he rose to distinction as a Royalist poet, and received a pension from Louis XVIII., and years afterwards a peerage from Louis Philippe. He had, in spite of the love of his father for Napoleon I., depicted France as "Rachel weeping for her children, for they were not," and in half-a-dozen ballads he had proved his loyalty. But at heart he was free and republican.

Mirecourt, still gushing, tells us that in the midst of poverty the young couple, whose united years only reached to middle age, retired to a "ravishing little house, No. 42, Rue Notre-dame-des-Champs, built like a convent, and hidden like a bird's-nest in trees." "And there there was," says this miserable scribe, striking a pose as if he was making an epigram, "there there was a summer dining-room, with a terrace, and a winter dining-room." "On était reçu par Madame Hugo, l'ange du foyer." It would be odd if anyone else but a man's wife should welcome you, or be "the angel of the hearth," or, to be quite French, of the stove. Suffice it to say that in this little house, to which the profits of "Hans of Iceland" brought comfort, there came a circle of friends, and that Sainte Beuve formed there a club, of which Hugo was chief. This club consisted of Dumas, Paul Foucher, Hugo, Méry Arnold, Fleury, and Sainte Beuve; and sometimes met with another club, with Thiers, Mignet, Piesse, Armand Carrel, and others.

Then the two clubs combined, upon which our French author bursts into an epigram, "On opérait une fusion des deux cénacles. *La poésie accueillait la politique et la traitait en sœur !*" Is it not sweet ! We do not write like that *yet* in England.

In 1826, the "Odes and Ballads" of Victor Hugo betrayed the political change of his spirit. In 1827 he published a drama called "Cromwell," in which he, by a preface, demolished Racine and the sticklers for unity, and asserted the freedom of the modern and Christian drama against the rules of Aristotle. Henceforth there was a struggle between these Unity-arians and Victor Hugo. The genius of Hugo was victorious; and we need not say what an effect this had upon England, where *all* our plays are taken from the French, more or less *en gros ou en détail*. In "Cromwell," in "Ernani," "Marian de Lorme," "Le Roi s'amuse," "Lucréce Borgia," "Marie Tudor," "Angelo," "La Esmeralda," "Les Burgraves," and especially in that very great drama, "Ruy Blas," Victor Hugo carried out his principles with triumph.

Let us now for a moment look at his poems, of which, by the way, some of the most beautiful have been very finely translated by Robert Brough, in the *Train*; and it is there that the genius of the man will more especially be found. We here subjoin a few of the verses of "Sara la Bagneuse," translated with exceeding delicacy by Robert Brough :

"SARA LA BAGNEUSE.

Sara, indolent as fair,
    In the air,
Pois'd upon a hammock, swings
To and fro above a pool,
    Limpid—cool—
Watered by Illysees' springs.

And the glassy sheet below,
    As they go,
Shows them swinging fro and to ;
Tiny car and burden fair,
    In the air !
As she leans herself to view.

She, with timid foot, in play
    Taps the spray ;
Ruffling thus the mirror still,
Redd'ning quickly, back it shrinks,
    While the minx
Shudd'ring, laughs to feel the chill.

Hidden lay within the bow'r,
    In an hour,
You shall see the maiden go
From the bath in all her charms,
    With her arms
Cross'd upon her breast of snow.

Pure as a drop of morning's lymph,
    Shines the nymph,
Stepping from a crystal brook ;
Wet, with quiv'ring shoulders bare,
    In the air,
Glancing round with anxious look.

Watch her ! how her bosom heaves ;
        Crackling leaves
Sound to her like knell of doom ;
Should a gnat her shoulders brush,
        Mark her blush,
Like a ripe pomegranate's bloom.

All that robe or veil conceals,
        Chance reveals ;
Deep within her cloudless eyes
Shines her as shines a star,
        From afar,
Through the blue of summer skies.

Water from her rounded hips,
        Raining drips,
As from off a poplar tall,
Or as if the heedless girl,
        Pearl by pearl,
Down had let her necklace fall."

In every one of his poems there are signs of genius and
marks of grace; there is also a neatness of workmanship which is admirable in contrast with our
careless writers.   Take, for instance, this little gem,
which we have translated line for line :

"THE FLOWER AND THE BUTTERFLY.

The lowly flower to its airy guest
                Whispered, ' Oh, stay !
How different are our lots, while here I rest
                Thou fliest away !
Fliest and comest back, and fliest again,
                To play elsewhere ;

Yet at each morn thou findest me the same,
Bedewed with tears.
Ah, that our love may pass in faithful days,
Oh, my heart's king !
By me take root ; or, if thou will not stay,
Let me take wing !"'

"Les 'Chants du Crépuscule' sont remplis d'une multitude de petits chefs-d'œuvre," says Mirecourt, and here
we agree with him. Everywhere one finds the hand of
a master. *Les chansons des rues et des bois* have, however, an eroticism which pleases the Swinburian fancy;
and " Les Travailleurs de la Mer," says our gusher, is
a veritable insult to Providence ; but then Mirecourt
does not live at Jersey, and has not seen the struggle
of the elements.

But it is as a prose writer that Hugo is by far the
greatest, greater than as a poet or a dramatist. As
chief of the romantic drama, he pushed the meaning
of the word to something far higher than it had ever
covered before. In his wonderful story of " Notre
Dame," in the veritable creations of the hunchback
Quasimodo, the priest Claud Frollo struggling with
his guilty love, the innocent gipsy Esmeralda, the
young author had given a proof of his genius; but his
greatest strength was reserved for his years of exile,
of banishment, of reflection, of the struggle of a giant
against his fate. As an exile, a blind Homer, he has
sung of man's struggle not only with the elements, but

with education and society, as an Æschylus has pictured and sung of the fore-doomed troubles of Orestes.

We have said that Hugo was made by the citizen
king, Louis Philippe, a peer of France. In England
we put our men of genius in a melancholy ruin of a
Poet's Corner in a huge lump, where the fame of one
may neutralise that of the other, and the memories
and reflections that arise from the grave of Dickens
may effectually be driven away by glancing at the
busts of Shakespeare and Thackeray. In France,
either in persecution or in reward, they do recognise
their genius. Made a peer by Louis Philippe, Hugo
was elected by the Republicans first to the Consti-
tuent and then to the National Assembly, wherein
his eloquence was noted. He wrote certain very war-
like "Lettres du Rhin," and with consistent inconsis-
tency was president of a Peace Society. The crime of
December—when Louis Napoleon's troops shot down
some hundreds of the people and some ten of the
elected of France, going in their perfect legality to
meet in their National Commons House—set Hugo
in violent opposition. He flew first to Brussels,
then to England, where he wrote a somewhat violent
letter to the Queen upon some criminal very properly
condemned to death; then he fled to Jersey, and
has since resided in a sister island at Hauteville
House. Here he lives with his two sons, Charles
and Victor, and a daughter, Mdlle. Adèle Hugo, with,

of course, the mother, Madame Hugo, as tenderly
loved as ever. From his island he sent forth his
scorching satire "Napoleon le Pêtit" and "Les Chati-
ments;" but paper pellets cannot move one who relies
only upon *chassepôts* and *armes de précision.*

His great works since his exile have been "Les
Misérables" and "Les Travailleurs de la Mer." In one
he pictured man struggling against social wrong; in the
other in his struggle with fate and the elements. In
many respects faulty, these are yet in many others
the greatest tragic and romantic works of the century.
We are promised another "1793," which will complete a kind of trilogy. Madame Hugo also promises
a life of her husband, detailing not only his great
works, but his many unostentatious acts of charity.
Perhaps Victor Hugo, by his weekly dinners to poor
children, —dinners of meat and bread and wine,—
was the first to give the impulse to the movement
for feeding the poor, which the English have since so
thoroughly and systematically caught up. If, as the
dull ones say, genius is mad, it is with a benevolent
fine madness that Hugo is rightly possessed. Hugo has
never ceased to protest against wrong and tyranny;
never ceased to hope in the grand future of the world.

We have not here room for criticism ; it would be
either insufficient, or far too long. We must, therefore, end with a sketch of the poet. Years ago—for
he triumphed when young—he had introduced the

taste for old armour, tapestry, painted windows, mediæval costume, and those admirably beautiful relics of old furniture, which is now so prevalent in Paris and in London. Herein we authors are really of some use to you prosaic upholsterers and architects; you fat and greasy citizens are made to understand how nice your country-box may be made, *through* the author, if you please, Mr. Pugwash. And Mr. Chasuble, to Walter Scott and Hugo *you* owe some of your chances of bringing back lecterns, singing boys, processions, introits, and other church matters. Yes, here we are of use. In a mediæval hall in an ancient hotel, garnished with arms and massive furniture, the young poet and his wife, with their children playing before them, looked the true grande dame and seigneur of the old time that their friend Louis Boulanger, portrait painter to the family, has represented them. In their little English house at Hauteville, in the sea-worn island won by the English from the Normans, and still retaining its Norman customs and its singular rights, a vigorous white-headed man of nearly seventy, with an iron grey beard, hair cut short, broad chest and shoulders, face marked with the frequent foot of time, eyes that stare out eagle-like from the bold countenance, is a man, like John Florio of Elizabeth's time, still resolute, still hoping for the federation of the peoples; still dreaming those dreams which you and we have forgotten, and weaker people never had. By him is an ancient lady, once his bride of fifteen, but now his consoler, his counsellor, and his guide. To them come the haters of kings, the political implacables, the tribunes of the people, the exiles from many lands, the poor, the broken-hearted, the hopeless. But Victor Hugo has for each and all some heart-stirring noble words, some deep feeling to appeal to ; and as the silver-haired lady clasps his hands and looks into his face, as he still fulminates against the triple-anarchy (Nature, and Government, and Fate) which bind down aspiring man, she repeats his own noble lines *(Le poëte en des jours impies)*, which we have here attempted to translate:

> " The Poet in these days of Wrong
>   Moulds and prepares a better time ;
> Utopian is this man of song,
>   Earth-bound his feet, his thought sublime !
> He looks above our little heads
>   To all time ! Prophet-like he stands,
> And holds, or scorned or praised or blamed,
>   A torch upreared in sacred hands.
> The light he trims in days of crime
>   Will brighten all our Future Time."

CHARLES READE.

CHARLES READE.

"PUT YOURSELF IN HIS PLACE."

Such is the title of a story now running through the pages of the *Cornhill Magazine*.

That story is about a skilled workman who loves above him, and has a hard battle to rise in the world and win his sweetheart. In this noble struggle he is so unfortunate as to come into collision with certain Trades' Unions, in that populous district of England where the Unions prefer crime to defeat.

Thus the story treats the great question of the day, and handles it pretty fairly. The writer is neither a manufacturer nor a workman, and has no prejudice in the matter, but sees the virtues and the faults of both, and what he sees he says.

To save this subject from unworthy treatment on the stage, the author has dramatised his own work, and the drama will shortly be produced in London, and played by an admirable company selected from various first-class theatres to do justice to a theme so important and so real.

May the 28th.

"PUT YOURSELF IN HIS PLACE"

A drama in four acts, by the author of the drama "It's Never too Late to Mend," will be represented at the Theatre Royal Adelphi.

May the 23rd.

"Put Yourself in his Place," by the author of the novel "It's Never too Late to Mend," will be published by Messrs. Smith and Elder, complete in three volumes, and can be ordered in advance at any respectable library throughout the kingdom.

THE curiosity of literature with which we have commenced this biography is in its way unique, and it is only by understanding it that the reader will fully comprehend the marvellously vigorous novelist who wrote it. It sounds like a puff, but it is not so. It looks like an arrogant piece of self-assertion, of which, by the way, strange as it may seem, Charles Reade would not be guilty—not even in spite of those italics, "to save this subject from unworthy treatment." And as this announcement was stuck upon one of the *affiche* boards of the Adelphi Theatre, the last paragraph looked uncommonly like a Moses-like advertisement of a new pair of trousers ; and the suggestion that it could "be ordered in advance at any respectable library in the kingdom "—what book cannot?—seems to be the neatest bit of buncombe advertising that could possibly be indulged in. What Mr. Charles Reade does intend to say—and we hold that he is a man of true genius, and has the modesty of true genius—is, that he has written a very powerful, very earnest, and very honest novel ; that he believes that it treats of the most vital question of the day ; that while it does so with the interest of a fiction, it also does so with the clearness of a statesman suggesting a remedy for a terrible national disease. He intends, further, to let the public know that having written a good novel, he intends to sell it; that a man of letters, although a thousand times a more valuable man, and a much rarer production, has the right of making money by his talent, equally with the butter-man, the iron factor, or the speculator in the stocks. That the public believes in tall-talk advertisement and brag, and that it must be hit full in the face before it is awakened. In this age of competition Mr. Reade believes that the silent man has no notice taken of him. It is no use crying fresh herrings in a whisper, and being so proud as to "thank God nobody hears you." You must not be ashamed of your *métier*. If you write a story of the day, you must make it bear upon the day in the heaviest pos- sible way. You must circulate widely, and hit the public as hard as you can.

But the author of "Put Yourself in his Place," which golden maxim we have been following as we write, while he enters with full vigour into all we have pre- viously said, really, and with good cause, believes in his own genius, and is bold enough to say so. Take for instance his motto to his last book: " I will frame a work of fiction upon notorious fact, so that anybody shall think he can do the same; shall labour

and toil attempting to do the same, and fail;—such
is the power of sequence and connection in writing."
—*Horace : Art of Poetry.*

And very readily and generously does the public
accept the writings of this generous, impulsive egotist,
which designation must be understood in an entirely
good sense.   Mr. Reade believes thoroughly in himself.   He has no doubt as to his vocation, and whatever he finds to do that he does with all his might.
The faults that he has are not the faults of this
generation.   He does not doubt and hesitate ; he is
not feminine, except from the surplusage of his
manliness ; he does not despise the means by which
he makes money ; he is no trimmer ; he believes in
goodness, and yet knows what wickedness is ; he is
entirely human, and yet in his aspirations far in
advance of the ruck and vulgar herd of humanity.
He is *sui generis ;* he has formed a school of his own,
in which he has no pupil.   His career has not been
a very rapid one, nor are his works—which are so
very easy to read, and in which one has such a rapid
interest—at all easy to write.   He does not produce
quickly, but what he gives us is so finished and
so natural that it looks as if it were done without
any trouble.

Mr., or rather Dr., Reade, for he is D.C.L., is the
son of the late John Reade, of Ipsden House, Oxford-
shire.   He was educated at Magdalen College, and

graduated B.A. in 1835, having been born in 1814. He studied at Lincoln's Inn, and was called to the bar in 1843 ; but literary barristers seldom practice, and, indeed, literature is so jealous a mistress that she will allow of no other service—at least, in most instances. In the year 1852 a little work, half dramatic, and served up afterwards in a dramatic form, was presented to the public, called " Peg Woffington," founded on the story of that generous but semi-virtuous actress. This had at once a great success, and deserved it. In 1853 another novel, also in post-octavo (10s. 6d.), was published by Mr. Bentley, called "Christie Johnstone," and this, too, made a hit. In a short time there followed upon this a very pretty story of a bloomer, called " The Course of True Love Never did Run Smooth;" then "Jack of all Trades" (the autobiography of a thief) ; then, in or about the years '55 and '56, Mr. Reade wrote for the *London Journal* a capital story called "White Lies," and it says much for the despised readers of that journal that they, most of them, recognised its extreme cleverness, while, when published by Mr. Trübner in 1857, in three volumes, it did not attract the public of Mudie's and the libraries in an equal degree, nor according to its deserts.

In the year 1856 Mr. Reade published a work which had a highly moral and politico-social aim— that of calling attention to the condition of our

prisons, and also to the far more important, because
eternal truth, that

> " Men may rise on stepping stones
> Of their dead selves to higher things."

The name of this was, "It's Never too Late to Mend,"
and it created a sensation indeed. The cruelties
practised in gaols were looked into ; a governor of a
gaol removed and suspended, and various new brooms
were set in work through the vigour of this *exposé*.
" It's Never too Late to Mend," may be taken as
Charles Reade's typical work. The writing was so
strong that it was painfully vivid ; it was as true as
lightning, but it hurt your eyes, and it hurt especially
those lazy sensitive men who feel for and yet never
help the poor, and who try to believe that our
humane system is all *couleur de rose*. This was so
much the case that Mr. Reade was bullied and
scolded in a most amusing way by the old termagants
of the press; they scolded like fish-fags, but the
author little recked of their scolding. The fun of
this thing—and to a properly satirical person it is very
funny—consists in both persons meaning the same
thing, and neither being able to convince the other
of that not unimportant fact. When, after the lapse
of some time, the death of the offending governor of
the gaol, and the cleansing to some extent of our prison system, " Never too Late to Mend" was produced
at the Princess's Theatre, an old critic and dramatist,

Mr. Tomlins, who is since dead, and who never rose
to a position of weight or of eminence in literature,
arose on the first night and protested, with his back
to the terrible scene, against the cruelty and exaggeration of the play. There was quite a row in the
house, and the author, we believe, attempted to address the audience from the private boxes. Then in
the papers there was, first, Mr. Tomlins' criticism,
and Mr. Reade's indignant protest that he spoke the
truth; then came Tomlins' denial, and as both
authors were exceedingly impulsive and vivid, they
emptied the slang dictionary with immense vigour
upon each other's heads, greatly to the amusement
of the public and to the beneficial advertisement of
the play. Both meant well; both were for serving
truth honestly, but each was so *entêté* that he scorned
to listen to the other.

The next novels that we had from Mr. Reade were
" Love me Little, Love me Long; " " The Cloister
and the Hearth," an ambitious work in four volumes;
" Hard Cash," written for Charles Dickens's weekly
magazine, just as the " Cloister and the Hearth " was
written for *Once a Week* under the name of "A Hard
Fight." Next to this succeeded "Griffith Gaunt,"
written for a magazine under the stupid name of *The
Argosy;* and then one of the very best of his stories,
the plot of which was furnished him by Mr. Boucicault,
called "Foul Play," which appeared in *Once a Week;*

and next and last, this admirable, vivid, and over-head-and-heels work, " Put Yourself in his Place," which has been for some months running through the pages of the *Cornhill Magazine*.

Mr. Charles Reade has also written some very successful plays, " Masks and Faces," &c., and has worked in conjunction with Mr. Tom Taylor as a dramatist. Whatsoever he does he does most earnestly. He is no half-hearted workman; and he knows his own ability as a literary artist so well that he always succeeds.

Charles Reade is, as an author, very well worth studying. He is so thorough in what he does, so determined and so intense, that he falls into exaggeration, and yet it is doubtful whether he over-paints the truth. It is the languid age that is in fault, and *not* the vivid author. In his last work he has described the effects of Unions in the Sheffield trades, and he has not gone one bit out of the record of that terrible Commission which sat and revealed to us exactly how matters stood. So great an artist is this writer, that one feels towards the murderer by deputy, Mr. Grotait, a kind of sympathy, just as Shakespeare makes you feel a human heart beating even in Iago or Richard III. Grotait is, of course, drawn from the life; he is none other than our friend Mr. Broadhead, who, somehow, in spite of the Commission, and in spite of forcible articles of the press, and in spite of Mr. Roebuck, to whose courage Charles Reade bears a generous and well-merited tribute, carries with him the sympathy of hundreds of working men. Added to this effect of exaggeration, heightened by a dramatic mind, this author has an overheat and vigorous fertility in his invention that requires to be moderated, and a determination to paint so exactly what he feels, that people turn away from the sight in terror, fright, or disgust. He has quoted the "Ars Poetica;" let us recall two or three lines which warn an artist not—even in the heat and excess of his admiration for mere art—to show too much to the public. Flaccus says :

" Ne pueros coram populo Medea trucidet ;
  Aut humana palam coquat exta nefarius Atreus,
  Aut in avem Procne vertatur. Cadmus in aquem.
  Quodcunque ostendis mihi sic, *incredulus odi.*"

And in those two last words, or rather in the last line, is the secret of the enmity of a great part of the press for Charles Reade. Even critics cannot appreciate what they cannot understand. Not only is Charles Reade true, but he is too true. His reality is beyond realism. Compare Charles Dickens and his pantomimic touch with Charles Reade, and you will see how infinitely superior the latter is as an artist. Take, for instance, those two sailors in "Foul Play," which are as true to life as anything drawn by the great masters, Fielding, Smollett, or Sterne, and

put them side by side with any of the minor characters of Charles Dickens. Those sailors will "stand
out" all alive, while Dickens's work will look faint,
sketchy, unreal, comical, and yet caricatured and
pantomimic. Take, too, as a direct proof of master-
dom in art, the creation of female character. Place
side by side Charles Reade's women with Charles
Dickens's pretty little marionette company of rag
dolls beautifully painted to the life.

Finally, there are two matters to remark. Reade
has quarrelled with the press, and has set it at defiance; he does his own plays that they may not be
unworthily treated; he insults and contemns the
critics. The result is that, on the whole, he is perhaps better treated than any other writer. At any
rate, there is from this, this lesson to be learnt,—
either the press is very generous, or it is very power-
less. When an author is strong enough to trust
himself—and he *is* strong enough when he thoroughly
believes in himself,—he can walk alone without criticism. The opinions of a few weaker professional
brethren are nothing to him. It is the public who
appraises *his* value.

Secondly, there is this last observation, which shapes
itself into a congratulation both to the author under
review and the public. It is a matter of honest ex-
ultation to reflect that one, whose impulses are so
true and so noble, who loves what is good, thorough,

and laborious, and hates what is effeminate, weak, and mean, is so popular and so well appreciated. We are delighted when Reade begins a new story; we know it will be angular and singular, but that it will be bold and true. In circumstances of great danger, his latest hero, Henry Little, gives a toast, "Here is quick exposure, sudden death, and sure damnation to all hypocrites, thieves and assassins." It is just what Charles Reade would do before the most blood-thirsty critics. His motto should be, "Quod vult valde vult." May he live long to teach us that what we vehemently desire should be only that which is noble and true.

JOHN RUSKIN, M.A., D.C.L., &c.

JOHN RUSKIN, M.A., D.C.L., &c.

THERE is a story told of a gentleman-farmer, not unaccustomed to the outsides of books, that he took down to his farm with immense gusto, Ruskin "On the Construction of Sheepfolds." It was foreanent the lambing season, and our Bucolic wished to provide. His rage will be imagined by those who love to hug a book to read after dinner, and to debate with an architectural author the proper form of some building. Ruskin's "Sheepfolds" is a pamphlet on the discipline of the Church! There are a thousand other ridiculous stories told. A person bought "Table Traits" to read as a cookery book; the "Gentle Life" was caught up as a disquisition on fishing, and a hunting man carried away the "Recreations of a Country Parson" as a work which should be full of delightful chapters on pastoral sports, — shooting, fishing, and fox-hunting. What more, bleated the poor deceived one, what other recreations can a country parson have?

But Ruskin's titles will give one an insight into the

man. Earnest, honest, full of love for his fellow-men, all that he does has some end in view, and this end is to make men better and wiser. We can well believe him when he writes : " In these books of mine, their distinctive character, as essays on art, is their bringing everything to a root in a human passion and a human hope. Arising first not in any désire to explain the principles of art, but in the endeavour to defend an individual painter from injustice, they have been coloured throughout—nay, continually altered in shape, and even warped and broken, *by digressions respecting social questions, which had for me an interest tenfold greater than the work I had been forced into undertaking.* Every principle of painting which I have stated is traced to some spiritual and vital fact."

Our readers will now see what Ruskin is, a great social and political writer, who has been turned for a moment, and by a generous impulse, to write upon art. What he wrote he wrote well, from his soul, as so good and great a man must write ; and even when he generously undertook the defence of that mean and selfish old genius Turner, he did not wholly lose himself in his subject. Perhaps no one was more astonished than Turner at the turn things took. Here were the English, who are mostly ignorant of art, buying greasy, sticky, and dark old masters, and worse, wretched copies from old masters—things so black that one could not see. Ruskin, a young graduate, comes and waves his magician's pen in "Modern Painters," and our newspaper critics, more ignorant even then than now, which is saying much, are converted, and the reign of modern art comes in. We begin to love daylight, real drawing, colour, light, cheerfulness; not fusty old saints, miserable friars, and impossible apotheoses of saints that never existed. And yet no one loves the old masters more than Ruskin and this writer—when they are masters, look you! However, the reign of Turner and modern painters was established, and thousands upon thousands of pounds were laid out upon English artists who, but for Ruskin, would have starved. As a rule, and we know them well, our more fashionable artists are an ill-read, unthinking, over-paid and over-praised set. Has any one of them ever thought of giving Ruskin a dinner, or subscribing to any testimonial for his gigantic work? Does Mr. Birket Foster believe that without Ruskin he would get three and four hundred pounds for those little bits of water-colours? No; he would still be working on blocks of wood with a H.H.H. pencil. Do the pre-Raphaelites reflect that without him their angular drawings, flat painting, and want of atmosphere, would have become famous? If they do, they are still conceited muffs. They have forgotten Perugino, Bartolomeo, and the rest of the old Italians, now that they have made their name— thanks to Ruskin. Thanks also to him for having improved the whole of our art and art-knowledge. He is a great man; we hardly know yet how great.

Look at him at the Royal Institute. Leave the country by an early train, dine in London, and then, favoured by a Fellow, present your ticket to Ruskin's lecture. A long, thin, shambling gentleman, like a country clergyman, with hair red and after the "pound of candles" style in its method of tumbling over his face; a Scotch face, full of shrewdness; very ugly if we believe some photographs, very winning, bright, and clever, nay, sweet and charming, if we trust to George Richmond's portrait and to reality. The mouth is small, the nose somewhat *retroussé*, the forehead small, but so is the whole face; yet the head is capable, and the fiery soul seems to work upwards and flash out of the windows of those eyes, as the eloquent words, hurried onward in a torrent, flash too, and light up whole tracts of darkness. A word, a hint, a slight reference to some gargoyle or spandrill, some carved work in stone, and you see it all. A dry subject becomes luminous; the cold dead stones of Venice begin to move and raise themselves to life. After hearing Ruskin you understand how it was that Apollo made the stones dance and form in order to build Troy walls—which you never did before. But Ruskin has tried higher game than art.

Born in 1819, Ruskin is the son of a London wine-merchant, who had the good sense to send his son to

Oxford, where, at the age of twenty, he took the New-degate Prize for English Poetry. This is worth while bearing in mind, for Ruskin's style is very flowing and buoyant, and full of poetic imagery of a high order. Then taken with a love of art, the student, after taking his degree, studied under J. D. Harding and Copley Fielding, excellent artists, who have a great love of nature very apparent in their works. Having learnt to paint, to know what a palette is, what scumbling, what the difference between a tube of megilp and a tube of paint, and being indeed practically no fool of an artist, the graduate wrote a book to tell the world—which, Heaven knows, wanted it—something about art. The reception of his book " Modern Painters," when first issued in 1843, was simply contemptuous.

Art critics—who have been admirably sketched by Thackeray as Fred Bayham—were ignorant reporters, who did not know a mahl-stick from a walking-cane, and who, in the plenitude of their ignorance, could not see that they were killed outright, run through the body, by Ruskin's rapier. A Turk had a scimitar so sharp that he used to pass it through a man's neck without hurting him. The victim used to grin with delighted surprise. " Sneeze," said the *Sabreur Turque*. The executed one did so, and his head rolled on the floor. Most of our stupid art critics are dead;

some have exhibited the crick in their necks; but a great many of them have not yet sneezed, and go on writing about Parmegiano, Claude, chiaro-oscuro, and the corregiosity of Corregio, with distressing simplicity. Quietly and triumphantly "Modern Painters" made its way; a second edition was called for within a year; Turner was enthroned (poor mean old man, he had tumbled into decadence, painted pictures full of varied colours like a convalescent black eye, and still quoted his own MS. poem, the " Fallacies of Hope"), and the public's idea of painters and painting was revolutionised.

The great writer—for the style, and the style is the man; it is God's gift, as colour is to the painter— was then away to Italy studying. Mark this, not one step does Ruskin take without study. He records, in a simple unaffected way, a striking instance of this. " The winter," he says, " was spent mainly in trying to get at the mind of Titian,—not a light winter's task,—of which the issue, being in many ways very unexpected to me, necessitated my going in the spring to Berlin, to see Titian's portrait of Lavinia there, and to Dresden to see the Tribute Money, the elder Lavinia, and girl in white, with the flag fan. Another portrait, at Dresden, of a lady in a dress of rose and gold, by me unheard of before, and one of an admiral, at Munich, had like to have kept me in Germany all summer." So conscientiously does Mr. Ruskin work. In 1846, another volume of "Modern Painters"followed, and another was promised. In the interim he had been studying architecture, and we had his "Seven Lamps of Architecture," 1849; the "Stones of Venice," 1851; and the second and third volumes of the same in 1853. All these were large volumes, *editions de luxe*, for Mr. Ruskin's fortune is a sufficient if not a very large one. He appears to have thought that only a large price would repay books of that character. Like Rogers's "Italy," published at a heavy price, the works paid capitally.

We must now rapidly sketch the work of Ruskin, to show what he has done, and afterwards we will say a few words upon how he has done it. In 1851, Ruskin wrote in favour of the pre-Raphaelites, a set of ardent and admirable young painters, whose forcible ignorance was needed to bring us back from the schools of Chalon and Collins, and the poor creatures who had given up their mean souls to the aristocracy and the "Book of Beauty." All of the P. R. brethren have recanted practically; not one paints as he then painted, but infinitely better. In 1853, Ruskin lectured in Edinburgh on Pre-Raphaelitism and Gothic Architecture, and in 1854 he gave, in London, three lectures to working men on the Art of Illumination. He then advocated the sublime art of going backwards, so that we might get more forward, *reculer pour mieux sauter*. He had written for the *Quarterly* in 1847.

H

In 1851 he issued his pamphlet on Church discipline—
"The Construction of Sheepfolds;" in 1854 he wrote
on the opening of the Crystal Palace at Sydenham, anent
the protection of Art Antiquities throughout Europe.
For the Arundel Society he wrote a notice of Giotto
and his works, and, in 1855, he showed the *Times*
critic and others how to write, in his "Notes on the
Academy Exhibition." We have, besides, the "Two
Paths," the "Harbours of England," the "Political
Economy of Art," and then the idea of Political
Economy became strong upon him. "Unto this Last"
were essays in the *Cornhill Magazine;* "Sesame and
Lilies," "The Ethics of Dust," "Kings' Treasuries
and Queens' Gardens," and three lectures on "War,
Commerce, and Work," and afterwards "Letters to a
Working Man," which were first published in the
Manchester Examiner, and which will sink deeper and
deeper in men's minds, till they in some measure
revolutionise our ideas of property.

For Ruskin's words are weighty, socialistic, Christian, and yet revolutionary. We who believe in
Christ do not stand still; in word and deed we utter
something for the sake of the brethren; we are on the
hill top here in England, but the light shines from
other hill tops too. Let us explain ourselves. In
"Unto this Last," Ruskin had penetrated the fact that
the terrible want and poverty, want of sweetness and
light, is only to be remedied by more justice to the

workman, by lifting him up and taking his children
out of the dust. But how to do this? Leaving
poetry, Ruskin comes here to common-sense, and
puts down four axioms with, as he finely says, "a
plausible idea at the root." They are (1) "That
labour should be considered as elevating. (2) That
all reform should be conducted in the spirit of love.
(3) That all *workmen should be paid as soldiers are,
regardless of excellence* or greater capacity of production; literally, as in the parable, 'unto this last.'
And (4) One of the most important conditions for the
establishment of a healthy system of social economy
*would be the restraint of the properties and incomes of the
upper classes beyond fixed limits.*" Study that sentence,
because its spirit is now abroad; if you have a right
to divert the incomes of a church, a much greater
right have you to meddle with the unearned wages
of the rich. In Ruskin you will find the politics of
the future.

For his style, we give but one, a description of
Verona, which, for the benefit of his hearers, he contrasted with Edinburgh when lecturing in that city:

"I remember a city, more nobly placed even than Edinburgh,
which, instead of the valley now filled by lines of railroad, has a
broad and rushing river of blue water sweeping through the
heart of it; which, for the dark and solitary rock that bears
your castle, has an amphitheatre of cliffs crested with cypresses
and olive; which, for the two masses of Arthur's Seat and the
ravages of the Pentlands, has a chain of blue mountains higher

than the haughtiest peaks of the Highlands ; and which, for the
far-away Ben Ledi and Ben More, has the great central chain of
the St. Gothard Alps ; and yet, as you go out of the gates, and
walk in the suburban streets of that city—I mean Verona—the
eye never seeks to rest on that external scenery, however gorgeous ; it does not look for the gaps between the houses ; it may
for a few moments follow the broken lines of the great Alpine
battlements ; but it is only where they form a background for
other battlements, built by the hand of man. There is no neces-
sity felt to dwell on the blue river or the burning hill. The heart
and eye have enough to do in the streets of the city itself ; they
are contented there ; nay, they sometimes turn from the natural
scenery, as if too savage and solitary, to dwell with a deeper
interest on the palace walls that cast their shade upon the
streets, and the crowd of towers that rise out of that shadow into
the depth of the sky. That is a city to be proud of indeed."

In 1870 Mr. Ruskin was appointed Slade-Professor
of Art, at Cambridge, and has recently issued his
lectures in a volume from which we quote this noble
passage :

" So far from art being immoral, little else except art is moral ;
that life without industry is guilt, and industry without art is
brutality : and for the words ' good ' and ' wicked,' used of men,
you may almost substitute the words ' Makers ' or ' Destroyers.'
For the greater part of the seeming prosperity of the world is,
so far as our present knowledge extends, vain ; wholly useless
for any kind of good, but having assigned to it a certain in-
evitable sequence of destruction and of sorrow. Its stress is
only the stress of wandering storm ; its beauty the hectic of
plague : and what is called the history of mankind is too often
the record of the whirlwind, and the map of the spreading of the
leprosy But underneath all that, or in narrow spaces of dominion
in the midst of it, the work of every man, ' qui non accepit in

vanitatem animam suam,' endures and prospers ; a small remnant or green bud of it prevailing at last over evil. And though
faint with sickness, and encumbered in ruin, the true workers
redeem, inch by inch, the wilderness into garden ground ; by
the help of their joined hands the order of all things is surely
sustained and vitally expanded, and although with strange
vacillation, in the eyes of the watcher, the morning cometh, and
also the night, there is no hour of human existence that does
not draw on towards the perfect day.

"And perfect the day shall be, when it is of all men understood that the beauty of Holiness must be in labour as well as
in rest. Nay ! *more*, if it may be, in labour ; in our strength,
rather than in our weakness ; and in the choice of what we shall
work for through the six days, and may know to be good at their
evening time, than in the choice of what we pray for on the
seventh, of reward or repose. With the multitude that keep
holiday, we may perhaps sometimes vainly have gone up to the
house of the Lord, and vainly there asked for what we fancied
would be mercy ; but for the few who labour as their Lord
would have them, the mercy needs no seeking, and their wide
home no hallowing. Surely goodness and mercy shall *follow*
them, *all* the days of their life ; and they shall dwell in the house
of the Lord—FOR EVER."—*Lectures on Art.*

Here is a writer after our own heart ; no dreamer
after Arthur and his knights, no searcher after Holy
Grails, no petty describer of sensation trials for murder or adultery, no mere painter of comic people who
never existed, of " character " which boils and bubbles
only in his own too humorous brain. For while
Ruskin tells us of Function, bé sure that he honours
the function of the writer, and that is *not* merely to
distract nor to amuse, not to take us now to Thebes,
now to Athens, as Horace has it, to make us weep,

laugh, or creep all over at mere ghosts—no, ten thousand times No! It is—this noble function of a writer which John Ruskin has nobly discharged—to bind our hearts closer to our brothers, and to lift our souls nearer unto God!

THE ETHICS OF RUSKIN.

THE ETHICS OF RUSKIN.

HESE are the times," wrote Thomas Paine, the infidel and agitator, in No. 1 of *The Crisis*—"these are the times that try men's souls." That was a forcible sentence, worthy of the title of the paper—*The Crisis*. But we all live in a "crisis," and all times try men's souls; indeed, each age adapts its trial and its pressure with abundant care, so that each soul finds the burden and the sore weight, nor need complain when others are tried as well. But these *are* times, we will say, that have peculiar trials. Such is man's conceit. Before the births of conquerors and kings, Nature—fond nurse of these fortunate great ones—had given note that the future has something worth seeing behind her veil. Before great Julius died, as Shakespeare, musically repeating Plutarch, lets us know, old Beldame Earth was in strange taking: hurricanes toppled down towers, in the sky floated ashes and stars of fire, comets flew eccentrically here and there, and the sheeted ghosts did squeak and gibber in the Roman streets! To what purpose were these warnings, if

they ever existed ?   A miracle twice repeated becomes
no miracle ; nay, we shall have learned men who will
just look again into that miracle and prove that it is
but a law.   So we, of a sceptical age, are rightly
sceptical as to these peculiar times.   The exordium
may do for the ordinary preacher who wishes to wake
up his drowsy flock; but it will not serve us.   The
present times are fraught with severe lessons, big
with the future; but not more so than others.   We
have had the most brutal revelations of cold-blooded
murders plotted in peaceful, Christian England, by
those lamb-like martyrs, the working men.   We have
had a congress of idle men, sitting like a secret
society, a band of assassins, or the *Vehme Gerichte*,
and decreeing that one of their number shall be
maimed, wounded, put out of the way, or shot to
death, because he dared to try and gain a free and
honest living.   We have had popular teachers and
writers, who yelled like angry madmen at Governor
Eyre for saving an English colony by the court-
martial trial of a rebellious negro, silent as to the
murderer Broadhead, because he was and is a so-
called working man, and so-called working men take
in their papers.   We have had organised bands of
roughs who broke down the Park palings, and a
member of Parliament who apologised for them.   We
have had a meeting of Conservative working men
mobbed, hooted, hounded, and beaten out of a public

hall, in which they had legitimately called a meeting, by Radical Reformers, who, at the same time, claimed liberty of speech, and shrieked with comic indignation because not allowed to speak in Hyde Park, which never was intended but for recreation. We have had organised desperadoes rob sixty, or seventy, or a hundred people in the open day in London streets; and a Protestant lecturer stir up a Romanist mob to riotous ruin in Birmingham; and yet these are not extraordinary times. Our union murders have existed for one hundred years, and we have lived through them. Our workmen have been so ill-advised, so petted by goody books and ignorant editors, that at the Paris Exhibition we were beaten on our own ground. While the workman strikes and starves for fancied wrongs, while our teachers have for twenty-five years been ashamed of Protestant feelings and Bible teachings, our newspaper writers have been ere this more ignorant than they are now; and this is all the comfort we can give anyone—we have lived through all this, so we are actually not living in strange times. But this is certain, there is a great change coming; and John Ruskin, one of our greatest modern teachers, has been the first, or one of the first, to warn us of it. As an Art critic, he has done much good. He brought love, truth, honesty, vision, knowledge, to bear on Art. He cut deep into that shameless obstruction, the Royal Academy; he exalted new men. Mr.

Millais owes much to Mr. Ruskin; he made the pre-Raphaelites; indeed, his success made them foolishly conceited, and spoilt them somewhat; but this he intended not. A singularly quick and fertile thinker, he produced some noble works very rapidly, and in these he scattered such wonderfully eloquent thoughts, such noble vindications of God's works, that no one English writer, save Jeremy Taylor, can be cited, who can show such blood, life, colour, motion, passion, and reality in his sentences. Ruskin's words live; they are not merely bits of type—there they are, and there they will be. But it is not to these, which will remain great monuments for artists to refer to, that we would point at present. We have other work to do; for Ruskin, abandoning now for some time the province of Art teacher, in which he is first, has taken to a wider school, perhaps the noblest that a mere modern prose writer can take up, that of teacher of Political Economy to a nation which boasts of its economists, and believes itself to be, rightly or wrongly, the foremost nation, as regards that science, in the world.

Now, Political Economy has a name to young ladies and vapid young gentlemen which is the most deadly and tiresome, and yet it is the most vital, sweet, and interesting. It resembles that philosophy of which Milton sang that it was charming and divine—

> " Not harsh and crabbèd, as dull fools suppose,
> But musical as is Apollo's lute."

The mission of Moses was economic, for he propounded the *Oikonomia*, or house-law, whereby every
man should go in and possess the land, and every one
in the vast tribes of Israel should dwell at peace, and
no one should hurt his neighbour ; or if, by mischance,
he did so, he should atone for it, if by crime, should
suffer ; so that goodness should abound, wisdom
should be exalted, peace should ensue ; the ways of
the Lord should be known as pleasant ways, and
their sons should " grow up as the young plants," and
the daughters should be chaste, pure, and beautiful
" as the polished corners of the temple." True
economy, then, is the science of life ; it comprehends
the best knowledge of the world, it concerns itself
with the happiness of man, it makes life sweeter and
better ; it restrains the evil, exalts the good, banishes
selfishness, makes us understand the luxury of virtue,
and undertakes to supply the greatest happiness to
the greatest number. It must be founded not on selfishness, but on religion ; not on mere political *dicta*,
or the garbled, ill-conceived maxims of the trader ;
not on the interested notions of either the consumer
or the producer, but on certain canons, which, generously conceived and wisely interpreted, in giving
good to one, will give it also to all.

It is not too much to say that Mr. Ruskin's political
economy aims at all this. He is a great man and a
wise thinker ; but we must not suppose that his

doctrines are therefore received at once by the political quidnuncs who patch up old ideas of selfishness,
which they call Political Economy.   Mr. Ruskin's
essays are full of forcible, eloquent writing.   They
were received partly with ridicule, partly with a
vacant non-comprehension, partly with indignant
denial; but they have, as he himself says of Political
Economy, "a plausible idea at the root."

Of course numbers 3 and 4 are propositions* which
have been received with loud denials and indignant
protestations; and it is but fair to say that Ruskin
has hardly developed his theory, since certain letters,
published in a Manchester paper, are not yet republished by himself, corrected and annotated; so that
even in these deductions, except in the last, which
we quote in his own words, we may be guilty of some
error.   However, his ethics have made a very great,
and very deep and wide sensation.

A correspondent, writing to us to request our
opinion on these things, says: "I send you these
letters, but I still retain a few, which are really unfit
for perusal, having been well thumbed by 'greasy
mechanics' in a mechanic's greasy workshop during
meal and leisure hours, when the hands are rather
black, and the reading-desks are massive but dirty
castings.   We believe you to be a leader of thought
and opinion in England; and there are not a few of

* See page 99.

us here who desire to have your opinion upon these as soon as possible." Now, papers that are read by working men at Ancoats, will be read and pondered over by working men all over the world, and working men now have the position in their own hands. The relations of capital (which we take here to be mere money and possessions, not brain capital, which the labourer also has) and labour are undergoing a revision, and it would be mere cowardice to shut our eyes to the fact. Mr. Ruskin earnestly desires to "remove the temptation to use every energy for the possession of wealth," and in that we have long been with him. He desires earnestly to benefit mankind, and he believes that this gentle spoliation of the too rich classes will be gradually brought into force from beneath, without any violent or impatient proceedings. These are weighty words; and among all our weekly and daily teachers we have not yet found a man able and willing to tackle their author or confute his arguments, unfinished and inchoate as they yet are.

To state Mr. Ruskin's case fairly, we must first refer to our definition of true Political Economy as given above, and reiterate that the basis of his teaching is generosity or charitable (affectionate) feeling towards man. "You have seen long ago," he wrote to a friend on the 7th of last March, "that the essential difference between the Political Economy I am trying to teach and the popular science, is, that mine

is based *on presumably attained honesty in men,* and
conceivable respect in them for the interests of others,
while the popular science founds itself wholly on their
own supposed constant regard for their own" (interest).
This is perfectly true. To make as much as one
could, to govern by dividing others, to buy in the
cheapest and to sell in the dearest market, to rise
early so that one could anticipate others "in picking
up the worm," these were the destructive axioms of
Economy, falsely so called. But Mr. Ruskin wisely
puts all that aside as an error. "Your way of making
money so that you may be the head of a village, the
only rich man amongst hundreds of poor," he would
say, "is a selfish, vicious way; and, because vicious,
it is unwise. You corrupt yourselves, and you render
others envious. How dwelleth the love of God in you?"
Of course, this teaching of Ruskin, the lifting up of
the community, the cultivation of each and singular,
is not new. It is merely God's law, the Bible law,
and therefore Christian law, for Christianity is the
most levelling of all religions; it lifts the poor man
out of the mire to set him among princes, and the
great prince it makes low. Few people can quote the
Bible, as few people have so well studied it, better
than Ruskin: with him it is a force, a weapon—a
very two-edged sword. In the letter quoted he puts
forward the Bible to prove that song, and dance, and
wine, were given to man to make glad his heart in

religious ceremonies, not to be prostituted to the wretched *can-can* of the French, nor to the Covent Garden Pantomime with its "forty clever swells," young women half undressed, smoking forty bad cigars, neither to the drunkenness and stupid howlings of a Swiss harvest home. And then, taking the lowest human estimation of the Bible, he argues upon *that;* so that putting aside Divine authority, he proves " how peculiarly ghastly is our festivity in its utter joylessness, in the paralysis and helplessness of a vice in which there is neither pleasure nor art." And in watching and reporting on certain Parisian dancers who have since appeared in London, he says : " Nothing could be better done in its own evil way, the object of the dance being throughout to express in every gesture the wildest fury of insolence and vicious passions possible in human nature. So that, you see, though for the present we find ourselves utterly incapable of a rapture of gladness and thanksgiving, the dance which is presented as characteristic of modern civilisation is still rapturous enough, but it is the rapture of blasphemy."

The argument to be drawn from these powerful but somewhat raphsodical letters seems to be, that we are as much gone out of the true way in Political Economy as in dancing. We want recalling to true Art ; and whether we take the Bible as a book of mere wise sentences, or as a book every syllable of which is inspired, we are equally wrong. And here we may give

I

Mr. Ruskin's view of the Bible, which he so constantly studies.   There are, he says, four ways of regarding it.   The 1st, " As being dictated by the Supreme Being, and every syllable of it His Word."   This theory is, he adds, of course "tenable by no ordinarily well-educated person."   The 2nd is, " That though admitting verbal error, the Bible is absolutely true, furnished to man by the Divine Inspiration of the speakers and writers thereof, and that every one who honestly and prayerfully seeks for such truth as is necessary for salvation, will infallibly find it there." " This," he continues, " is the theory held by most of our good and upright clergymen, and the better class of the professedly religious laity ; " among which we may assuredly reckon Mr. Ruskin.   The third theory, denying the inspiration, allows the historical accuracy, the record of " true miracles," and of a " true witness to the resurrection and the life to come."   This is the theory held by most of the active leaders of modern thought.   The fourth and last possible theory places the Bible on a par with the best moral books of the Egyptians, Greeks, Persians, and Indians, and that it is with them to be reverently studied.   And so certain is Ruskin of the truth of his Economies, that he addresses this fourth class of thinkers, and appeals to the Book which for some 1,500 years has been the chief guide of Europe, which forbids pride, lascivious-ness, and covetousness—which enjoins truth, temper-

ance, equity, and charity. Now, all great thinkers have
done the same; *ergo*, on that humble basis and premiss
Ruskin builds up his theories, and from that small coin
of vantage they will assuredly go forth and conquer.

His faults are not many, but we may mention them.
He preaches a kind of Communism, which, although
practised by the Apostles and early Christians, was
in no way commanded, and which nowhere, except in
Utopian Cloud Land, could exist beneficially. He
believes too much in worldly prosperity *for the mass*,
while he rightly tells us how miserably evil it is to
almost all individuals. He talks very proudly and
cruelly of those who, like us, have "dared to inso-
lently preach contentment to a man with thirty
shillings a-week;" and he is hasty in his denuncia-
tions of follies which arise from education, from a long
peace and prosperity, and from the cowardice of our
preachers and our writers for many years, and from
the selfishness of the ministries of all parties, who
have given all the honours and rewards to rich men,
and have therefore made riches the only incentive.
But Ruskin has a very noble heart, and one that is
very tender, too; is most nobly eloquent, and will be
listened to; he sympathises with poverty and ignorance, but is tempestuously moved at vice and folly,
forgetting that they are the saddest phases of poverty
and ignorance. He raises up a warning voice at a
time when change has come upon us, and tells us to

go back to the old times of earnestness, of trade guilds,
of honour, obedience, reverence; of industry and
work in each man; "every youth in the State, from
the King's son downwards, should learn to do something finely and thoroughly,"—not forward to mere
wallowing in wealth, and corrupting, selfish ease.
And Ruskin must be listened to; or else, so surely
as we allow thousands to starve in ignorance and
want, to fester in slothful ease, to plot and plan
selfish murders, to die starving and helpless while we
are full of meat and wine, to go on in the wretched
ignorant way we allow our lowest classes to do, we shall
pass away as Persia and Greece and Rome have passed
away, with more guilt to ourselves and less excuse.
"Take unto yourselves heed," says Joshua, "that
ye love the Lord your God; else if ye do in any wise
go back, know for a certainty that the Lord your
God will no more drive out any of these nations
before you; but they shall be snares and traps unto
you, and scourges in your sides, and thorns in your
eyes, until ye perish from off this good land which
the Lord your God hath given you." These, simply,
are the ethics of John Ruskin, even the ethics of the
Bible. Let us be just, and fear not; let us follow
this great teacher; but alas! how can we be just,
when out of one thousand children in Manchester,
barely four hundred can read, and the rest are
ignorant, and know not good from evil?

ROBERT BROWNING.

ROBERT BROWNING.

I**N that marvellous opening of "Faust" where
the Poet, the Manager of the theatre, and
Mr. Merryman** *(der lustige Person)* **debate**
as to the proper thing to put before the public,
the Poet demands for his art the chief admiration ;
the Manager, on the contrary, thinks of the scenery,
and Mr. Merryman of fun and frolic. The Poet says
of himself, and quite truly, that

> " His voice is fame ; he gives us to inherit
>   Olympus and the loved Elysian field.
>   The soul of man sublimed—man's soaring spirit
>   Lives in the POET gloriously reveal'd."

Whereto Mr. Merryman makes a very wise and
beautiful answer :

> " A poet yet should regulate his fancies ;
>   *   *   *   *
>   For oh the secrets of the poet's art,
>   What are they but the dreams of the young heart ?
>   Oh, 'tis the young enjoy the poet's mood,
>   Float with him on imagination's wing,

> Think all his thoughts, are his in everything,
> Are, while they dream not of it, all they see !"*

And then Goethe launches out into one of those marvellously subtle, daring, and tender expositions which make him what he is.

We need this reference when speaking of Robert Browning. With him we feel that a poet gives man something to inherit, while at the same time he makes us repeat with Mr. Merryman that sentence about "regulating his fancies." Half the English-speaking world could not understand Browning; let us say two-thirds, or three-fourths; or what do you say to nine-tenths? Take all the people who really can read Shakespeare with pleasure, and comprehend that clear, deep, intense writer; not one-half of these could understand Browning. And yet he is a great poet, deep, intense, but seldom quite clear. He thinks

---

* The Poet *der Dichter* seems also to feel this, and in one of his bursts of intensely beautiful but egoistic poetry says :

> " Gieb ungebändigt jene Triebe,
> Das tiefe schmerzenvolle Glück
> Des haffes kraft, die macht der Liebe
> Gieb meine jugend mi zurück!"

Thus translated by Dr. Anster :

> " Give me, oh give, youth's passions unconfined,
> The rush of joy that felt almost like pain,
> Its hale, its love, its own tumultous mind ;
> Give me my youth again ! "

too quickly; and he involves the reader in a crowd
of similes and expositions, which come tumbling over
one another as "the water comes down at Lodore."
He is a fit instance of the "palpable obscure." He
affects titles to his books as strange as does Ruskin.
Shakespeare gives his works plain, bolt-upright
names,—"Julius Cæsar," "Macbeth;" or gently
sweet and modest titles cap his works,—"A Winter's
Tale," "A Midsummer Night's Dream," or "All's
Well that Ends Well." But our cultivators of the
palpable obscure—much as we love what is good in
them, we hate their folly—launch out into such titles
as "Pippa Passes," "Bells and Pomegranates,"
"Idylls of the King," "Oriana," "Ethics of Dust,"
"Kings' Treasuries and Queens' Gardens"—and so
on. They do this to attract attention, because they
are weak, not strong, because they are affected with
their weight of poetry; whereas the true giants bore
their burden of genius modestly, and were all the
better poets for not exhibiting the modern poetic
strut.

But of modern poets we are, for many reasons,
inclined to rank Robert Browning as the first, before
Tennyson, Swinburne, or Morris; and he is one that
has played a waiting game, and has never been
crowned by elated crowds like Tennyson. Moreover,
Browning is a poet with poets; he grows upon us.
There was a time when he said truly, that of his

books the writer and the reader were one and the same: he himself was all the public that he had. But now he can venture upon the wildest thing that any modern poet ever did; that is, he can publish a poem in four volumes, at 7s. 6d. each, telling in each volume the same story three times over; and he can command a public for this extraordinary work of art.

Robert Browning is, as may be seen from his portraits, a handsome, bold, defiant-looking man, with somewhat of a poet's earnest gaze. He does not possess the super-essential outward mask of a poet, as did Robert Southey, of whom Byron said that he looked more like a bard than anyone he ever met. He has not what is vulgarly called a "poetic" appearance, that is, he wears a well-made coat, and does not muffle himself up in a cloak; and yet he looks quite sufficiently a poet. He is of mature age, having been born in 1812. He was educated at the London University. In 1836 Browning published his truly poetic first work, "Paracelsus;" in 1837 he produced his tragedy of "Strafford," a subtle but not an acting tragedy; full of fine lines and subtle thoughts, but which no audience would now sit out. All that Macready could do to "mount" and produce the play was done; but it was a failure. The "Blot on the 'Scutcheon," produced in 1843, was a very fine acting play, but unsuccessful; for in those days there

were numbers of poetic playwrights, authors of unacted dramas of merit, who neglected the interests
and action of the piece merely to put into the mouths
of the actors fine sentiments in blank verse. The
"unacted drama" became then a synonym for fine
words; the acted drama was bald, devoid of merit,
and depended, as it does now, upon mere situation,
sensation, and farce. Since that time Browning has
not given us an acting drama, but has confined himself to dramatic poetry and to dramatic scenes. In
1840 he published "Sordello," a mysterious work;
in '46, "Bells and Pomegranates;" in '50, "Christmas
Eve and Easter Day;" in 55, "Men and Women."
In '62 Messrs. Chapman & Hall published "Selections from the Works of Robert Browning," a charming volume, not to be confounded with another
subsequent selection published by another firm,
which is comparatively worthless. In '64 the poet
issued "Dramatis Personæ," and in '69 the four
volumes called "The Ring and the Book," a poem,
as we have said, told twelve times over by different
people.

Now, what excuse have we to make for Robert
Browning's having so pertinaciously troubled the
public? For that is one way to look at it. Accursed
be those preachers who have nothing to say, and who
fill up the world with vain babblement and the strife
of tongues! Not every one has the divine gift of

song; and for some that have, and who have wasted
it in mere licentiousness, or in feminine folly, better
were it had they never been born.   As to Browning,
there is this to be said, that he felt deeply what was
poetic, and tried vigorously to express it.   He had,
too, some real merit about him ; but it was not of an
easy, popular kind; and although there was, when
he appeared in 1835, a great opening for a poet—
Shelley, Byron, Keats, and Southey being dead, and
Wordsworth beyond any new and fresh expression—
neither Browning nor Alfred Tennyson, who had
lately published his volume, filled the vacant place.
Both volumes were received by the robust public of
that day with contempt.   Tennyson had written in
puling accents about Adeline " sweetly smiling,"
Fatima, Oriana, and a dozen other pretty names,
and over the literary horizon there were signs that
the disastrous advent of Woman's rule was about to
come upon us.   Soft and sweet was " school-miss
Alfred "—" Low, low, whisper low," " Oh swallow,
swallow, flying south," &c.; " Let her wind her
milk-white arms about me; let me die," &c.; but
Montrose wrote a song a thousand times more
touching, aye, and one that would please a true
woman more, in that sweet " My dear and only love : "

> " But if thou wilt prove faithful, then,
> And constant of thy word,
> I'll make thee glorious by my pen,
> And famous by my sword."

Still it must be said of Browning that he is essentially manly. "In the region of morals," writes Mr. Austin, "women may have had a beneficent influence in modern times" (not all women; some of the most immoral novels in sentiment ever published have been written by women), "but in the region of Art their influence has been unmitigatedly mischievous. They have ruined the stage." (This is quite true; there is now no opening, so to speak, for a really good, mature actress; all that is demanded is supplied by pretty, painted young girls in silk tights, and with plenty of false hair.) "They have dwarfed painting till it has become the mere representative of pretty little sentiment—much of it terribly false—and mawkish, common-place domesticities; and they have helped poetry to become, in the hands of Mr. Tennyson, at least, and his followers, the handmaid of their own limited interests, susceptibilities, and yearnings." "Every-day evidence makes it clear," says Mr. Swinburne, "that our time has room enough only for such as are content to write for children and girls."

Now, Mr. Browning has not helped on this state of things; he has not cut down all things to the mere drawing-room standard. His "Paracelsus," a marvellously subtle and studious poem, was at least beyond that. Here is the history of it: Paracelsus—Theophrastus Paracelsus Bombastus de Hohenheim

—was a half-mad braggart and German physician of the Middle Ages, who discovered the use of opium, and did his best to rescue medicine from the disgrace of being the most ignorant "science" in the world. His history may be read in many a magazine article, for it has a strange charm. This braggart doctor (a great quack by the way, always vaunting himself) Mr. Browning took as his hero. He elevates him into a kind of Faust, without the superhuman machinery, and he contrasts this super-fine braggart with a simpler creation, his friend Aprile, and the motives of the two men are thus contrasted:

> PAR. His secret !—I shall get his secret, fool. I am
>   The mortal who aspired to KNOW ; and thou——
> APRI. I would LOVE infinitely, and be loved.
> PAR. Poor slave ! I am thy king indeed !

In the end, after various adventures and thoughts, poured out thick and slab, often in the most rugged verse that can be conceived—involved, knotted, twisted, and obscure—hard, and yet sometimes beautiful as the striæ and stains in malachite or mar-ble—the two ambitions are brought again into con-trast, and Paracelsus, chastened by defeat, and blinded even by the vast expanse of the KNOWABLE, beaten down by the infinity of God's work and know-ledge, and the wondrous purpose of life as yet behind the veil, dies, with his friend Festus kneeling by him. Aprile has died some time before, hoping and trusting in his faith in love; and Paracelsus, as he dies, reverts to him and to his doctrine, which he admits the wiser. Here are some sweet lines upon lost love:

> " 'Tis only when they spring to Heaven, that angels
> Reveal themselves to you ; they sit all day
> Beside you, and lie down at night by you,
> Who care not for their presence. Muse or sleep,
> And all at once they leave you, and you know them.
> We are so fool'd and cheated ! "

And the dying words of Paracelsus are as beautiful as they are wise. He finds that *love* should always precede *power*. With much power should always be more love, or man becomes a tyrant. His own failure was because he did not understand this. He failed—and why ? Because—

> " In my own heart love had not been made wise :
> To trace love's faint beginnings in mankind ;
> To know even hate is but a mask of Love's ;
> To see a good in evil, and a hope
> In ill success ; to sympathise—be proud
> Of their half-reasonings, faint aspirings, struggles
> Dimly for truth, their poorest fallacies,
> And prejudice and fears, and cares and doubts ;
> All with a touch of nobleness, for all
> Their error, all ambitions, upward tending,
> Like plants in mines, which never saw the sun,
> But dream of him, and guess where he may be,
> And do their best to climb and get to him,—
> All this I knew not, and I fail'd."

This is very beautiful, *O, si sic omnia!* The critics, who have done much harm, received it not as Hamlet bids us receive strange truth,—" And therefore as a stranger give it welcome,"—but served Browning almost as they had served Keats. "We can assure our readers," says the *Quarterly Review* (of Keats), "that this young man's poems were received with all but a universal shout of laughter!" Contemplate the Philistines laughing at Sampson! Critics did not understand Browning; so they abused him.

One, however, did understand him, and she was Miss Elizabeth Barrett, unquestionably the finest female poet that England has produced. She married Browning, and lived with him in Italy for many years most happily. She was but of delicate health, a learned poetess, of equal calibre with, some say higher than, her husband. She herself did not think so; nor do we. There can hardly be conceived a more beautiful or enviable life than that of these two singers, each aspiring for the freedom of Italy, the progress of knowledge, the higher exaltation of the soul. Gradually the public came round to their way of viewing matters. One rich gentleman left them, it is said, a legacy, £5,000 each, for their good work; and editions of their poems began actually to be published without loss! At last, a few years ago, when the fame of both was established, the health of Mrs. Browning gave way, and she died at Florence on the

29th of June, 1861, leaving her love but a memory, and to her poet husband, as he tells us in these lines, her memory but a prayer for help and strength. Thus he speaks to her spirit in his last poem :

> " O lyric love ! half-angel and half-bird,
>   And all a wonder and a wild desire—
>   Boldest of hearts that ever braved the sun,
>   Took sanctuary within the holier blue,
>   And sang a kindred soul out to his face—
>   Yet human at the red-ripe of the heart—
>   When the first summons from the darkling earth
>   Reach'd thee amid thy chambers, blanch'd their blue,
>   And bared them of the glory—to drop down,
>   To toil for man, to suffer, or to die—
>   This is the same voice : can thy soul know change?
>   Hail, then, and hearken from the realms of help ! "

Beautiful as this is, the reader will find it very obscure. No one, for instance, could parse it or render it grammatical. That is a grave fault. Besides " Paracelsus," and other hard thought-out dramatic pieces, Browning has become celebrated for his Lyrics—" How they brought the good news to Ghent," &c., and for a certain ethical, philosophic, and even theologic kind of verse,—" Mr. Sludge, the Medium," " Caliban on Setebos," " Bishop Blougram," in which the poet, entering into the soul of his character, a half brute, a Yankee rogue, or a Roman Catholic bishop, makes him think out and reveal in involved speech the nature of his character.

K

These poems are simply entrancing to those who love (and we are of them) the studious, reflecting method of the author. To the vast public they are perhaps obscure ; in all probability they are not quite true, not so true as the inner searchings of Iago into his own villainy, or of Cassius into his own ambition, but they are very fine. Caliban, in his island, reflecting on the nature of God, reasons just as an utterly selfish, untaught savage would ; Bishop Blougram as an educated priest, from whose heart all real faith in his calling had disappeared, but who yet thought it necessary to keep up appearances. As poets live chiefly by a reflected fame, and as the sweet small-meaning of Tennyson begins now to pale, there has arisen a party which places Browning at the head of modern poets, and is glad to objurgate its former idol, Tennyson. There are people who believe that eccentricity is genius, and that if they think differently from the crowd, they think better than the crowd. These, of course, joined the new sect ; and, without belonging either to the one group or the other, we confess that we think with them.

Browning is a much deeper, more manly, and more subtle thinker than Tennyson ; both hold their own office in high esteem ; Tennyson, it seems to some, cherishes an overweening conceit of his own work. The first is analytic ; the poet is with him, to quote his own head-lines, "Epoist, dramatist, or, so to call him, analyst, who turns in due course synthesist;" the other is equally proud of his singing robes, and so much worships not only old times, but the nobility of man, that in effect he is a pantheist. But both of them lack the highest *status* of the poet, of Shakespeare, of Robert Burns, of a dozen other smaller in size, but equal in quality, who sang out of the nature of the heart, because music, love, veneration, worship, and wonder were in their souls, and they became poets as larks soaring up to heaven become singing-birds—because God puts the song into their throats, and they can't help rejoicing in the sweet expression, the *exosmosis*, flowing outwards—to use a chemical term—which they find it impossible to repress.

Such poets are not laborious and involved. Knowing their innate strongly natural power, they do not brag about it, nor write laudations of their office,—they best praise it by practising it; but some of our modern bards, who are not so great either, strut and talk loudly, pretend that they are within an ace of comprehending God and Infinity (as in Tennyson's "Flower in the crannied wall"), and run off from obscurity to obscurity, to produce poetry by art (of which, too, they talk a good deal), forgetting that the Art itself is Nature.

K 2

MR. ANTHONY TROLLOPE.

MR. ANTHONY TROLLOPE.

E protest that in the reference to Tennyson we have not been unjust. We love him as well as most young ladies; perhaps we understand him better. But it is a sign of a weak age when living men of letters are puffed up with a flatulent laudation, and are exalted above the illustrious dead. Any one knowing English literature will recall the dull time when Alexander Pope was elevated above that poor creature, Shakespeare, who was looked upon as a wildly-luxuriant clownish genius who wanted improving—as he has been improved by Tate and Cibber. There still was a galaxy of poets all revolving round one central star—Garth, Tickle, Spratt, King, Eusden, Sheffield! How dreary read those names now, and yet each man had —egad, each man has—merit. They were very pretty fellows, but flattery in their day slew them. Before you condemn them wholly, read them. They were not entirely without some good; yet in their days their flatterers made them gods. Now, Tennyson

is just as far from Shakespeare as ever Tickle, or
Garth, or Eusden is from him;—and Mr. Anthony
Trollope is about as far from Fielding.

Yet we all like Trollope much. He writes "as
a gentleman for gentlemen," as the phrase of the
day has it, as if Homer, the led-blind man as they
called the nameless one, wrote only for one class.
But in this picked age, you see, we label our works
of genius. Every vapid shilling's worth *testibus*
Tyburnia or *The Best Society*—you could not go farther
from good literature, nor fare worse on the whole—
describes itself as a "first-class" magazine. That
is why such are purchased only by third-class pas-
sengers, and those flunkeys and housemaids who
shoulder us poor Bohemians in the second-class.
Every paper is a first-class organ, and essentially in
this meaning Mr. Anthony Trollope is a first-class
novelist, and yet he is very clever, and has had an
effect on this age. "Sir," says a character in Jerrold's "Housekeeper," "I am a student of human
nature." "Yes," retorts his interlocutor, "you
study human nature as a housebreaker does a house,
to take advantage of its weakest parts." Trollope has done
this with our parsons. Of him we may say that he

"To parsons gave up what was meant for mankind."

For from the Bishop and his wife in "Barchester
Towers" to that good old fellow, the Rev. Mr.

Crawley, who puts the noble ballad of Lord Bateman into. Greek verse, preserving the measure and the rhyme, Trollope is never tired of introducing us inside the clerical waistcoat. Do we think anything better of the parsons? We know parsons well, and, upon the whole—though we find them men like ourselves, sometimes not too elevated, not too self-sacrificial, not too noble—we can only think that the clerics drawn by Trollope are a disgrace, and almost a libel. We do not say that they are not true. They are photographically true, but they are never so from the highest and noblest sight-point. Van-dyke, whose portraits are true to nature, and Lawrence, in a lower way, never painted anything but a gentleman or a lady. So some few of our photographers elevate their photographic sitters. They take them at their best. They look clever, well, at ease, capable. Other artists stand on a lower ground, and give us those sombre, hard-featured, commonplace English men and women who make our photographic albums a horror, and the portraits of our actresses in the shop windows a sin and a disgrace. Mr. Trollope hath dealt somewhat after this fashion with our clergy. He has not done any better with our dukes and men in office; he has not flattered our pretty commonplace English girls, and as for our equally commonplace young Englishmen, let Johnny Eames bear witness that he pictured them

as very ordinary Philistines and fools. And yet we all
read him, and like him. What is the power he has
over us? Simply there is but one answer. It is art—it
may be commonplace art, but it is art. Mr. Trollope
is a literary workman of a sort; but a true workman.

His outward appearance symbolises, or rather
pictures, his inner. When you look at his face, you
exclaim, with Addison's Cato, " Plato, thou reasonest
well." For, as that great one said, the soul chooses
a fit house wherein to dwell, you must own that the
soul of Trollope has fitted itself with a proper and suggestive tabernacle. His portrait is gaunt, grim, partly
grey, and looks taller than he is; his eyes are notice-
able, dark, and brilliant; two strong lines down each
side of his mouth, lost in a tufted American-like
beard, give him a look of greater ill-nature than he
possesses. He is unquestionably a gentleman, but
of the middle-class look, by no means of the *haut
école.* He gives one an idea—that is, if one knows
life and town pretty well—that he has seen hard
service in the drudgery of some government office;
he has a cut-and-dried official look, and seems capable of scolding and otherwise irritating his juniors.
He looks his age—about fifty-five—and is a man one
would hardly choose to confide in. A Winchester,
and afterwards a Harrow boy, he gave little promise
of inheriting any of the brilliant caustic genius of his
mother, whose most truthful pictures of the United

States made the Americans hate her; while her immortal figure of the widow Barnaby caused her sex never to forgive her.

His inherited genius is of a different kind, less incisive, much less vulgar, as people have it, but, as we think, far inferior. The sons of great ones generally show this. There are living men of letters who inherit the *nomen et preterea nihil* else of the father, and who yet pick up a decent living on their intangible estate. Neither Anthony, nor his brother Thomas Adolphus, who is five years his senior, owe anything to their mother's style or manner. Both are educated gentlemen, who have been too much and too well taught to be copyists. They both write well; in his way the historian, T. A. Trollope, perhaps the better of the two, but we repeat there is not even a *soupçon* of the old flavour of Mrs. Fanny Trollope.

Anthony has been a most industrious writer. He never made a big hit or a sensation, but he has hit the public continually in the same place, and has succeeded in making an impression. From "Barchester Towers," "The Bertrams," "Castle Richmond," by far his wittiest story, to "The Small House at Allington," "Rachel Ray," "Can You Forgive Her?" "Phineas Finn," and his "Vicar of Bullhampton," which was originally bought for *Once a Week*, and now walks alone on its own hook, there are many novels, but only two distinct grounds, Irish

and clerical. The "clothes" which Trollope "occupies" are chiefly clerical, a very shabby clerical suit;
and it is hard to say whether his bishops or his
bishops' wives are the more distasteful. We don't like
either. What students in the lower life think of their
pastors and masters in the higher life, so repeated
and photographed by Trollope, we forbear to say.
They must regard them with infinite disgust. Selfish,
very meanly small and narrow, without strength
enough to be positively hateful, they amuse us, flatter
our vanity skilfully by showing us how much better
we are than they; and then they are forgotten. There
are not many notes in their music; bloodless, passion-
less, highly genteel, they are content to live and to be
fed——and their talk is like them.

These true pictures of an age very poor and weak
in its nature, very much subdued, sceptical, lym-
phatic, and with an eternal need of "prodding" and
"goading" to make it stir; of an age which could
believe in Lord Palmerston as a God-guided minister;
have found an excellent illustrator in a man who has
great merit, but which the age persists in accepting
as an illustrative artist—you might as well call him
a balloonist—John Everett Millais. He is as well
fitted to Trollope as Phiz is to Dickens. When Phiz
tried to illustrate our author, as he did in "Can You
Forgive Her?" he failed miserably; he absolutely
put life and humour into some of the figures under

which Trollope had written such subscriptions as these—dry, empty as old nuts, but singularly descriptive of the author and his mind.   Here are the titles, taken haphazard: "And you went at him at the station?" (two backs of young men, a shawl and a bonnet in the distance—*Millais*).   "Won't you take some more wine?" (old fogies drinking—*Millais*). "Would you mind shutting the window?" (young doll and withered old doll in petticoats—*Phiz*). "Bell, here's the inkstand" (female model on a ladder, back view; side view of a ditto, holding ladder—*Millais*). We will not go on.   When you look at these, you will think that the author and artist have conferred a sweet boon upon you, but your blood will not run more rapidly, nor your heart bound with nobler expansion.   At least, ours don't.   Some of our modern wooden artists, *elevés* of the great manufactory of Dalziel Bros., are *raffolent* about these cuts. "Look," they will say, "at the folds of that gown, sir!   Ah, Jove! what a coat sleeve!" Well, but what about the figure inside?

"I've seen much finer women, ripe and real,
Than all the nonsense of their stone ideal,"

said Byron.   Of course he had *not*, but that's neither here nor there.   One could not well surpass the Venus, Hercules, or Apollo in flesh and blood; but if you were to put Millais' gowns and coats into Regent Street, one could match them.

The same may be said of the author's personages.
They are made to pattern, and to supply a demand.
The public wants a commonplace English girl, and it
gets Lucy Robarts or Lilly Dale. The tone is low,
quiet; the study solid, repeatedly painted, and round;
the ideas, the manners, the very words of the day are
reproduced. Will they live? No, not twenty years!
Live! Why should they? Who would care to load
his shelves with paper and print containing such
words as these: "'Mamma, dear, give me a postage-
stamp.' 'There is one, Lilly. Are you going to the
post?' 'No, I think old John Boston will come
this way. He may as well take it.' 'So he may,'
said Mrs. Dale, thoughtfully"—and so on for pages.
But it is so real! Now is not the postage-stamp real?
Yes, as real as his women, Lady Glencora Palliser,
Mrs. Proudie, Mrs. Crawley, Mrs. Gazebee, and
the rest; as real as his men, Mr. Plantagenet Palliser,
the Duke of Omnium, Mr. Fothergill, Johnny Eames
—we need not particularise. Some of his vulgar
sketches are very clever—Mr. Scruby and the man
who travels with iron furniture, Captain Bellfield and
Mr. Chesacre. They are British Philistines proper,
and have not an ounce of nobility among the lot, and
what Mr. Trollope does not find he certainly does
not put in. His stories are drawn from such a
realistic standpoint, that the effect of reading his
books is as deadening as a photographer's glass door-

case full of ordinary men and women. Have these
people souls? Do they possess hearts and brains?
Should we be proud of belonging to such a race?
They are the true pictures of the age; can we re-
joice in the times we live in? They have not goodness enough in them to be saved. Heaven, unless a
heaven of gigs, nice clothes, and five hundred a-year,
would be utterly superfluous, they are so much lower
than the angels; neither have they force or strength
enough to be damned. An utterly relentless annihi-
lation is all that we can demand for them; practically, we give them that; we read on and on, and
forget.

Is it worth while being a novelist, however clever,
to produce so small an effect? Are clergymen always
but walking respectabilities in white chokers? Are
our mothers and sisters such quiet, shadowless dum-
mies? Have we no hopes and fears, no tears, laughter,
rejoicings, no death, no future hope beyond this earth,
no heroic feelings which lift us beyond this earth's
sphere? Thank God, good people, whose goodness
is confined to the fact that they do not swear, commonplace bishops and vinegary bishop's wives, squires
and their educated do-nothing sons, girls who feebly
intrigue as they play croquet for a good match, and
are utterly regardless of good men, are passing away.
If Mr. Trollope paints—and he paints firmly, consis-
tently, and with a quiet obstinate kind of art—all

that can be found in English society, the sooner that society is changed for something of a more decided pattern the better. No one can care for the faint and obscure outlines, and the colourless sort of wool, with which Mr. Trollope weaves his human and his faded tapestry.

MR. ALFRED TENNYSON.

L

MR. ALFRED TENNYSON.

ALFRED TENNYSON, is he not the luckiest man of letters in this very lucky age, this day of small things, this money-seeking, veneer-loving time? "Sir," said a gentleman in the stalls at the Olympic, "I can't understand 'Little Em'ly' at all." "You seldom can comprehend a dramatised novel," said we. "Have you not read 'David Copperfield?'" "Why, no; we young fellows"—he was about ten years younger than his collocutor—"have not time for *deep reading;* we are engaged in *picking up the sixpences !*"

An age that calls Dickens *deep* reading, and picks up the sixpences, will appreciate Alfred Tennyson. Look at his photograph. Deep-browed, but not deep-lined; bald, but not grey; with a dark disappointment and little hopeful feeling on his face; with hair unkempt, heaped up in the carriage of his shoulders, and with his figure covered with a tragic cloak, the Laureate is pourtrayed, gloomily peering from two ineffective and not very lustrous eyes, a man of sixty,

looking more like a worn and a more feeling man of
fifty. His skin is sallow, his whole physique not jovial
nor red like Shakespeare and Dickens, but lachrymose
and saturnine; lachrymose! and yet, as regards
fame and reward, what a successful man he has been!
At the age at which Shakespeare was holding horses,
he was a pensionary of the Court. When he was very
young the critics killed a far greater poet, John
Keats, so that they might shower down repentant and
self-recalcitrant praise on the successor. When he
was but young, an old worn-out poet—a true prose
man, but a poet still—contended for the Laureateship
after years of toil and pen labour, but the young
singer was crowned, and received the Laureate's
wreath, the Laureate's fame and pension—the glory
of which wreath was made purer and higher from that
of his predecessor, Wordsworth.

Tennyson's access to fame was sudden. " Lorsque
Tennyson publia ses premiers poëmes," says M.
Taine, " the critics spoke mockingly of them," and
let us say the critics were right. " He was silent,"
continues the French author, " and for ten years no
one saw his name in a review, nor even in a cata-
logue, his books had burrowed their way alone
(' *avaient fait leur chemin tout seuls et sous terre*'), and on
the first blow Tennyson passed for the greatest poet
of his country and his age." It was because the age
had been sinking in verve and true poetic feeling that

Tennyson, great as he is in some points, at once rose to the level of its highest appreciation. He had one or two things about him, not of him but exterior to him, which pleased the public. He was a gentleman, the son of a Lincolnshire clergyman of good family, and of a melodious and high-sounding name. His uncle, Charles Tennyson, assumed the name of D'Eyncourt, to mark his descent from that ancient Saxon house. He was a 'Varsity man, as the slangy people of to-day call those educated at Oxford or Cambridge; he was not political nor enthusiastic; he "was excessively much" of the drawing-room, and smelt of the "Keepsake" and "Friendship's Offering" so strongly that the very names of his heroines seem to come out of gilt leaves, red silk or morocco covers, and their portraits to have been drawn by Boxall or Chalon, and engraved by Heath. Sweetly smiling Adeline, Eleänore, Lilian, "airy fairy Lilian," St. Agnes, Clara, Fatima, Maud, as Taine has it, "toutes les choses sont fines et exquises." Even a lady cannot frown without pleasing so well-bred a poet :

> " Frowns perfect-sweet along the brow,
> Light-glooming over eyes divine,
> Like little clouds sun-fringed."

This is pretty, pretty, very pretty. The *Quarterly*, which had done its best to kill Keats, strode up to Tennyson as did the mad Ajax after slaying the

sheep, and laughing, strode away, saying indignant
things of this puling poet. What an effeminate thing,
in effect, says the *Quarterly*, to write thus :

> " Oh ! *darling room*, my heart's delight;
> Dear room, the apple of my sight ;
> With my *two couches*, soft and white,
> There is no room so *exquisite ;*
> No little room so soft and bright
> .   Wherein to read, *wherein to write.*"

Possibly not, as to the room ; but if one wants to get
manly poetry, we would rather have it from the worn
deal desk of Scott, and from the plough-tail with
Burns, and from the rough mountain stone whence
Wordsworth communed with Nature.

It has cost long years for Tennyson to free himself
from the drawing-room style of poetry. Indeed the
" Keepsake " and " Book of Beauty " haunt him for
ever, and have effectually forbidden him to be a *great*
poet. And yet he had something of a chance that
way once. There is the divine *afflatus* perceptible,
but he has been educated too much, and is too careful
and too timid. They write of him as of one who lies
on the sofa all day, and smokes cigars : he has a soft-
ness and an effeminacy which is altogether false ;
even Bulwer has twitted him about being " a school-
miss Alfred " when he was a great bearded rough
fellow of forty:

> " Even in a love song man should write for men,"

said Bulwer, in reference to the Laureate. But from

off that mental sofa Alfred Tennyson never has risen.
He is a retired recluse and somewhat sulky gentleman, that is but *one* kind of man ; a true poet should
be of all kinds. His very passion is theatrical, and the
great heart of the man who weeps or cries out does
not beat sufficiently to rumple the starched shirt
which covers his manly chest.

> " O my cousin, shallow-hearted ! O my Amy, mine no more !
> O the dreary, dreary moorland ! O the barren, barren shore !
> Falser than all fancy fathoms, falser than all songs have sung ;
> Puppet to a father's threat, and servile to a shrewish tongue !"

You see that while he curses the false girl, this
young gentleman remembers apt alliteration's artful
aid. Mark well those f's and the s's. Compare this
with the mad rage of Hamlet, when he believes that
Ophelia is playing false with him, and with the wild
rhapsodies he indulges in at her death.

Tennyson's popularity, as a poet, grew down from
the higher classes. A few young people of high life
began to admire him, and Moxon sold his books
slowly ; then the next stratum of society under these
took the fever, and found in the Laureate's poems
easy things to understand; and then again, and again,
a wider but a commoner circle took up his songs.

By his books he made at last much money. His
brothers Charles and Septimus, both singers, were at
one time rivals, but he soon distanced them and
others. It was whispered that the Queen admired

and that Prince Albert read his poems, and then
with the loyal English-speaking people his fame
was made.   Moxon died, and the house paid Tennyson all that his books brought, save a percentage of
fifteen per cent., so that for some years the poet found
his lines golden.   When *Macmillan* and the *Cornhill*
magazines were started, their proprietors wanted
names · to attract, and they paid the Laureate a
guinea a line for some weak kickshaws :

> " I stood on a tower, in the wet,
>   When the old year and new year met,"

and a weak story about a City clerk, which were
hardly worth printing.   The magazines did themselves
good as regards advertising, but much harm to the
Laureate.   It is not well to drag a great name about
on an advertising van ; yet, in spite of this, the poet
step by step grew in popularity, and critics wrote of his
great wisdom, and reviews praised the Cambridge prize-
man, and spoke with bated breath of his high genius.

It will be as well to look to some few dates to see
how his fame had culminated.   Tennyson was born
in 1810 ; educated at Cambridge at the same time at
which Thackeray was there ; Thackeray never graduated, one of Tennyson's poetic themes gained a
·prize.   In 1830 the Laureate published poems, chiefly
lyrical, with prose notes full of egotism, which were
properly laughed at, and since then, it is said, Tenny-

son has abandoned prose for ever. In 1832 this little book of poems again appeared, with most of the silly ones cut out, and the others very greatly improved. In 1842, after ten years of polish, appeared a larger and fuller edition, and the very reviews which had laughed at him began to praise him. In 1847 he published the " Princess," which was somehow thought to be connected with Royalty, but was only a pleasant medley, not too strong, and full of feminine sweetnesses. The public was delighted with it ; the "Book of Beauty" flavour pervaded it like vanilla : how touchingly superior must a man, a college-man, have felt as he read :

> " Pretty were the sight
> If our old halls could change their sex, and flaunt
> With prudes for proctors, dowagers for deans,
> And sweet girl-graduates in their golden hair.
> I think they should not wear our rusty gowns."

In 1850 Tennyson made a great step in advance as a poet, but not as a thinker, by writing—or rather by publishing, for he keeps his works a long time by him —" In Memoriam." The friend, celebrated and regretted so much in that poem, is Arthur H. Hallam, son of the historian. In 1851 occurred the Great Exhibition, and the Laureate, who had done no Laureate's work, might have greeted it as he did that of '62, but it was left to a volunteer laureate, Mr. Thackeray, who, in the columns of the *Times*, wrote

a May-day ode with mòre true " grit " in it than anything Tennyson has done.   In 1852 died the Duke of
Wellington, and Tennyson reported his funeral in
noble verse, perhaps the noblest he has ever written.
In 1855 he published " Maud," which he believes to
be, as he has told certain friends, the best thing he
has ever written, and which certainly has in it more
passion of the kind felt by the Baker Street and West-
bourne Grove classes than any other of his pieces.
In 1861 came his contribution to a great epic on the
theme of King Arthur, " Flos Regum Arturus," and
in 1864 " Enoch Arden " and other poems.

For nearly forty years, then, Alfred Tennyson has
been before the public ; for twenty years he has been
the Laureate, taking the laurel

> " greener from the brows
> Of him that uttered nothing base ;"

for nearly ten years his bust has stood in the vestibule
of his college, Trinity, as the somewhat genius of the
place ; and for all that time at least he has been
accepted as the greatest living poet.   Lately two
concordances to his works have been published, an
honour only yet accorded to the Bible, Shakespeare,
and Milton, and only last year an enterprising publishing firm is said to have given the poet £4,500
a-year as the calculated profit of publishing his
works !   Poetry pays, then, even now ; the Queen
salutes the Laureate with respect ; it has been said,

and has been denied, that he has been offered and
refused a baronetcy. Can grateful England be more
profuse to her singer and her son ?

Yes, Tennyson is a greatly successful, but he is not
a great poet. The next age will surely reverse the
verdict of this. He is sugar sweet, pretty-pretty, full
of womanly talk and feminine stuff. Lilian, Dora,
Clara, Emmeline—you can count up thirty such
pretty names, but you cannot count any great poem
of the Laureate's. Shelley has his Ode to the Sky-
lark, Keats his to the Grecian Urn, Coleridge his
Geneviéve, his weird Ancient Mariner, Wordsworth
that touching, yea, aching sublimity on the Intimations
of Immortality—where is there one thing of Tennyson which can approach that ? He has kept himself
aloof from men ; he has polished his poems till all are
ripe and rotten ; he has no fire and no fault ; he has
never lifted one to Heaven nor plunged us to the
lower depths. He has no creed, no faith, no depth.
When another poet would bare his heart he talks of
his pulses :

> " My *pulses* therefore beat again
> For other friends that once I met ;
> *Nor can it suit me to forget*
> The mighty hopes that make us men."

What a grand line is that last, and what a feeble
beast crawls on its belly before it ! Can we forgive
a poet " suiting to forget " Heaven, Hell, Christ and

His Death upon the Cross, His agony and bloody sweat ?—Heavens, that a Christian poet should be found lisping out *that !*

No, he is no great poet.   Mr. Tennyson has been very discreet, and a very good Court poet,—for a manufactured article really none better; but he is like the lady who did not want to " look frightful when dead," and so put on the paint and the fucus, and he will take no deep hold of the world.   What did sweet Will Shakespeare do ?   Did he not say that he had

> " *gored* mine own thoughts ;
> Sold cheap what is most dear,
> And made myself a motley to the view."

Did he not give us blood and passion with his poetry ? But what says Tennyson: " Nor can it suit me to forget "that I am admired by all young ladies, and am a Laureate.   Further he adds,

> " I count it crime
> To mourn for any overmuch."

And posterity will count it folly to place a half-hearted and polished rhymster amongst her shining great ones who were fellows with poverty and dis-respect in this life, and who learnt in suffering that they might teach in song.

MR. GEORGE AUGUSTUS SALA.

MR. GEORGE AUGUSTUS SALA.

OOKING, with a merry, audacious, bold look, out of your photographic portrait-album, which contains so many vile slanders upon yourself, your wife, and your friends, is one whose name stands at the head of the present paper, a Bohemian writer of a bad school, but yet a brave man ; one that has done very little good, and yet one full of capabilities for good ; a writer of sound English and a scholar, and yet a driveller of tipsy, high-flown, and high-falutin' nonsense ; a man of understanding when he likes, and yet of bosh and nonsense as well when he chooses to debase himself; one of keen intellect, high qualities, prodigious memory, great picturesqueness, and a photographic accuracy, and yet so utterly careless of his own reputation, of the dignity of letters, of what is due to himself, that he can sell his pen to describe a Jew clothier's, an advertising furniture dealer's, a Liverpool draper's, a Manchester hatter's, or a St. Paul's Churchyard bonnet-shop. A man who ought to have taken the lead on any paper, but one who, clinging to the old traditions of our pen profession, has done but little upon one only. There is an odious Americanism, " reliable," meaning that those to whom it is applied can be trusted, or leant upon. In ninety cases out of the hundred G. A. S. will bring up his copy with the accurate regard to time which newspapers require, but at the last number in every decennial he will have failed. This has gained him respect with the dullards who generally conduct and start papers, who believe that a man of genius cannot but be irregular and eccentric. If the " genius " gets into the hands of the Jews, is often drunken, always in debt, sometimes in prison, and is totally disreputable, living *à tort et à travers* the rules of society, these newspaper proprietors think more and more of him, and go down on their knees and bribe him to write.

> "Great wits to madness sure are near allied,
> And thin partitions do their bounds divide."

When the " great wit " writes a novel, draws all the money, gets in a mess with it, and asks somebody else to finish it whom he is unwilling to pay; or when he starts on his travels, leaving a proprietor of a periodical with a half finished serial on hand, the admiration of Bohemia, printer, and public, is enormous. The recalcitrant author is afterwards pardoned, and received with open arms. What a clever fellow he must be for these people to stand this!

Like this has been the reasoning with regard to Mr. Sala, of whom we, of course, do not narrate all these little fables. Yet such men exist, and the offences of such are condoned with wonderful ease by the public whom they do not touch, just as a reference by Mr. Charles Matthews to his little escapades with his creditors raises a merry laugh. To the stupid public it is a matter of dubious yet unmeasured admiration, this juncture of social unfitness and fluent verbiage which they take for wisdom. To think that you may see, let us say, Theodore Hook and Dr. Maginn rolling drunk in Fleet Street, and peacefully reposing in the kennel over night, and the next day read those highly-flown articles in the *John Bull* condemnatory of Queen Caroline, in which it demonstrated that that poor lady had not one rag of virtue left to cover her, and that they (the writers) had a chestful of virtuous blankets and undergarments, besides the superfine, double-milled, thick clothing they stood upright in— to think on this, is it not wonderful indeed! But reflect, oh, British public—those Pagan Romans did not choose *their* Censors thus!

Mr. Sala, who in the flesh is *goguenard*, jovial, and externally something like Bardolph, is a very severe censor when he chooses. He is of a mature age— let us say forty-five—and has worked for the press nearly thirty years out of that, for he began early, and it is whispered wrote at one time for the excelling

M

Mr. Edward Lloyd, of Salisbury Square, certain romances of the Mrs. Radcliffe school, which our best novelists of to-day have copied, such as " Adah, the Betrayed; or, the Murder at the Old Smithy," "Julia, the Deserted," and the like.   These penny romances were not vicious, though morbidly exciting; one called "Sweeney Todd; or, the String of Pearls," related how a certain barber in Fleet Street cut the throats of his customers, and then sunk them down a trap to a kitchen, where they were made into, and whence they issued, as mutton-pies!   We doubt if our eccentric genius wrote such stories, but certainly he worked hard and honestly at whatever came up, and we wish to heaven that some of the superfine, satin-wove, hot-pressed, gilt-edged, and fashionable novelists worked half as well and had had the same practice.   Nothing in the world is there like it for style.   Do you think, young author, that those easy incisive sentences, those quiet sly touches, those pretty turns of Sterne, or Fielding, or Thackeray, came by chance?   If you do, you are as big a blunderer as Dogberry, when he declared that reading and writing were the gift of Nature.

When Dickens established his *Household Words*, with its unattainable motto,

" Familiar in their mouths as household words,

which it certainly was not, a dozen young knights of

the pen rushed to aid the Arthur of the literary Round Table.   Our hero was one, and as Mr. Dickens, with singular generosity and blindness, determined that everybody should "gush" as he gushed and write Dickenese as he wrote, the facile pen of Sala was in great request.   Sketch after sketch of real verve and merit, each of which was attributed to the great Dickens, and many of which were republished in his name in New York, proceeded from Sala, notably "Captain Quagg's Conversion," "The Key of the Street," and others of the same sort.   They were fresh, sparkling, and fast, written with abounding spirit and that sort of devil-may-care cleverness which is so pleasing to young men.   When an author lets you into his confidence, and knows everything, is equally familiar with a sailors' home in Wapping, a thieves' cellar in Liverpool, the Queen's palace at Berlin, the Emperor's cabinet in Paris, the Eleusinian mysteries, and the game of Knur and Spell, you know that you are reading the remarks of an uncommon clever fellow.   The implicit confidence which young readers, and old fellows, too, of the middle class, place in the dissertations of the young lions of the *Daily Telegraph* is founded on the love they have for the bold buc- caneering style in which the latter write.   We have it from a certain Camarilla that sits upon the wild lucubrations of some of these famous leaders, that the grammar is very bad indeed, and as to the Latin, we know that even the lynx-eyed supervisors cannot keep *that* right. But what then—*Que voulez vous mes amis ?* You get your lurid leader, all blue fire and glitter, and wonderful of its sort. Well, it *is* nice to read; but, after all, what does it mean ? You begin a dissertation on the Virgin Mary, and you find that, ere you have read three lines, there is a learned essay on the Paphian mysteries and the wondrous rites of Venus. As for policy and study of the constitution of this great country, Heaven only knows whereto the D. T. has led us ! When that fine property was in the market, after the gallant Colonel Sleigh had brought it out and failed, there was a perturbation among the band of Bohemians who wrote its articles. Sala was among them, of course ; does not everyone know his style ? He had gone to Russia for Dickens, and was always talking of the Nevskoi Prospect and eternal snow. He has been here, there, and elsewhere, and he lets you know it. Happily for the band of penmen, astute gentlemen of an ancient but exiled people bought the *Daily ;* its sale went up ; advertisements made it pay, and Sala was very wisely made a special correspondent.

Perhaps, for a cheap paper, there is no man better fitted for this work. He cannot understand politics, but he is well up in art; he cares very little about religion, but he has a photographic eye. He does not write the blatant untruths and braggadocio of

Mr. Dash, the Parisian correspondent; but he does give you an insight into the manners of the people. Some of his touches are simply admirable. Take the second volume of " From Waterloo to the Peninsula:" the description of the laziness, misery, sunshine, rags, pride, and folly of Spain were never better given. A master of words, he paints a figure at a touch, as that of the beggar, proud and sturdy, whose "rags were flamboyant behind, while his worn plush inexpressibles were *rayonné* in front." Gustave Doré, whose illustrations of Spain in *Le Monde Illustré* are in his best style, has no touch like it.

While doing all this hard work, and, according to his lights, doing it honestly and well, with no high aim, but giving the public what it asked for, and no more—trifle and whipt cream—not teaching the people, nor preaching to them, nor incidentally even reproving them, but amusing and tickling them, Mr. Sala republished many of his sketches, and one or two tales and stories that he had written. His books are not very successful. They have been issued cheaply or at a high price, but when the facile author removes to a higher class of writing or of readers he somewhat fails. Not more than one of his books can be said to have achieved a decided success. Mr. Sala's published works are as follows :—

"How I Tamed Mrs. Cruiser," 1858; "Journey due North," 1859; "Twice Round the Clock," 1859;

" The Baddington Peerage," 1860 ; " Gaslight and
Daylight," 1860 ; " Lady Chesterfield's Letters,"
1860; "Looking at Life," 1860 ; " Make your Game,"
1860 ; " Dutch Pictures, with some Sketches in the
Flemish Manner," 1861 ; "Seven Sons of Mammon,"
1861 ; " Accepted Addresses," 1862 ; " Ship Chandler,
and other Tales," 1862 ; " Two Prima Donnas,"
1862 ; and since that time, at intervals, " After
Breakfast ;" " My Diary in America in the Midst
of War ;" " From Waterloo to the Peninsula," and
" A Trip to Barbary by a Round-about Route."

Of these books his light London sketches are the
best and most successful, such as " Twice Round
the Clock," published first in the *Welcome Guest*, and
illustrated by a very wooden and angular young
artist, since dead, William McConnell. Perhaps it
is unfair to call the poor fellow an artist, for most
assuredly he understood little art ; he was a wooden
wood draughtsman, very hard and full of lines, but
he had the merit of drawing the scenes from reality.
Next in merit are the travels, which are full of observation and curious reading, for Sala, if a desultory
student, is in some sort a scholar. He once talked
of some poor woman " in a sleazy (thin and worn)
shawl," whereon a pundit in the *Saturday Review*
asked what is " sleazy," and did not know that
ancient and perfectly correct but provincial word.
He is a curious and out-of-the-way reader, and not

to be sneered at. Next follow his touch-and-go social articles, beautifully calculated for the meridian of Cockneydom and the intellects of virtuous publicans, intelligent greengrocers, and the readers of a certain class generally ; and last of all in merit are his novels. Small wits talked of the " Badly-done Peerage " and the " Seven Tons of Gammon," and not without reason were these names given. There are, however, pages of admirable writing in both, but a sustained plot and well pourtrayed characters seem to be beyond the author's painting. His women are dolls, his men the tinselled theatrical figures we are all acquainted with as boys, and that is all.

And so we part with G. A. S. There has been the making of many a good author in him. As Thackeray once said of him, he is " a horse big enough to pull any shay about," but he is a horse that does not go well in harness. To some his tipsy writing is odious ; to few even his very best work can be of use. His face, as one can see in a coloured photograph, is an index to his style. He is bold, ready, and Bohemian. He is grateful to Dickens, and says, in a touching memorial of that author, " the first five-pound note I ever earned in literature came from his kind hand." His career is a *coup manqué*, and if he leave a name to survive till his youngest Bohemian admirer be an old man—for it will survive no longer—it will yet carry with it no affectionate reverence, and will not be conducive to much good. He is a man of potentiality, not of accomplished fact. In the meantime, reckless writing has produced money, recklessly gotten and, it would seem, as recklessly distributed, and so far the end which the vivacious writer has aimed at in literature is answered. A nobler purpose would have achieved a nobler and far higher result.

MR. CHARLES LEVER.

MR. CHARLES LEVER.

THE " Prince of neck-or-nothing novelists,"
as he is called, Charles James Lever,
Esquire, Her Majesty's Consul at Florence,
is *not* a Waterloo officer, nor a Peninsular veteran.
It is well to assure the reader of this fact, for Mr.
Lever has told so many stories about fighting and
fighters, told them, too, with so much art and truth,
and has so thrown himself into military life, that
when we first read his entrancing books as boys, we
always believed " Dr. Lever," as we called him—for
we had an inkling of his *status*—was a surgeon-major
to the most dashing and ubiquitous corps in the
British army, and had been wounded at Waterloo,
and (would have been, if in a foreign army) decorated
on the field.

But you see how fancy plays with us. That somewhat fair, rotund, farmer-looking gentleman, with
round shoulders, broad and massive; with the good-
humoured face, twinkling eyes, thin hair, and capa-
cious head, which looks as if it had done nothing else

but superintend agricultural produce, is a physician, and has never been in the army. He is the son of a builder; was born in August, 1806, at Dublin, and for some time taught at home. But during those eventful years of our lives in which boys learn most, when John Leech and William Makepeace Thackeray, nor must we forget their school-fellows and contemporaries, Martin Farquhar Tupper and George—we will spare the rest of the names, *the prenomina* in this case—Reynolds, the penny blood-and-thunder novelist, were at the Charterhouse, Charles Lever was being educated in France. Thackeray has thrown tender recollections about his school. Colonel Newcome, you remember, dies as a poor brother of the Charterhouse, as many a good man has died; but we don't think that Leech, Reynolds, or Tupper has said a word about it. That is a good sign in a boy and a man when he takes to his old school, and lets his imagination play fondly about it. The Charterhouse returned the love. We were present at Thackeray's sale when a huge price was given for an old school dictionary of the dead author's, and that was bought for a relic by his old school. Moreover, the authorities have put up two tablets, one to Leech and one to Thackeray. In fifty years John Leech will be forgotten, but Thackeray's name will be greater than ever. Tupper and Reynolds are still alive—the first a scholar and a gentleman, though no poet, the second a most mischievous writer. We don't think the Charterhouse will ever put up tablets to either.

After studying and passing, young Lever was sent to the North of Ireland on a medical commission, and distinguished himself as medical officer in the district of Londonderry, Coleraine, and Newtown Limavady, so that, not long afterwards, he received the appointment of physician to the Embassy at Brussels, where Sir George Hamilton Seymour was then envoy to the Belgian Court. Here he met with many military men, and seems to have made that study of the life of a soldier which has stood him in such good stead.

While at Brussels Mr. Lever made a sudden plunge into literature, and with such success that he "awoke up famous" after a fashion. His first venture, which seems to have been issued by Orr in 1840, was "Harry Lorrequer," a tale of dash and devilry, which may, in some measure, be regarded as an Irish pendant to Dickens's "Pickwick." The amount of "spirit" in each of these novels is hardly to be estimated in these sober days. Fun, frolic, adventure, doings which by some would be called vicious, and by others who do not object to the vice would be stigmatised as snobbish, are chronicled with tremendous glee. Drunkenness is a virtue, sobriety a folly, lovemaking an amiable pastime; and to be surrounded by debt and duns, to set the law at defiance, to duck a sheriff's officer, and to frighten an attorney out of his wits, is the normal state of the Irish Bayard, who is significantly described as "the man for Galway." This fun came upon our cold English intellects like a pleasant douche bath of warmed and perfumed water—or rather whiskey and water. We were refreshed while we were slightly intoxicated, and bought eagerly the monthly instalments in pink covers, which were rendered even more *couleur de rose* by a symbolical design by Phiz. You saw Ireland, not as a dejected damsel, but as the prettiest little shepherdess in the world. Donnybrook Fair, then fast dying out, did not represent faction fights, with the hatred of generations fomented rather than healed by the priests, but a few friendly contests with the shillelagh, in which Irish knights, not in steel armour but in long frieze coats, took part, while Biddy as a Queen of Beauty stood ready to crown the gentle, the courteous, and above all the humorous champion.

It is asserted that all Lever's stories are drawn from the life. If so, what wonder that we Saxons don't understand the Irish? If not the very safest people—for they are represented as being prodigiously handy with their duelling pistols—to live amongst, they are in Lever's novels certainly the very pleasantest; and if an Englishman will only put up with the good-humoured jest of having day turned into night, and be prepared to jump any amount of stone walls upon an Irish blood horse of prodigious speed and bone, he can live in Paradise in the Green Island.

It is difficult for us to say what contemporary critics thought of Lever's successes, for the *Quarterly* does not notice him, and Mr. Cordy Jeaffreson, who has spoken with adulation of forgotten writers, is silent. As for his popularity, it is undoubted. "Harry Lorrequer" paid, and was speedily followed by some charming novels—stories which have poetry, sensation, purity, and extreme interest, not without a dash of history and a certain knowledge of society and high life in them very cunningly mixed. We know of no novels which are at once so interesting and so harmless. Great skill as a *raconteur*, vivacity, wit, humour, in a small degree, and broad fun in a very full degree, distinguish them all. And with the knowledge—saddened by events—that Charles Lever possesses of his countrymen, it is astonishing how cleverly he has concealed their many faults and vices, and how prominently he has put their virtues before the world, and yet without a suspicion of flattery. He is not an old man, but as full of wisdom and spirit as ever. If his judgment be equal to his insight, we should say that he of all men living is the one to be consulted as to the best way of governing Ireland. For years he has lived at a distance from his country, and is not to be deceived by party glamour and that intoxication by excitement which seems to turn the best brains at home. "Papæ! Papæ!" you cry with the Chelsea philosopher, "wonderful indeed!" What, make a novelist a statesman! But let us remember that the most prosaic people in the world, the Spartans, made an old, blind, song-making school-master their general, and that he led them on to glorious victory.

After "Harry Lorrequer" there followed in quick succession "Charles O'Malley," 1841; "Jack Hinton, the Guardsman," 1843; "Arthur O'Leary," 1844; "The O'Donoghue," 1845; "Tom Burke of Ours," 1846; "The Knight of Gwynne," 1847; "Con Cregan, the Irish Gil Blas," and "Roland Cashel," 1849; "The Daltons," 1852; "The Dodd Family Abroad," 1852; "The Fortunes of Glencore," 1857; "The Martins of Cromartin," 1859; "Maurice Tiernay, the Soldier of Fortune," and "One of Them," 1861; "Tales of the Trains," by Tilbury Tramp, "St. Patrick's Eve," and more lately, in the *Cornhill Magazine*, "That Boy of Norcotts"—a capital story—and in *Blackwood's Magazine*, the various conversations, notes, epigrammatic turns, and reflections of Cornelius O'Dowd, Esquire. All these have been valuable works—to the booksellers. As to the public, it has been amused and delighted in a very gentle, honest, open way. Mr. Lever is a gentleman, cleanly and honourable; and, though he has not "eschewed sack," yet he admits no scurrilous lines in his tunes. He has ripened as he has grown older; and got wiser and better as time wears away. He does not write those rattling works now, and even dear old Thackeray, whom we are about to quote, would hardly find anything salient enough to sketch. We quote Thackeray, chiefly to give a picture of what Lever can do, for, as that famous hand wrote "George de Barnwell" with greater verve and learning than Bulwer, and surpassed Disraeli in his mock novel of "Codlingsby," so he threw even Lever into the shade in his burlesque story of "Phil Fogarty." Don't you know "Phil Fogarty"—perhaps the best bit of good honest humorous fooling out? "Phil" is a genuine brother to "Tom Burke" and "Harry Lorrequer." We quote Thackeray as the best possible means of conveying in one minute the method of Lever:

* * * * * * *

"The gabion was ours. After two hours' fighting, we were in possession of the first embrasure, and made ourselves as comfortable as circumstances would admit. Jack Delamere, Tom Delancy, Jerry Blake, the Doctor, and myself, sat under a pontoon, and our servants laid out a hasty supper on a tumbril. Though Cambacères had escaped me so provokingly after I cut him down, his spoils were mine; a cold fowl and a Bologna sausage were found in the Marshal's holster; and in the haversack of a French private, who lay a corpse on the glacis, we found a loaf of bread, his three days' ration. Instead of salt we had gunpowder; and you may be sure, wherever the Doctor was, a flask of good brandy was behind him in his instrument case. We sat down and made a soldier's supper. The Doctor pulled a few of the delicious fruit from the lemon-trees growing near (and round which the Carabiniers and the 24th Leger had made a desperate rally), and punch was brewed in Jack Dela-

N

mere's helmet. 'Faith, it never had so much wit in it before,' said the Doctor, as he ladled out the drink. We all roared with laughing, except the guardsman, who was as savage as a Turk at a christening."

Here, too, follows one of the songs in imitation of Lever, who, by the way, writes a capital ditty:

> " You've all heard of Larry O'Toole,
>   Of the beautiful town of Drumgoole ;
>   He had but one eye,
>   To ogle ye by—
>   O, murther, but that was a jew'l !
>   A fool
>   He made of de girls, dis O'Toole.
>
> 'Twas he was the boy didn't fail,
>   To tuck down pitaties and mail ;
>   He never would shrink
>   From any strong dthrink
>   Was it whiskey or Drogheda ale ;
>   I'm bail
>   This Larry would swallow a pail.
>
> O, many a night at the bowl,
>   With Larry I've sot cheek by jowl ;
>   He's gone to his rest,
>   Where there's dthrink of the best,
>   And so let us give his old soul
>   A howl,
>   For 'twas he made the noggin to rowl."

Mr. Charles Lever has long become a moderate Conservative, and his opinions upon the Irish Church Bill, and his prophetic foreshadowing of the very troubles Ireland now suffers from, are well worth studying. The society he pictured has long passed away. We have now no Mickey Free, any more than we have Pickwick's servant, Sam Weller. Happily, too, for us, Stiggins in the lifetime of his portrayer, has died out; unhappily, too, the good old Father Tom, the Irish priest who was a gentleman, educated at St. Omer, and with a smack of Parisian breeding in him, has died out, too. Instead of that, we have priests educated at Maynooth, the sons of cottiers and the brothers of the poor peasantry who are so misguided and misled. These, too, with an unerring pen, Mr. Cornelius O'Dowd has portrayed, but the pen lacks the old fun; we have grown gradually duller in these serious times.

" Ridentem dicere verum quid vetat ? "

How many times will that be requoted ? What Horace demanded has been permitted to Lever, who has not only told the truth with a smiling face, but has brought the tears into many eyes, and with all his fun and frolic has never brought a blush to any cheek. He has not attempted to preach; he has not been either a stoic or a cynic. His philosophy is rather of the garden of Epicurus, and the enjoyment he teaches is that of manliness and reason, and for good, clean, wholesome reading, which will leave no headache nor heartache, and no dregs within the mind, commend us to Charles Lever. Messrs. Smith and Son seem to have a monopoly of his novels, and they are to be bought on every railway stall. Reader, instead of the new prurient half-crown's worth, buy "Tom Burke" or "Harry Lorrequer" for two shillings—and be happy.

MR. GEORGE GROTE.

MR. GEORGE GROTE.

IT speaks well for the Republic of Letters that, when Mr. Grote was leading the *Oi polloi* of Reform and Democracy, and writing in the *Edinburgh Review*, the Tory *Quarterly* hailed the writer of the "stirring and stately narrative" as "not merely *a* historian, but *the* historian of Greece." And this title, it must be remembered, was given while Mitford and Dr. Thirlwall headed the Greek historians, while Müller and Ranke investigated, while Niebuhr took up ancient stories, and tried to reduce, or did reduce them to mere legends. "The works of these men," says the generous *Quarterly*, "look thin and blasted beside the full proportions of the long research which unfolds the rise and progress of the Athenian democracy."

In writing of George Grote, then, we shall have to write of a truly noble man of letters, and it says very little for Toryism, or Conservatism, or whatever a great party may now be termed, that it has never

honoured Literature as it should be honoured. Of
course, in these degenerate days, and in the reigns of
the Brunswick, the patronage of the Court is but
small. No men have been more wisely loyal than
men of letters; no men have been more scantily
recognised. A fourth-rate Academician—by which
we mean a painter—showed us, the other day, a
picture, four of such as he could well paint in a year,
and for which he asked and got a price larger than
most first-rate authors get for the work of their lifetime. But then a painter furnishes your house, and
makes your walls look grand; an author only furnishes your brains—if you have any. We do not
complain; we only urge that the scantiness of pay
should be a reason of more honour from the Court.
It would be ridiculous to institute a comparison of
the value of an author in comparison with a painter,
towards the State. In educating, in leavening, and
ennobling, or in degrading a people, the author has
almost infinite power. Mr. G. W. M. Reynolds,
with his "Mysteries of the Court" and his mischievous novels, which sell so largely in America,
was of more consequence than twenty Landseers and
forty Ettys, and did more harm than two hundred
such Academicians could do good. Once upon a
time, when John Leland wrote a certain novel, which
we shall not name, and painted "in glowing colours,"
as he terms them, a career of vice, the Government

paid the too clever rogue a pension *not* to write again.
Wise persons those. Our Court has let the people
tumble and trudge on through mud and mire, and
infinite chaotic folly and filth, and has neither
punished nor rewarded. The consequence is——
well, " Formosa ; " the likenesses of courtesans in
our most chaste shops, a general corruption, and—
girls of the period.

As for any rewarding of intellect, that has chiefly
been done by the Whigs or Liberals. Lord Houghton,
or, as they call him, *Haut-ton*, a good plain poet ;
Macaulay, with his cock-sure and subjective style,
which will, as soon as we get to be scholars, stink in
our nostrils ; even Bulwer helped to his Baronetcy,
attest the fact that the Whigs do try to ennoble genius
or talent. Here, again, is a rumour, and we believe
a perfectly true one, that Mr. Gladstone did offer to
make Mr. Grote, once the leader of the " Rads," and
the one to whom was entrusted an annual motion on
the ballot, a baron ! Would he have been Baron
Sedgmoor ; or would he, having overthrown Mitford
and Thirlwall, boldly hail from Greece, as does
Lesseps from Suez ?

Here, indeed, is an admirable man of letters ; a
true scholar ; a learned, patient, excellent writer of
the good old fashion ; a man celebrated, not notorious;
too wise to be subjective, like Macaulay and his
enemy but imitator Hepworth Dixon ; too truthful

to describe scenes of which he only found a hint, with the vivid falsehood of the *Daily Telegraph* correspondent, who described the resplendent effulgence of a full moon *when she was perfectly hidden in her first quarter.* Of such writers we shall shortly have to speak enough. Here we have one who is indeed good; whom to admire is to prove your taste, and this is the banker-scholar—as Rogers was the banker-poet—George Grote, D.C.L., F.R.S., who was born at Clay Hill, near Beckenham, Kent, in 1794. Nearly seventy-six years old; the white hair very thin and scant, the eyes dimmed with poring over many books, the head bent with study more than by age. Seventy-six years old, say near eighty! a long time to wait for honour, and it is nearly fifteen years since his *Magnum Opus* was written. Some time since the Queen drove up to town to visit Dean Stanley—Arthur Penrhyn Stanley—a dean and a courtier. Her Majesty honoured him with her presence at luncheon, and it was arranged that two illustrious men, both old in years and honours, untitled and unrecognised, however, by any gazette, should be found chatting with Stanley when the illustrious and widowed dame dropped in. One of these men, found in learned ease on this truly regal visit—for Windsor Castle is not so large, of course, as Dean's Yard, Westminster—one of these men was Thomas Carlyle, philosopher of Chelsea; the other

George Grote, historian of Greece.   Her Majesty no
doubt enjoyed the luncheon !

When History is written philosophically, as by
Mr. Grote, it becomes much less interesting, but it is
eminently more true. After a long study of all the
best writers of that little peninsula, which at one
time contained an army of great men and philosophers, and now seems but to hold a segregation of
the acutest sharpers of all Europe, Grote set himself
to study the meaning of words. "The modern historian," he says, "strives in vain to convey the
impression which appears in the condensed and
burning phrases of Thucydides," and, of course, all
that is left him is to expand, to amplify, or to con-
dense. We all know how Lord Macaulay and his
school used history. They made it a picture book,
after the manner of Walter Scott, with or without
leave or license, with or without a hint in the bare
chronicle which they expanded. We heard how the
sea roared (when it was a calm) ; how some hero
shouted (when he never said a word) ; how the
heroine lifted up her voice and wept (when she was
silent in terror, or dumb from contempt). This is
history with a vengeance ; nor was the historian
content with this untruthful and shameful perversion.
What is legitimate with the novelist is contemptible
and detestable cheating with the historian. "Why,
dear Sir Walter," said an old lady to Scott, "you

seem as if you had lived in these times and saw all
you describe. Where do you get it all from ? " " I
read a great deal," replied the novelist, " and I
imagine the rest. I am like the theatrical manager,
when I can't snow white I snow brown." Perhaps
there never was a more annoyingly untrue and inar-
tistic book than Dixon's " Life of Lord Bacon." He
introduces people as present who were absent ; he
lets us hear them talk when they said nothing ; he
attributes motives, sets up and pulls down characters,
and moves his puppets about in a most theatrical
manner. People who reflect and who know are
disgusted, and truly one gentleman has taken the
trouble to write a volume to expose the so-called
historian's follies and misrepresentations, but the
public is gulled. In the meantime the real actors in
history denounce it and laugh at it. " Don't read
me history," said the sick Sir Robert Walpole to
his son, " for that I know must be false."

It is the greatest praise of Mr. Grote, that he has
kept strictly to the letter of his brief. If he " ex-
pands " it is learnedly, and with reason. When
Thucydides or a chronicler uses a peculiar phrase,
Grote, finding out the meaning, will properly turn
his narrative. We do not have the " lurid smiles,"
" the slow and cautious step " of accord or approach
which we have in inferior novelists, but we do have
a solid structure, and not a barley-sugar sham.

If it were worth while to dwell on trifles in this short sketch, one might applaud or object to Mr. Grote's method of nomenclature. Personally, we think that he is right, but nationally we are bound to think him wrong. He will write Alkibiadês, Sôcratês, Peisistratus, Héraklês, Skiônê, and the like. The Greeks wrote them so. So the Latins talk of Pompeius Magnus, while we talk of Pompey. But the whole "kit" of classic names will one day have to be rewritten. Nikias does *not* look so well as Nicias, but it is more like the original, and let us be as near truth as we can. Some day we shall say Kikero and Kaisar, instead of Sisero and Seizer. At present we are bad enough, but the French are worse. Aristidês is pronounced *Airêstcêd*, and Tullius Cicero is reduced to *Toole* (Tulle). Why Grote should talk of the people always as a *demus*, a soldier as a *hoplite*, and a founder as an *ækist*, is not so clear. We want the history of Greece written in English, not in Greek.

After all, the very best painting, because the truest, is portrait-painting, and the very best history is biography. This is especially true in Grote's case. His later work on "Plato and the other Companions of Socrates," is the most entertaining of all that he has written. And the subject is worthy of him. The history of no mere man that the world has seen is equal to that of the little stone-mason figure-cutter of Athens who used to ask questions. The noble galaxy of great spirits who surrounded him—Plato, Xenophon, Critias, Crito, each a king of men—was only fitted to be crowned by the philosophical monarch, who died as he would have slept, the chief actor in a tragedy without the strut of the tragedian, the victim in a martyrdom without the song and crown of the martyr. We need not recommend Mr. Grote's work, but we will urge our readers to get it. If they want to get rid of contemporary nonsense, and to clear their minds of cant, while they fill them with great and sublime images, they should read of Plato and Socrates in the pages of Grote.

Mr. Grote has written on the ballot, has contributed to the *Edinburgh* and *Westminster;* has issued a pamphlet on Plato's theory of the Earth, and another on the Republic of Switzerland. A philosophical republican and yet a despiser of *demus*, an ardent supporter of the ballot because, we fancy, he fears the corruption of the people, a man of learned ease and yet a most laborious scholar, this great historian seems to be a contradiction, and yet is a whole-hearted, honest, wise man. To give a specimen of his great history—a large work, in twelve volumes —would be to bring a brick from Babylon under the notion of picturing the elevation of the houses and plan of the streets. Let the reader dip into it whereever he may, he cannot go wrong, and will be abundantly rewarded. For the scholar there is an interesting and masterly discussion on the myths and legends of early Greece; for the student of literature the disquisitions upon Homer, and all the poets, historians, and philosophers, from Æschylus and Herodotus down to Plato and Plutarch ; for the statesman, the remarkable descriptions of the legislation of Lycurgus, the object of ostracism, the working of the Athenian constitution, the influence of the democratic form of government, and the causes of the decline of the once invincible republics of Greece ; and for the "general reader," the narrative of the war against Xerxes, the battles of Marathon and Thermopylæ, the retreat of the Ten Thousand, the expedition to Syracuse, and a hundred other episodes, any or all of which he will follow with breathless and sustained interest. Mr. Grote's work has revolutionised our notions of ancient Greece. It is a wonderful story, and is wonderfully told.

THE RIGHT HON. B. DISRAELI,
P.C., D.C.L., M.P., &c., &c.

o

THE RIGHT HON. B. DISRAELI,

P.C., D.C.L., M.P., &c., &c.

ANKIND, then,' said Vivian Grey, 'is my great game. At this moment how many a powerful noble only wants wit to be a Minister; and what wants Vivian Grey to attain the same end? That noble's influence. When two people can so materially assist each other, why are they not brought together? Shall I, because my birth baulks my fancy, pass my life a moping misanthrope in an old chateau? Now let me probe myself. Does my cheek blench? I have the mind for the conception, and I can perform right skilfully upon the most splendid of musical instruments—the human voice—to make others believe those conceptions. There wants but one thing more—courage, pure, perfect courage; and does Vivian Grey know fear?' He laughed an answer of the bitterest derision."

This extract from "Vivian Grey" will show why Mr. Disraeli has been at once feared, distrusted, and hated. When he was Prime Minister two literary

gentlemen, both partially disagreeing with his politics, desired, for the honour of their class, to give him
a dinner, whereat authors of all shades of opinion
should join to celebrate the accession to the highest
post of this Royal Republic—for England is by far
more truly republican in its fairness and openness of
career than America—of an author who had written
some brilliant novels, who had said some of the best
epigrams in political life, who had written leaders for
the *Times*, conducted the *Representative*, and who at
least was never ashamed of his craft.   The answers,
let us say so far, revealed respect for the motives of
the senders, but bitter animosity to Disraeli. People
seemed to be unable, if in common fairness only, to
separate the man from the minister; and noble
authors, politically of his own way of thinking, wrote
four sides of note-paper in which they bespattered the
very clever politician and author with caustic abuse.
The dinner was obliged to be renounced, but a certain
number of scholars and gentlemen succeeded in getting
him on the committee of a literary dinner, in taking the
chair of which, Vivian Grey made a most clever and
charming speech, and worked his way with undaunted
courage, with singular *bonhomie* and unflagging pluck.
    Another cause of his being disliked and mistrusted
is his singular cleverness. We know what Byron
said about the dull world which loves not those who
are too clever for it. " He who surpasses or subdues

mankind," said the noble author, "must look to garner up a pretty fair share of hatred." He must, indeed, and a reputation for cleverness is as fatal as the thing itself. Now, clever as Mr. Disraeli undoubtedly is, his reputation for talent exceeds that which he holds. Country members, and the dulness of the House, if we may presume that there are such in that brilliant assembly, look with suspicion upon a man of such reputation, and, like certain banks, Mr. Disraeli's paper currency far exceeds the weighty bullion of real worth that he keeps at home.

It is because he has written a book, aye, and ten books, all clever, wild, and nonsensical too; for this, people cannot forgive him; and the reason they cannot do so is because these books have an air of insincerity. The ordinary Britisher has the feeling of Herr Philister about him, so far as this, he cannot separate mental from moral character. Those who best know Mr. Disraeli, let us say his wife, Lady Beaconsfield, and his late brother, James Disraeli, loved him, and love him with a devotion which does honour to both. The man *is* a hero to his valet-de-chambre, but as he has never concealed his hatred of shallowness, his knowledge of the pretence of great courts, his belief, a thousand times proved to be well founded, that "a good cry" will move the English people very much better than a noble cause, people hate him. He has let the world know how clever he

is, and the world has discounted his sincerity. He
has touched the right nail on the head very often, and
people have cried—What a happy *guess!* He has
done that dangerous thing about which Lord John's
misquotation from Job—" Oh that mine enemy had
written a book!"—has passed into a proverb, and
people have judged him very severely by those very
books. He has never had fair play. He has been
looked on by his party as a clever mercenary, a sort
of political Bashi-bazouk, useful for skirmishing and
for getting killed. He has been treated as the later
Roman Emperors used their Saxon and barbarian
body-guard, as capital defenders, fighters, flesh for
Dacian swords or Persian arrows, but *not* as of the
old Roman stuff. He has been at least as true to
England and to his party as Lord John, who often
plays the worst of all tricks to England and to Pro-
testantism (" Johnny's upset the coach-again," said
the late Lord Derby), but people believed in that
bumptious little statesman, and *not* in Disraeli. He
has had a marvellous amount of *un*luck, but he never
deserted his leader after once settling down, and was
never ashamed of his race or people. But in spite of
all difficulties, and an unjust and superabundant
hatred, he has been Prime Minister, *is* leader of the
oldest party in Europe, will be honestly and sincerely
mourned when he dies—and be buried in Westminster
Abbey.

After this exordium the reader may perhaps be surprised to find that we do not admire his novels, believe that they are very much overrated, that they will not live twenty years after his death, and that if Messrs. Longmans give £10,000 for his " Lothair," they only *mis*calculate on the curiosity of novel-readers and the elasticity of Mr. Mudie's subscription. The rumour is, however, an advertisement—and Mr. Disraeli is *not* properly a novelist, nor a man of letters *pur sang*, any more than a firework-maker is an artilleryman.   He is actually a free lance in politics, using literature as a sword, revolver, culverin, bow and arrow, or any offensive weapon a free lance would carry.   Cleverly he has used it ; but it is because his service to letters—great Goddess ! who art so jealous that no half-worshipper gains thy full smile—is insincere that his readers have formed the idea that he is not sincere.   *Le style c'est l'homme !* That truth, too, has betrayed him ; a silly, affected, tinselly style, a "damme how clever " method of writing, fine but without eloquence, distressful but without pathos, glittering but without humour or fun —a shaft that strikes but does not remain—this, too, has ruined him, or at least carried away from him the glory which his young ambition desired.

You can see him near Grosvenor Gate walking in the sunshine, an old man who looks older than he is, bent down, with his hands behind his back, thoughtful, sallow, his face lined with care. You can see him, too, after a triumph in the House, youthful almost, very good-natured, genial and wise-looking, with a tender face, and a statesman-like look, a worthy chief to follow, something of the *old* young Disraeli who used to be found, in black velvet breeches, by the way, at the Countess of Blessington's assemblies, side by side with the present Emperor of the French. Or you can see him walking briskly along, talking to a man whom he wishes to convince, eager, active, and well-looking; one who was until late in life called young Disraeli, and whom, in spite of his sixty years, it is difficult to think of as old, who has the gift of a renewed youth, as some actors have; who when seen in the House, always contrasts with the ideal formed of him; one who has gathered from those with whom he lived an air of *haut ton* which his brothers never had, and which old Isaac Disraeli never had either, although he had an universal mind in its way, literary, but petty literary; the mind not of the poet nor of the noble prose-man, but of the book collector and *dilettanté*. Would, by the way, that we had more such book-men now.

A short time ago an old gentleman, who still lives not far from the British Museum, related to the author that he was intimate with the grandfather of the present Prime Minister and the father of old Isaac Disraeli, the author of " Curiosities of Literature." This old gentleman—himself of that grand Faith, in which alone Unitarianism is philosophic and epic in its sublime beauty, the faith of Judaism, which peddling critics would call the Jewish *persuasion*—is remarkable for having been at one time the successful rival to Rothschild; for to him and to his house was offered the gigantic loan of 1815 by Russia, on which the greater fortunes of the house were built. He refused it; Rothschild took it, and went up into the skies like a balloon. This, however, by the way. Our friend knew Disraeli's grandfather, a poor man, who was an Italian descendant of "one of those Hebrew families whom the Inquisition forced to emigrate from the Spanish Peninsula at the end of the fifteenth century. His ancestors had dropped their Gothic surname on their settlement in the Terra Firma; and grateful to the God of Jacob who had sustained them through unheard-of trials, they assumed the name of Disraeli (a name never borne before nor since by any other family), in order that *their race might be for ever recognised*."

This is a turgid sentence, written when the author was a mature man; and yet the "race" which is to be "for ever recognised," bids fair to be known but for a short time. Benjamin Disraeli had but one brother, James, who died unmarried, while the great leader of the family has no children. His grandfather was named Benjamin, "the son of the right

hand," and came to England in 1748, resolved to
settle in a country where the dynasty seemed established, and where public opinion seemed definitively
" averse to persecution *on* matters of creed and conscience." One may notice, as we pass them, the
strange use of prepositions in these sentences. Mr.
Disraeli's ancestors " settle *in* terra firma," and he
talks about persecution " *on* matters of creed." However, he has reason to be proud of his descent. His
family was of the Sephardim, that is, of those children of Israel who had never quitted the shores of
the Mediterranean, and who looked down upon all
other Jews as of an inferior caste. To the claim of
ancestry of such a man as this, that of our nobles and
ourselves must seem absurd. Ours is but puddle
blood compared with that of the noble Jew. Date as
we may, as a Stanley, a Percy, or a De Vere, from
the successful soldiers who regenerated the cause of
the robber William with the baptism of success, what
is a descent of eight hundred years compared with
that which must have run a thousand years before
the time of Christ, and which stretches beyond that
at least two thousand years? Mr. Disraeli has
always felt this. Unlike the Laureate, who wrote—

> " Trust me, Clara Vere de Vere,
>   In yon blue heavens above us bent,
>   The grand old gardener and his wife
>   Smile at the claims of long descent"—

he has put forward the value of race, the "generosity" (*generosus*, of good birth) of long descent, and has urged to the utmost the claim of his own people for hereditary talent. Let us especially note that he has never been at all ashamed of being a Jew in race and blood, and never would join with the silly Hebrews who write to the *Pall Mall Gazette* to complain that in the police reports a man is often described as "a Jew."

A Jew, then, a believer in the old covenant, old Benjamin Disraeli left the falling state of Venice one hundred and twenty years ago, and settled in England. After a prosperous life, he died at the age of ninety-six, leaving a studious, brown-eyed boy, a lover of books, a connoisseur, a *dilettanté*, and one not at all likely to advance the fortunes of the family. This was Isaac Disraeli, the author of "Curiosities of Literature," an amiable, learned, and excellent man, who aimed at uniting the style of Horace Walpole with the universal book-learning of Peter Bayle, and who has produced a most amusing and valuable work; shreds of other works, but one which will live. The literature of Isaac Disraeli lifted him into fashionable society. He knew the men of the day, and came westward a short step, moving from Red Lion Square into Bloomsbury Square; at the south-west corner of which his son Benjamin was born on the 21st December, 1805.*

This gentle, admirable old man of letters, certainly never made the family richer. That it was not very well off in the world's goods may be proved by the fact that Benjamin Disraeli, after an education at a suburban academy, was articled to a firm of city attorneys, dwelling most appropriately in the Old Jewry. But this apprenticeship he did not complete. The young man, ambitious, full of fire, an alien in blood, stamped with much of the peculiar facial qualities of his race, yet learned, fashionable, a marked man, had this problem set him: how to make *himself* the foremost man of the country he had adopted. Had not Joseph been sold into slavery three thousand years before, and had he not risen to be the Prime Minister of the Pharaohs, and the saviour of his people? Could not Benjamin, though

---

* Some Christians scoff at him as a Jew, with a singular disregard of all they owe to the Hebrew race. Now the fact is, that (in plain English) Disraeli is neither an apostate nor a Jew. He was born of Hebrew parents, but his father, thinking fit to quarrel with his synagogue, failed to teach his child Judaism. One day Rogers, the celebrated banker-poet, happening to visit at Isaac Disraeli's house, at Hackney, when Benjamin was five or six years old, and regretting to find so intelligent a youth without religious instruction, took him to Hackney Church. From this event dates his absolute and complete severance from the Jewish communion. He became a Christian, and a great genius was lost to us.—*Jewish Chronicle.*

of a scattered race, do much the same? His grand-father had, with an admirable foresight, chosen the nation wherein this problem was to be worked out. It was by political daring that he (Benjamin) would rise to political power.

Some such thoughts must have run through Mr. Disraeli's brain: we say *must*, because, although pictorial biography is, in most cases, deplorably false, yet in this one instance it is absolutely true. Mr. Disraeli has written many novels, and in more than one of these he represents himself as an ambitious youth, of foreign extraction or of Eastern birth, who, in answer to such dreams as these, does make certain advances, which bring him to the top of the tree. In the heroes of his own fictions, Mr. Disraeli has prophesied and foreshadowed his own political life; and, as we read this biography, we may just cast away for ever the foolish assertion that any man is "held down" or oppressed in free England. Given ambition and talents—and these not always of the highest—an attorney's clerk shall rise to be the leader of the Government of the proudest and most ancient monarchy of Europe. The uncertainty of a presidential election in the United States is a mere shadow to the certainty of this. Remember, we do not say that the position is worth the winning to certain pure yet ambitious minds; but we do assert that the chance is given, and that it may be won.

The future Prime Minister soon threw off the trammels of the attorney's desk, that dull prelude to so brilliant and so variegated a career, and stripped himself for the encounter. He started, just as he was twenty-one, a kind of Tory-Liberal paper, the *Representative*,* with just as much Toryism in it as a man of ancient blood might want, and just as much Liberalism as the readers might demand. But this soon came to grief. It was in truth very badly written, bombastic, vociferous—pot-valiant, as it were; for Mr. Disraeli's style as a writer is, in our opinion, far from good; whereas his style as a speaker, or a writer of vindicatory and vindictive letters, is excellent. Like a French soldier, he is always admirable, and full of fire in his attack. Not at all disheartened by his political failure, our hero then tried his pen, which he had flashed in politics, in romance, and wrote a series of political novels; each, we may be sure, with a deep meaning. They won for their author a certain renown. They took the town, and were everywhere talked of. They were accepted as very clever, brilliant novels, written more for the purpose of showing the views of a party, and for exhibiting the undoubted talent of their author, than

---

* Mr. Disraeli, in returning to a writer a biography of himself, made an elision of the passage concerning this paper. Mr. Murray started it, and Mr. Lockhart edited it. It lived five months.

for anything else. They were " Vivian Grey," the " Young Duke," " Contarini Fleming," " Voyage of Captain Papanilla," "Henrietta Temple," "Venetia," " Coningsby," the " Wondrous Tale of Alroy," a prose poem, &c. These have been often reprinted, but we doubt whether any of them will long survive. " Coningsby " is the best, and exhibits political life in anything but admirable colours. We may linger awhile over these stories, more to study the character of them and their author than for anything else. Every one of them is written in a bombastic and stilted style, but very pretentious, and certainly " taking," just as any novelty (ritualism, for instance) is taking at the time. They are præ-Raphaelite in effect, in rawness and brightness of colour; that is, in just the faults, and not the virtues, of the remarkable young painters ; they are, or rather were, *new*, just as the turgid " Guy Livingstone " was new; and they, one and all, bear witness to the intention and ambition of the author. To one of them Mr. Disraeli had prefixed the motto, " Why, then, the world's mine oyster, which with my sword I'll open ; " and with the same courage as that of an adventurous knight in the Middle Ages, it is evident that in the early part of this century the young author intended to go into the great lists and win. We have said the style is bad. It is that of a Byronic and Ossianic prose, not like the sweet simplicity of

our best writers, and some of it fairly sets our teeth
on edge, though we are ready to confess that it may
please others. Take, for example, this rhapsody
from "Contarini Fleming:" "Oh, inscrutable, in-
exorable destiny, which must be fulfilled!—doom
that mortals must endure, and cannot, direct! Lo, I
kneel before thee, and I pray. Let it end! let it
end! let it end at once!" [The young gentleman
is raving for his sweetheart.] "And shall it not be?
Do I exist? do I breathe, and think, and dare? And
I a man—and a man of strong passions, and deep
thoughts? And shall I, like a vile beggar upon my
knees, crave the rich heritage that is my own by
right? If she be not mine, there is no longer time,
—no longer human existence,—no longer a beautiful
and an everlasting world. Let it all cease; let the
whole globe crack and shiver; *let all nations and all
human hopes expire at once; let chaos come again, if
this girl be not my bride!*"

After this, superfine reviews may condemn penny
novels if they like; but we, who endeavour to be
fair, must own that many of the cheap novels boast
a purer style, and even tear their passions into more
effective tatters, when they do tear them, than does
the Prime Minister. But it was not all rant that
filled these novels. Disraeli claimed for his race the
supreme talent and the directing mind of the world;
and, although the claim is by far too wide, there was

something in it; and it was, and is, a noble sight to see a young David of an oppressed race stepping forward so boldly, with only the sling of his genius, and the stone of his bitter tongue, to slay the ugly Goliath of popular ignorance and prejudice. "Hath not a Jew eyes?" "If you prick us do we not bleed?" says the universal Shakespeare, anxious only to put a Jew on the same footing as ourselves. Is not a Jew the best musician in the world, the best financial minister, the best dancer, theatrical *entrepreneur?* asks Disraeli; in short, has not the Jew the oldest blood and the finest genius in the world? "The Jews," says Coningsby, "are essentially Tories;" "Race is the only truth;" "The Jews are of the purest race,—the chosen people; they are the aristocracy of Nature." You will find all these in "Tancred, or the New Crusade," published in 1847, in which year the author also argued the admission of Jews into Parliament against the views of his own political friends. This was brave, courageous, and to be applauded. Many of his assertions are bombastic, and his proofs futile. All the genius of the world does not, as he asserts, lie in the Jew musicians, Mendelssohn and Mozart; but his generous boldness is to be applauded; and as great an amount of genius and talent is to be allowed to the Jewish people now existing as to any other people; but certainly not more.

P

To go back to the novels. After the very rapid production of the earlier ones, Mr. Disraeli left England in 1829, spent the winter in Constantinople, and travelled in the spring through Syria, Egypt, and Nubia. He returned in 1831 with new views, as we have seen, of race, and of the Asian mystery, and found the people very much agitated about Reform. He put up for Wycombe, a nice little borough in Bucks, about five miles from his father's seat at Bradenham, and started with a recommendation from Mr. Hume and from Daniel O'Connell as something between Whig and Tory. All that is certain is, that he went in for triennial Parliaments and vote by ballot. He fought three electioneering battles here, got defeated each time, and then turned up at Taunton as a Conservative of Lord Lyndhurst's type; that is, as very much the sort of leader he is now. Here it was that he indulged in a sneer, not undeserved, at O'Connell, and brought down upon himself that coarse castigation which has become a familiar quotation. "He calls me traitor," said O'Connell; "my answer to that is, that he is a liar. He is a liar in action and in words. His life is a living lie." And, as if that was not strong enough, the demagogue went on: "When I speak of Mr. Disraeli as a Jew, I mean not to taunt him on that account. Better ladies and gentlemen than amongst the Jews I have never met. They were once the chosen people of God. There were miscreants among them, however; and it must certainly have been from one of those that Disraeli descended. He possesses just the qualities of the impenitent thief who died upon the cross, whose name must have been Disraeli. (Roars of laughter.) For aught I know, the present Disraeli is descended from him; and with the impression that he is, I now forgive *the heir-at-law of the blasphemous thief that died upon the cross.*" * (Loud cheers, mingled with laughter.)

This is very Irish, very wrong, and very shocking, and yet all the world laughed at it. Disraeli the Younger, as he was then called, stood against the jeers of the world, answered the agitator with invective, and as the latter could not fight, being precluded by a vow, he challenged his son, Morgan O'Connell, to resume " his vicarious duties of yielding satisfaction for the insults which his father lavished with impunity on his political opponents ! " The challenge was not accepted. Mr. Disraeli then wrote to O'Connell a wonderfully strong letter, before the brilliant style of which all the writer's novels pale and fade. "Although you," he wrote, " have

---

* Mr. Disraeli has been blamed for replying to these hard words, and Professor Goldwin Smith is very angry at being called a "social parasite ; " but did not Goldwin Smith himself just say something quite as hard in intention, something about a lackey in the guise of a statesman?

P 2

long placed yourself out of the pale of civilisation, still I am one that will not be insulted, even by a Yahoo, without chastising IT. * * I called upon your son to assume his vicarious office of yielding satisfaction for his *shrinking sire.* I admire your scurrilous allusions to my origin. I know the tactics of your Church ; *it clamours for toleration ; it labours for supremacy.*" Then, in allusion to O'Connell, he compares himself to him. " You say that I was once a Radical, and am now a Tory. My conscience acquits me of ever having deserted a political friend, or of ever having changed a political opinion. I have nothing to appeal to but the good sense of the people. A death's head and cross-bones were not blazoned on my banners." (This in allusion to O'Connell's disturbance in Ireland.) " My pecuniary resources, too, were limited. I was not one of those public beggars that we see swarming with their obtrusive boxes in the chapels of your creed. Nor am I in possession of a princely revenue, arising from a starving race of fanatical slaves. I expect, however, to be a representative of the people *before the Repeal of the Union.* We shall meet at Philippi."

The letter closed with a threatened castigation of the " big beggarman," who was then collecting " rint " from the deluded Irish peasantry, for the purpose of obtaining a " repale," which he knew he should never get. Mr. Disraeli sent also a letter to

O'Connell's son, in which he said, "I will take every opportunity of holding your father's name up to public contempt ; and I fervently pray that you, or some of your blood, may attempt to avenge the inextinguishable hatred with which I shall pursue his existence." This is strong language ; but it was forty years ago, when people were somewhat rougher than they are now. Mr. Disraeli, then writing in the *Times*, utterly extinguished the editor of the *Globe*, who took up O'Connell's cause. "An anonymous writer," he says, "should at least display power. When Jupiter hurls a thunderbolt, it may be mercy in the god to veil his glory with a cloud ; but we can only view with contemptuous lenity the mischievous varlet who pelts us with mud as we are riding by, and then hides behind a dusthole." Altogether these political attacks, although often unjust, did Mr. Disraeli an immense deal of good ; they brought him out ; they proved him to be a master of fence. "The editor of the *Globe*," he said (it is worthy of remark that the paper now is the staunchest supporter of the Premier), "has recorded in his columns a lively memento of his excited doltishness. · What does it signify? His business is to chalk the walls of the nation with praises of his master's blacking. He is worthy of his vocation ; only it is ludicrous to see this poor devil whitewashing the barriers of Bayswater with the selfsame complacency as if he were

painting the halls of the Vatican." Mr. Disraeli
was now a marked man, even as a politician ; and in
the next election (1832) he found that the first step
of the ladder had been mounted, and that he was a
British representative, as member for Maidstone.

When still a young man, and in the enviable position of the enjoyment of the fulfilment of his first
and young ambition, " I shall be," he wrote to
O'Connell, " a representative of the people before
the Repeal of the Union." His prophecy had been
fulfilled, and, happy in his quiet but " immense self-
sufficiency "—to borrow a phrase from M. Louis
Blanc—he set forward in his career as a member of
Parliament. Now, the House of Commons, like
every other large club where men congregate, and
where individual weight is felt, is just the place to
take the nonsense out of a man. Each member soon
falls to his natural level; and the good nature as
well as the good sense of the House is remarkable.
The whole House, it has been said, has always more
common sense and more genius than any single
member, or than any dozen members, even though
they were the best ; and it is curious to find how
every new man, however great he may promise to be
before his election, is absorbed in the House, and
becomes, excepting in the rarest instance, a very
small portion of it. Look even at the two greatest
and most popular men of the Manchester school, Mr.

John Stuart Mill and Mr. John Bright. Out of the
House, addressing a crowded assembly in the Free
Trade Hall, or on the hustings of Westminster, these
gentlemen seem intellectual and oratorical giants;
but in the House of Commons they are amongst
their peers, and though they have full weight allowed
them there, they are not the Kings of Men that they
appear to be outside its walls.

Hence we must not be surprised if the fervid and
Eastern eloquence of Mr. Disraeli fell upon dull ears
in the House, and that even derisive cheers were
heard to greet his maiden speech. "Gentlemen,"
he is reported to have said, "you will not hear me
now; the time will come when you shall hear me."
He was at that time a member of the *coterie* of young
aspirants in literature and art who were often to be
seen at the evening parties of one of the most brilliant, notorious, and beautiful women of her time, the
Countess of Blessington; and at her house, Gore
House (which has now disappeared to make room for
one of the speculations of Prince Albert and Mr.
Henry Cole), Mr. Disraeli met some very curious
characters: Mr. Duncombe, the "Radical" member, of the most Conservative notions as regarded
himself; the Count D'Orsay, the Beau Brummel of
his time; and a melancholy gentleman, who lived in
King Street, St. James's, and had ambitious dreams
about fulfilling the destiny of his uncle. This gentle-

man, well known simply as "the Prince," used to walk quietly in to those evening receptions, and would rather listen than talk. He was so quiet, so observant, that some likened him to a gloomy sporting man; and there yet remains a sketch of him, by D'Orsay, leaning against the folding doors of the countess's drawing-room, melancholy and contemplative, and dressed in the tight black trousers and swallow-tail coat of the period. What was that man revolving in his mind? Was he then contemplating an invasion of France with a few discontented soldiers and a tame eagle? Was he dreaming of the time when his word would shake the world and give peace or war? Count D'Orsay, Mr. Benjamin Disraeli, and last and greatest, the present Emperor of the French, were three of the most extraordinary of those men, great in fashion, literature, and art, that assembled at Gore House; and between two of them, Mr. Disraeli and Prince Napoleon, there sprang up a great friendship.

During his enforced silence, if little Benjamin held his tongue, he did not refrain from using his pen. He is more than suspected, although it is said that he does not acknowledge the fact, of having written in the *Times* the celebrated letters of "Runnymede," addressed to various people and ministers, alternately in a cajoling and an insulting mood. We know how celebrated Mr. Disraeli is for his invective, and we may in these letters trace two things to their head : the first, the source of the Minister's powers ; the second, the source of that intense dislike which is entertained by too many towards him, and which will pursue him to his grave. The letters in the *Times* were in imitation of those of Junius ; but they did not equal those effusions, either in cause or effect. What the Runnymede letters did was to sell the paper and amuse the Tories, while they affixed party names on Whig leaders, and did little else. Of Lord John Russell " Runnymede " said that he was "born with a feeble intellect and a strong ambition," " busied with the tattle of valets ; " that he was " a feeble Catiline ; " that he had " a propensity to degrade everything to his own mean level, and to measure everything by his malignant standard ; " that he had written " the feeblest tragedy in the language," &c. Lord Palmerston was " a great Apollo of aspiring understrappers ; " had " the smartness of an attorney's clerk, and the intrigues of a Greek of the Lower Empire ; " was " a crimping lordship, with a career as insignificant as his intellect ; " that " he reminded one of a favourite footman on easy terms with his mistress ; " that " he was the Sporus of politics, cajoling France with an airy compliment, and menacing Russia with a perfumed cane." These are happy sentences, but neither politic nor wise. We cannot wonder if the author of them made enemies. Our present political writers are more polite.

The election of 1841 placed the power of Government in a Conservative Ministry, headed by Sir Robert Peel, strengthened by Lord Stanley (the late Earl of Derby), and commanding a huge majority in both Houses. The Ministry had the confidence of the country, and Mr. Disraeli was one of their supporters. But in 1844 the Corn-Law agitation worked wonders. Mr. Cobden and John Bright "stumped" the country, and by their arguments, their brilliant oratory, their common-sense views, brought thousands to their way of thinking. The last and most illustrious of these disciples was Sir Robert Peel himself. ·During the years that this Ministry held sway, from 1841 to 1846, Mr. Disraeli had been rising in the public estimation. He had published some very clever novels—"Coningsby," "Sybil," and "Tancred,"—and was identified with Lord John Manners and others as the leaders of the "Young England" party. The "Young England" people were the ritualists of politics. Everything was to be regenerated by a restoration. Chivalry was good; therefore we were to dress in armour, and indulge in the Eglinton tournament. The working man was good; the peasant—the noble peasant—was the tiller of the soil and the man who made all the money; therefore lord and peasant were to be on the most friendly terms; the lord taking, as usual, the best share. The middle classes were passed over, or rather regarded as the enemies of both. Trade was condemned. In "England's Trust," a poem written about that time, Lord John Manners has gained an uneasy immortality by a couplet which was said by friends and enemies to embody the creed of the party:

" Let wealth and commerce, laws and learning die ;
    But leave us still our old Nobility."

Had he written the cleverest satire in the world, he could not have more thoroughly damaged his friends. But Young England did not perceive it. They thought that an advance was to be made by a retrograde movement. The Queen and Prince Albert gave a fancy dress ball, in which they were dressed as Edward III. and Philippa of Hainault; and the Earl of Eglinton nearly beggared his estate by a grand tournament, in which Lord Chesterfield and other noblemen, dressed in complete armour, tilted at each other as knights of old, and a Queen of Beauty gave the prize to the most skilful knight and the most gallant horseman. This was pretty, romantic, and foolish. The dead past is dead; you cannot galvanise Queen Anne to life again, much less a monarch who died upwards of three hundred years previously. It was significant, too, that while all

were doing it in reality, no young nobleman would
play the fool in a fancy dress. But Motley was
there,—a clever artist, one of the middle classes.
He rode on a donkey, clothed in a patched dress,
archæologically correct, cracked mild witticisms of
the *soi-disant* knights, and belaboured his particular
ass (he did not dare to touch the others) with a
bladder of peas hung at the end of his bauble.

In the meantime Ebenezer Elliott was writing the
Corn-Law Rhymes. People were starving in the
North, and carrying a big loaf about the streets,
crying for cheap food and the repeal of the Corn
Laws. The party of Young England shouted, " No
surrender! " and Sir Robert Peel, at the head of a
Tory Ministry, made a memorable speech, in which
he confessed that the time was come that his duty
to the people made him sunder all his old friendships,
but that when he was dead he prayed to be remembered " as one who had brought a cheap loaf to the
cottage of the poor." Poor Sir Robert! his very
pathos was prosaic, but he gained the day : the Corn
Laws were abolished ; and henceforward Mr. Disraeli
assailed him with the greatest bitterness. Of him
he had once said that " whether in or out of office,
he had done his best to make the settlement of the
new Constitution of England work for the benefit of
the present time and of posterity ; " but now he
said he " flung down the gauntlet at the feet of the

man he had once been proud to follow." He exhausted invective in his speeches. Sir Robert, he said, was at the head of an organised hypocrisy, a traitor to his party, "a great Parliamentary middleman, who bamboozled one party and plundered the other." It is useless to chronicle any more of these brilliant flashes of spiteful wit. "The Tories," said Mr. Disraeli, "had found the Whigs bathing, and had stolen their clothes;" they had passed a measure advocated by their opponents. The country was quiet; and instead of a follower of the great Sir Robert, Mr. Disraeli was at the head of a small but compact party, lecturing to mechanics out of the House, and telling them to "aspire," declaring that English history "was to be re-written," sketching a brilliant future for Young England; and in the House, making people wonder at his exhaustive invective and brilliant sarcasms, and admire his head if they did not love his heart. "Disraeli is up," was the cry from the Strangers' Gallery; "we are sure to hear something good, and galling to Sir Robert."

This was soon to cease. Sir Robert, abandoned by his party, left office in 1846; and henceforward he attached himself to no party, but tried to strengthen every Administration by his calm advice and his great practical wisdom. "He was," said M. Guizot (who, himself a Prime Minister, can well judge of the difficulties which beset a statesman), "a great and

honest servant of the State, proud with a sort of
humility, and desiring to shine with no brilliancy
extrinsic to his natural sphere; devoted to his
country, without any craving for reward. Severing
himself from the past without cynical indifference,
braving the future without adventurous boldness,
solely swayed by the desire to meet the necessities of
the present, and to do himself honour by delivering
his country from peril and embarrassment ;—he was
thus in turn a Conservative and a Reformer, a Tory
or Whig, and almost a Radical, more wise than
provident, more courageous than firm, but always
sincere." What a panegyric for an English statesman ! What glory to England, that by her Constitution she called to her councils such a man, the
grandson ('tis his greatest glory) of a rich Lancashire
cotton spinner ! In 1850, just as it seemed he would
again soon be called to power, Sir Robert, thrown
from his horse, died, after three days' illness, amidst
the regrets of the highest and the lowest, friends and
foes, who were alike proud of their English leader.
Working men who studied politics, and who loved
their country, crowded late in the night round the
door of the dying statesman in Whitehall Gardens,
as anxious to listen to the last message of the doctor
as were the owners of the coroneted carriages, as
they waited for the whispered news.

In 1847 Mr. Disraeli was elected for Bucks, and

he took as his leader that gentleman of a stable mind in more senses than one, Lord George Bentinck. In 1848 a sudden death deprived us of that honest nobleman, and Mr. Disraeli was left as the recognised leader of his party. In February, 1852, the Mr. Disraeli, whose star had been gradually rising, was for the first time invested with the insignia of office. The Russell Ministry had ceased to exist, and Lord Derby was called upon to form a Ministry, of which the popular novelist was Chancellor of the Exchequer.

Of course there were a thousand pens pointed against this: the "idea," said the Philistines, " of a novelist being a man of figures!" People shook their heads in the City; the wise and the prudent hesitated; the silly and the forward were loud and open in their sneers; but on the third of February Mr. Disraeli took the House by storm with a budget clearly and lucidly put, and so dexterously framed, that even his opponents complimented him, and his companions applauded him to the echo. What Mr. Disraeli had more than once said had been " looming in the future " (now an almost forgotten, but once a celebrated phrase), was all made clear; and in a speech of five hours' duration, the Chancellor, master of the situation, expounded his views. Though the speech was easy to listen to, the items of the budget were not so easy to digest. Mr. Disraeli had

been faithful to the country party: there was an
increase on the house-tax, and a decrease of the
malt-tax. "You must alter your budget," said
one, "like Mr. Pitt." "I do not aspire to Mr.
Pitt's fame," was the humble, though proud reply;
" but I will not submit to the degradation of other
Chancellors." The Opposition rallied; a want of
confidence was plainly exhibited; and in a few days—
in the autumn of the year—the Duke of Wellington
died, and the Tories were thus deprived of his wise
councils; the Derby Ministry was out of office,
and Mr. Disraeli sat on the Opposition benches to
Lord Aberdeen. Throughout the times that followed,
Mr. Disraeli, faithful to his party, adhered to Lord
Derby, doing yeoman's service, attacking the Ministry
in brilliant speeches, and proving to admiration the
use of a censor in a free Government, and especially
of that which we should always desire to have, "Her
Majesty's Opposition" in strong force. When Lord
Derby came in, in 1858-9, our hero was again his
Chancellor, and brought in a most ingenious Reform
Bill, which, although admirable in many points, was
thrown out by the Whigs, principally at the instance
and jealousy of Lord John Russell, who no doubt
believed that, having passed the great measure thirty
years before, he was born to complete and supple-
ment it. But the Whigs failed to bring in a sufficient
measure of their own; and in the parliamentary

session of 1864 the eloquence of Mr. Disraeli was turned against Lord Palmerston's Government, especially as to his foreign policy, and was outpoured in favour of peace with France, and especially with the Emperor of that great country, his old friend of Gore House.

In 1865 Earl Russell was called to the head of affairs, having Lord Cranworth as his Lord Chancellor, and Mr. Gladstone as Chancellor of the Exchequer; and Mr. Disraeli did little else than carefully, and for his party, wisely, act as the leader of the Opposition. Thus he vigorously opposed the Whig Reform Bill, showing how hollow it was. But in defeating the Whigs, the Tories only gave a promissory-note of a wider measure ; and when, in July, 1866, Earl Derby was again called to the head of affairs, with Mr. Disraeli as Chancellor of the Exchequer, the latter had the honour of preparing a wide Reform Bill, which it is said by some will revolutionise the country. This is, of course, an exaggerated statement; to us the future of England is full of promise. When in February, 1868, the ill-health of Earl Derby compelled him to resign, the " literary man"—Vivian Grey—was sent for by the Queen, and Mr. Disraeli's patient striving of many years was crowned with success : he was placed in the highest position that a subject can occupy—that of First Minister of the Crown ; the dispenser of

Q

favours, places, and pensions; the wielder of a far
greater sway than the President of the most far-
stretching power in the world, the great American
Republic—hedged round with striving, alien, and
often hated rivals and possible successors—can hope
to wield.

It is not our purpose here to trace Mr. Disraeli's
political career. He was, in more senses than one,
but a stop-gap; he held for a short time the reins of
power; introduced a Reform Bill far more sweeping
than that offered us by the Radicals; made some excellent speeches; presided at a Literary Fund dinner;
was beaten by Mr. Gladstone, and went out of office,
with the rumour, too, about his ears that the Tories
were seeking another leader.

It was in the spring of 1870 that the literary and
political worlds were startled by the announcement
that Mr. Disraeli had in the press a new and brilliant
novel, to be called " Lothair."

In due time the book was published, and the
rumoured high price given, and numbers of the novel
ordered—£10,000 and twenty-five thousand as a *first*
edition, though, of course, not true—served to awaken
the curiosity of the world.

After the book appeared there was immediate
criticism. The poor author, however meritorious, has
to wait for years before he meets—if ever in his life
he meets—with due recognition; but when a review

of a book pays for its insertion by attracting readers, the press is quite wise enough to help the author *and* itself.

There was, of course, much acute and much windy and wordy criticism published about "Lothair"—which dazzled people for a time, like a firework—which was of course the cleverest novel of the season—nay, almost of the century. This it is not; but it *is* a very clever, and in so far, remarkable production. Mr. Disraeli is like his own French cook, who makes a splendid new dish of the oldest materials, and expects to receive the utmost applause for his cleverness; but, unlike his cook, he gets that which is so dear to the soul of the artist. Knowing the love of the English for lords, he doses them with lord after lord, and duke after duke, in his work; so much of the miscalled aristocratic element do we find, that we, like the *Spectator*, almost fear to criticise it, "without having an impartial duke on our literary staff." "Lothair," adds the reviewer, is apt to give one "duchesses, jewels, and general splendours on the brain;" it does more, it not only sickens one with false images, joyous excitement, excessive flattery of rank and love of riches, but it reveals that which else the author is very careful to hide—his Eastern origin, and his gorgeous and warm Judæan imagination. It is written with the utmost good-nature, and with a youthful exuberance which will be found to be very entrancing after the cold scepticism, the *nil admirari* cynicism, and penny satire of the day. Young ladies are entrancingly beautiful and intensely virtuous ; they sing, in these pages, as well as professionals; when they open their mouths, "roses seem to drop from them, and sometimes diamonds !" When they are angry, they have "tumults of the brow;" if they are rich, they have possessions in six or seven counties, and in each of the three kingdoms ; if they are beautiful, they surpass angels that ever painter or sculptor dreamt of. The plotting priests, who in this world are very common, coarse, mean people, using the devil's weapons for the devil's end, and truckling to mean passions with mean souls and meaner bribes, are full of intellect—acute, subtle, commanding—giving the directions of generals of the Pope's army for the reduction of kingdoms, the reversal of the verdict of ages, the subversion of the purpose of God. His very lawyers and men of business ooze from their pores with wondrous talent, and with a fatty richness which is somewhat sickening. He has fitly described his own style as an "ornate jargon ;" we have been reminded that we must borrow from De Quincey a better expression, though itself disfigured with De Quincey's false symbolism—"a jewelly hæmorrhage of words." It is not "jewelly;" the lumps of glittering matter poured out in the dazzling cascade are simply bits of glass or wood covered with tinsel ; they look like the jewelled haunts of the gnome of the diamonds in a pantomime ; go near them, even as close as the orchestra, and you see what they are.

And let us add that, with unconscious satire, produced, no doubt, by a certain reflex action of his mind, Mr. Disraeli has far surpassed, in " Lothair," the good-natured and most admirable satire on himself, written by Thackeray in his " Novels by Eminent Hands." Let any reader compare the two works, Thackeray's satire, "Codlingsby," by the Right Hon. B. Shrewsberry, and " Lothair," by the Right Hon. B. Disraeli, and ask whether one is more overloaded than the other. How delicious in its gaudy and incongruous colour is this extract of Codlingsby's palace in Holywell Street, which, by the way, is at the back of an old clothes'-shop. Did not the spirit of Disraeli, while its author was in a trance, escape from its body to inhabit for a time the brain of the satirist ?

"They entered a moderate-sized apartment—indeed, Holywell Street is not above a hundred yards long, and this chamber was not more than half that length—and fitted up with *the simple taste* of its owner. ·

The carpet was of white velvet- -(laid over several webs of Aubusson, Ispahan, and Axminster, so that your foot gave no more sound as it trod upon the yielding plain than the shadow which followed you)—of white velvet painted with flowers, arabesques, and classic figures by Sir William Ross, J. M.˙ W.

Turner, R.A., Mrs. Mee, and Paul Delaroche.*   The edges
were wrought with seed pearl, Valenciennes lace and bullion.
The walls were hung with cloth of silver, embroidered with gold
figures, over which were worked pomegranates, polyanthuses,
and passion-flowers, in ruby, amethyst, and smaragd.   The
drops of dew which the artificers had sprinkled on the flowers,
were of diamonds.   The hangings were overhung with pictures
yet more costly.   Giorgione the gorgeous, Titian the golden,
Rubens the ruddy and pulpy (the Pan of Painting), some of
Murillo's beatified shepherdesses, who smile on you out of darkness like a star; a few score of first-class Leonardos, and fifty
of the masterpieces of the patron of Julius and Leo, the imperial
genius of Urbino, covered the walls of the *little* chamber.
Divans of carved amber, covered with ermine, went round the
room, and in the midst was a fountain pattering and babbling
into jets of double-distilled otto of roses.

'Pipes, Goliath!' Rafael said gaily, to a little negro with a
silver collar (he spoke to him in his native tongue of Dongola);
'and welcome to our snuggery, my Codlingsby.'"

It is in this snuggery that Rafael Mendoza lends
money to the Pope and the Czar, entertains dukes,
earls, bishops, and archbishops by the dozens; brags
about the eternity and nobility of his race, and talks
with his sister, who is thus described, seated at an
ivory pianoforte, on a mother-of-pearl music-stool:

"Her hair had that deep glowing tinge in it which has been
the delight of all painters, and which, therefore, the vulgar sneer
at.   It was of burning auburn, meandering over her fairest

---

* ·The burlesque is perfect; the incongruity of painters, *the
seed pearls*, *Valenciennes lace and bullion*, the mixture of colours,
and the showy display of knowledge, which reveals ignorance,
are all in the best style of *caricatura.*

shoulders in twenty thousand minute ringlets; it hung to her waist, and below it. A light-blue velvet fillet, clasped with a diamond aigrette (valued at two hundred thousand tomauns, and bought from Lieutenant Vicovich, who had received it from Dost Mahomed), with a simple bird of paradise, formed her head-gear. A sea-green cymar, with short sleeves, displayed her exquisitely-moulded arms to perfection, and was fastened by a girdle of emeralds over a yellow satin frock. Pink gauze trousers, spangled with silver, and slippers of the same colour as the band which clasped her ringlets (but so covered with pearls, that the original hue of the charming papoosh disappeared entirely), completed her costume. She had three necklaces on, each of which would have dowered a princess; her fingers glittered with rings to their rosy tips, and priceless bracelets, bangles, and armlets wound round an arm that was whiter than the ivory grand-piano on which it leaned."

Here, too, is a touch not to be left out, as it is the chief point and high light of the picture: "'My lord's pipe is out,' said Miriam, with a smile, remarking the bewilderment of her guest—who, in truth, forgot to smoke; and taking up a thousand-pound note from a bundle on the piano, she lighted it at the taper, and proceeded to re-illumine the extinguished chibouk of Lord Codlingsby."

This is fine caricature, but really the painting is not much more overlaid than the original novel is in many parts. Disraeli paints, as we have shown, with a full brush; he overpowers the imagination of the vulgar, and wins or compels admiration by proceeding like a Timbuctoo lover,—first knocking his future bride down. Here, for instance, from

"Lothair," is a piece of work combining a clever sketch of a Bond Street jeweller, which is marvellously like that written by Thackeray:

"' Very interesting,' said Lothair, ' but what I want are pearls. That necklace which you have shown me is *like the necklace of a doll.* I want pearls, such as you see them in Italian pictures —Titians and Giorgiones—*such as a Queen of Cyprus would wear. I want ropes of pearls.'*—' Ah !' said Mr. Ruby, ' I know what your lordship means. Lady Bideford had something of that kind. She very much deceived us,—always told us her necklace must be sold at her death, and she had very bad health. We waited, but when she went, poor lady I it was claimed by the heir, and is in Chancery at this very moment. *The Justiniani's have ropes of pearls*—Madame Justiniani, of Paris, I have been told, gives a rope to every one of her children when they marry— but there is no expectation of a Justiniani parting with anything. Pearls are troublesome property, my Lord.   They require great care ; they want both air and exercise ; they must be worn frequently : you cannot lock them up   The Duchess of Havant has the finest pearls in this country, and I told her Grace, " Wear them whenever you can ; wear them at breakfast," and her Grace follows my advice,—she does wear them at breakfast. I go down to Havant Castle every year to see her Grace's pearls, and I wipe every one of them myself, and let them lie on a sunny bank in the garden, in a westerly wind, for hours and days together.   Their complexion would have been ruined had it not been for this treatment.   Pearls are like girls, my Lord, the y require quite as much attention.' "

Now and then Disraeli's satire peeps out with a delicate and good-natured flash, as in this description of the present slang of society : "' English is an expressive language,' said Mr. Pinto, ' but not difficult · to master.   It consists, so far as I can observe, of four words—'nice,' 'jolly,' 'charming,'' and 'bore'—and some grammarians add ' fond.'"

And the author deserves much credit for the real good nature of that satire, which is never morbid and hopeless. Indeed, some persons think it is hardly bitter enough. In pointing out the enemies of England—the perverts who would lead her to perdition, the silent, deceptive, and oily-black soldiery of the Jesuits, from whom, as well as from their antagonists, the secret societies, Mr. Disraeli's gay and gilded society, his charming dukes, beauteous duchesses, and divine Corisandes, with stately parks and domains larger than ordinary counties, have so much to fear —the author does not betray any peculiar feeling, or any hatred. He loves England, he must venerate it as the home of civil and religious liberty, but he looks with marvellous good-temper upon those gentlemen who are quietly undermining the walls of that home, and are storing up their gunpowder, barrel after barrel, to blow all such liberty to the sky. This easiness gives an air of lightness and persiflage to his work. The feeling of unreality begotten by the overloaded style is strengthened by the calm easy manner in which Monsignore Catesby and his crew are described.* And when one has read the book, clever as

* One of the most conspicuous characters in the ecclesiastical intrigue which is the main subject of Mr. Disraeli's new

it is, it is soon forgotten. It makes no abiding impression. We move among a fantastic crowd of conspirators and great priests, wealthy converts and rich men, and we forget that he but paints the reality, and pictures Dr. Manning, and Cardinal Wiseman, and the Marquis of Bute, and other people of our day, because he has drawn reality with so unreal a touch. To the great people with whom he has lived intimately for years, Disraeli's conduct, in picturing his intimates in such a "high falutin" style, and in giving, in their own exaggerated language, their own portraits, doings and sayings, has seemed little less than base, or as they say, " exceedingly improper," for one who has been a Prime Minister. To the lower and dangerous classes—to whom such a book, filtered through demagogic papers, will seem but a proof that the stories of G. W. M. Reynolds and the *London Journal* are actual truths—Mr. Disraeli has

---

story, is a certain Monsignore Catesby. The name smacks of treason, conspiracy, and gunpowder. The inquisitive people who profess to see real and living persons under the novelist's masks have decided to their own satisfaction that Monsignore Catesby is a respected and accomplished English priest, very well known in London, Father Capel. By a strange oversight, Mr. Disraeli has in one instance allowed the name Capel to be printed instead of Catesby. The error will be found in page 254 of the third volume of "Lothair." We will not speculate as to the origin of the blunder, which, whether or not it proceeded from the author's pen, has certainly escaped his eye. But it is curious enough to be worth recording.—*Daily News.*

pointed out the plate-chest. The democrats who meet in Hyde Park, and who vote the instant demolition of the " lounging classes," the equalisation of property, and the extinction of poverty by making us all alike poor and destitute, must feel, after having read of some of Mr. Disraeli's fabulously rich dukes, like the thievish soldier Marshal Blucher, who, after walking through Cheapside and seeing the jewellers' shops and riches of the City, and mounting the Monument and beholding equally rich streets stretching on every side, could only ejaculate, " Mein Gott, what plunder!" Whether the author will succeed in awakening the Protestants of this sceptical age to their danger, we very much doubt.

Lastly, the unreality of Disraeli's novels carries away from them any kind of conviction. Their brilliance tires ; their knowledge puffeth up, but doth not " edify," or, in English—for our Bible there follows the Latin too much—their knowledge puffeth up, but the higher knowledge of the true writer buildeth up. That is an edification which is beyond Disraeli. " But, then," says the reader, " the publishers have given £10,000 for his new novel, and do you dare to pronounce his work not of the first class ?" Dear reader, listen and perpend. The publisher would give a large sum for a novel by Lady Mordaunt, if it was the greatest bosh in the world, because of the notoriety of her name : people would rush to read it.

What is good the publisher as a rule does not know; what will *sell* he does know. "One day," said a lady of rank to the author, "I was desperately in want of some money, and I mentioned my want. It was to relieve some poor relation of Lady C. B., a woman of title who wrote, and who had written herself out. She jumped for joy. That's just what I want; C. or B., the publisher, has been haggling with me about my last novel; I want three hundred; they offer me two, because I have written too fast. 'Why,' said I, 'you gave me seven hundred for my first.' 'Yes, my lady,' said the Tonson of the day, 'your name was fresh then; if you will get us a fresh name with a title, we will give you seven hundred again.'" And they *did*, too. Lady C. B.'s novel was published as by the Countess ——, *edited* by the real authoress, and the publisher netted a considerable sum from the extra attraction. The story is quite true; we could mention the book. It will show you why so large an amount is to be given for "Lothair." As a man of letters, then, to us, we must openly confess Disraeli ranks but as a mediocrity; we admire his pluck, but we cannot wholly admire his novels.

Let us add two pretty little stories which have been the round of society, and which prove the love and attachment subsisting between the late Premier and his wife. Some one was saying that his face was handsome. "Handsome!" cried Lady Beaconsfield, "it is beautiful; you should see him while he sleeps!" The illusions and the love of youth had survived even till the autumn of life in the heart that could thus speak! Again, driving down to the House to hear a great speech from her husband on an important occasion, he, full of his subject, and preoccupied as he jumped from the brougham, shut one of her fingers in the door. Agonising as was the pain, she uttered no cry till he was out of sight, and then called her footman to open the door. "My dear," she is reported to have said, to one to whom she told the story, "I would not have cried out for the world; in thinking of my pain he would have been so agitated that he would have forgotten all the chief points in his speech."

Let us, too, add, that in all his novels there is no incident more chivalric and graceful than that which belongs to history, of a Prime Minister who had made dukes, and added more than one historic name to the peerage, refusing all honour himself, and laying the coronet of a viscountess at the feet of his wife.

And, apart from his literary fame, it will be as well to consider the lesson of his life. Since the beginning of this century there have been, omitting Mr. Gladstone, twenty-three Premiers, and but two—save Disraeli—not of the patrician order. These were Mr. Canning and Sir Robert Peel. Mr. Disraeli makes a third; and his elevation M. Louis Blanc regards as "very natural, yet very singular; very sad, yet very fortunate." He is not at all rich; in fact, were it not for a recent legacy, he would be a poor man. "What is it, then," asks this able writer, "that has put England—and, to begin with, the English aristocracy—at the feet of this plebeian, this Jew, this cosmopolite, this man of so anti-English a character? There he stands, at the head of a party he had taken such trouble to educate! erect on the body he has so dexterously led to commit suicide." His intellect is no ordinary one; but his is not the triumph of intellect: he has been true to one party, and that is *himself.* "It is sad, therefore," concludes M. Louis Blanc, "for it is a fatal example of respect for political rectitude having no share in his success. It is fortunate, because it shows that henceforth, in England, power will be no longer the exclusive property of a few patrician families." This has long been the case, M. Blanc. From Mr. Disraeli's story we take a happier augury. We believe that he has risen because he has read surely and truly the lesson of events, because he had boldness, talent, pluck, and honesty on his side, and because he has determined to set aside conventional dulness, and to open the way to the aristocracy of mind. And it is incumbent upon us, in the present crisis of the world's history, to aid such men. Instead of barring the door with the dull impassible aristocrat, and the land or mill owner, we should rather open it to those who have spirit and *geist*. Mind assuredly will win the day; they who are dead to it will soon be themselves dead in a dead nation. We must be a foremost nation in Europe ; an active nation, a busy and somewhat meddlesome nation in the politics of the world, or it is clear enough to all that we shall cease to be. With us, apathy means death. Either in the forefront of the race, or else in what Carlyle calls " ocean-abysses," England will arrive. And it is clear that she will achieve her foremost place, not by sneering and undervaluing hand-work and clever brain-work. Nay, to be commonly just, we must own that it is the vulgar mind that attributes to low means and base appliances the successes of great men. Shakespeare's dictum is ever to be borne in mind if we wish charitably to judge of others. Corruption wins not more than honesty ; fair dealing and hard work are at the bottom of a larger percentage of the successes of this world than the ill-natured imagine. But more than all, Mr. Disraeli's history is cheering, because it proves the thorough liberty of Englishmen, and that the brightest career is open to the poorest youth. " God," said poor Shelley, " has given man arms long enough to reach heaven, if he will only put them forth." Here, then, is a man who has put forth his arms : the grandson of an alien, of a despised race, educated at no public school, with no fortune, and a tongue that made enemies rather than friends, he placed a daring goal to his ambition ; and through the heat and turmoil of a long race, through accident and chance, he distanced by a head his more favourite competitors, reached the winning-post, and governed the country which received his wandering grandsire as its guest. Who shall prophesy the fall, who shall set bounds to the glorious future of a nation, which holds out such a prize to the aspiring youth she nourishes in her bosom ?

LORD LYTTON.

R

LORD LYTTON.

B Y birth Bulwer-Lytton was (is) *above the class* from which the ranks of the literary profession are filled; for, though not of a dazzling lineage, he was, on both sides, of *gentle* origin." It is very easy to copy from the "Peerage." Is it necessary to tell of a certain Bolver, son of Thunder, a Dane who came over with the Conqueror, and was descended from some Danish Viking? You can read that in Bulwer-Lytton's genealogy in Sir Bernard Burke's "Peerage." The truth is, Bulwer is a gentleman, and he looks it; a man of good blood and sound breed; his hands, feet, hair, and air show it. But Mr. Jeaffreson ought to know that our best writers are almost all of "gentle" origin, *testibus* Milton, Dryden, Addison, Sterne, Waller, Shaftesbury, and Shakespeare. However, let us back to Bulwer. It is a long way from Shakespeare to Bulwer; let us take the leap!

This "gentle" origin, falling upon the offspring of two families, each of which had money, led to

our author's custom of changing names. At one
time he was Lytton-Bulwer; at another he was
Bulwer-Lytton. His eldest brother, William Bulwer, the only one undistinguished out of three,
holds the ancestral house at Heydon Hall, Norfolk,
as fine a specimen of the architecture of the time
of James I. as one can see, and in the village there
is to be found one of the neatest of little inns, with
the "Bulwer Arms" as a sign. As Bulwer, too,
this great author—for he is great, in spite of his
shortcomings and his vanity—made himself known;
as Bulwer he won his first fame by novels full of
precocious wisdom and a dangerous finesse; as
Bulwer he wrote those famous plays, full of wit,
point, cleverness, sparkle, and miserably gilded, or
rather lacquered, poetry; as Bulwer he gave us
boys those admirable sentiments from the mouth
of Claude Melnotte, which we took for poetry, and
spouted till the tears came from our eyes. Do not
we all remember them?

> "Nay, dearest, nay, if thou would'st have me paint
> The home to which, could love fulfil its prayers,
> This hand should lead thee—listen!
> A palace *lifting* to eternal summer
> Its marble walls from out a gloomy bower
> Of coolest foliage, musical with birds
> *Whose songs should syllable thy name!*"

Well, they were pleasant days when we believed in
this very clever writer's poetry. He gave it us raw,

but it had such a glamour of cleverness over it that we accepted it as something very rare, and did not quite relish the unconscionably loud laughter into which Thackeray threw us when he tore the mask off the " Sea Captain " in *Fraser's Magazine*. Some tender soul, who has a love for poetic pruriency, and thinks that God-given talent should be used for the corruption of God's creatures, has written to us, shocked at our treatment of Swinburne. We will show him, who has read little and understands less, how Thackeray and Tennyson could handle (critically, of course) Bulwer-Lytton, and how Thackeray could carry the attack on the fair possessions of Tennyson. Remember, we are only on the side of Truth. We allowed all due appreciation for Mr. Swinburne's poetry. We wish that he, in carrying out his fine cookery of Greek and French dishes, had done that which the English gentleman requested the Irish waiter to do—served them in separate plates, and had allowed us to mix them ourselves. But enough. " Strike and spare not " is our motto here, when the blow is deserved. Praise, and praise generously, is but a pendant to it.

To our subject. Walking, let us say, up the hall of the Freemasons' at a Literary Fund dinner, there is a gentleman, rather feeble, doddering, a Cousin Feenix, with tumbled hair, a face rouged, flushed, a noble forehead and high aristocractic nose, a gentleman unmistakably, a gentleman with "the true nobleman look" that you do not find one man in a thousand has, and of which Pope spoke. He is not very strong, this gentleman, and has a scared kind of stare—that, indeed, of a student out in the world. In this living face, and in photographs from it, there is a suspicion that it is "got up" to what its owner thinks its best; that Pelham would be younger than he is. Vain struggle with Time; what gentle waggoner can put a "skid" on his wheel when he is going down hill, "or with a finger stay Ixion's wheel," as Keats has it? Look at the hair brushed forward and manipulated, the eyebrows, whiskers, and hair somewhat darkened, the moustache and imperial! The whole look of the man has just the clever *artistry*—not insincerity, for Lord Lytton is a true man—which is the little bit of bad taste which has prevented its master from being the very first in his rank. The little reft within the lute, and little rotten speck of garnered fruit—you know the rest. How wonderfully like his books every man is! Noble Charles Kingsley; superfine Lord Lytton; rocky Ben Jonson, with the "mountain belly and the rocky face;" gentle Shakespeare; pure and biblical John Milton; and "wicked" Lord Byron, as vain as wicked, and as wicked as vain— how you throw your own shadows and lights upon your pages!

This man, Lord Lytton, who has writen a most acute essay on the difference between Genius and Talent, has so high a share of the latter that he touches on the confines of the first. His industry is marvellous—as great as his genius. Let us rapidly see what he has done. He was born in 1805. His father, General Bulwer, died in 1807. In 1810 the little precocious fellow wrote verses in the Percy ballad style. In 1820, at the mature age of fifteen, he sent out " Ismael, an Oriental Tale," with other poems, one on Waterloo, in which Corporal Shaw, the Life Guardsman, figures as a hero :

> " Meantime brave Shaw usurps the martial plain,
> And spreads the field with Gallic heaps of slain."

" Ismael " is not bad stuff ; many a poet of fifty worries his face into wrinkles because the press will not praise worse verses. The young poet went to Cambridge after a course of private tutorship, and became a swell at Trinity Hall. In 1825 he won the Chancellor's Prize Medal, and, after another volume of verse, gave us, in 1827, his first novel, " Falkland," the hero of which is, of course, Byronic, wicked, Satanic even. So much harm had the Byron fever done. To laugh sardonically, to hate men much and women more, to scorn the world, and yet to hunger for it, was then thought fine and strong. His next work was " Mortimer; or, the Adventures of a Gentleman," which the publishers, with their usual insight, rejected. However, the word "Mortimer" was altered to "Pelham," and the effect was magical. The publishers issued it, and the public bought and praised it. It is a wonderfully clever novel for so young a man (published in 1828) of the superfine kid-glove and silver-fork school. Bulwer had used his education as well as his observation, and sarcasm and quotations are pretty well mixed in the result. In 1827 Bulwer graduated B.A. In the same year he married Rosina Wheeler, daughter of a gentleman of Limerick, and the marriage has not been a happy one, *testibus* Lady Lytton's spiteful novel of "Cheveley; or, the Man of Honour," and others; but from this marriage sprang the Hon. Edward Robert Bulwer (born 1832), a poet of no mean order, known as Owen Meredith.

In 1828, after "Pelham," came the "Disowned," and then, in quick succession, "Devereux," "Paul Clifford," "Eugene Aram," a drama on the same ghastly subject, the "Siamese Twins," "England and the English," "Last Days of Pompeii," "The Crisis" (politics), "Rienzi," "The Duchess de la Valliere," a drama, "Lady of Lyons," ditto, "Richelieu," ditto, "Money," ditto; then "Ernest Maltravers," down to "My Novel," "The Caxtons," "What will he do with it?" and others. From 1828 to 1869, we have thirty-one years, and, counting pamphlets and plays, more than forty volumes! Nor must we, in justice, forget his more ambitious works, such as "Athens: its Rise and Fall," (1837); "King Arthur," a poem (Colburn, 1849); and "The New Timon," a trenchant satire, written in admirable verse. All these called loud plaudits from the press at the time, and we are not of those who take simply to novelty, and abuse an old and an excellent servant. "The New Timon" had, unfortunately, a romantic story interwoven with its satire; had it not *that*, had it been a satire *pur et simple*, it would have nearly equalled those of Pope, or, let us say, Gifford. In style, it was between the two.

Some moral obliquity of vision, too, made Bulwer write those thrice damnable highwaymen stories, wherein we have gentlemen highwaymen, scorning society, and philosophic footpads. If his lordship spent all the money he ever had from all his novels and plays put together in reformatories—and the sum has been a very large one, Routledge paying him for a stereotyped edition £15,000—he could not undo a tithe of the evil he has done, by giving an impulse, with that much worse writer, Harrison Ainsworth, to the Penny Murder and Robbery Novel, which has filled our gaols with some of the brightest boys of England. "Gentleman Jack" and the "Boy Highwayman" are the true blood descendants, if illegitimate, indeed, of " Clifford " and " Jack Sheppard." The deductions were as odious as the sentiment was false. Thackeray, who seems to have hated Bulwer's works with an honest scorn, and to have pursued him with the pertinacity of a bloodhound, lashed him as no man has ever been lashed for his " Sea Captain," and in *Punch* wrote perhaps the wisest, wittiest, and best parody ever seen, on " Aram," in " George de Barnwell." Well might the romantic Bulwer have blushed and writhed ; but, unfortunately, the people who would be corrupted by " Paul Clifford " and " Aram," are just those who have not the wit to read the satire, nor the open daylight knowledge (loving darkness rather than light) to feel that a rogue can never be called a wise, witty, or a truly clever man. This, Bulwer could not see. It is not too much to say that the whole of British society is at present disturbed by the result of such teachings, infinitely diffused by the talk and reproduction of inferior minds.

In 1831 Bulwer was member for St. Ives ; then, in '.32, for Lincoln, till '42 ; was rejected till '52, when he became member for Herts ; in '35 he took his M.A. degree ; in '38 was made a baronet. In '44 his mother died, and he took the name of Lytton ; in 1853 he was made honorary D.C.L. of Oxford ; in 1856 Rector of Glasgow University ;

in the same year he was offered a seat in Lord
Derby's cabinet; in 1866 he was created Lord
Lytton of Knebworth. He won his baronetcy, we
believe, from the Whigs, and his barony from the
Tories, but his whole weight and popularity from
his capital and clever novels, so suited to a rest-
less, ambitious youth of readers, so seducing, so
dangerous, and yet in many parts so wise. On
the whole one cannot deny the highest crown one
can bestow upon the next-step-to-genius to Bulwer.
He ripens as he goes on, but his art is imitative
rather than original. He is too clever by half.
His best works are often echoes, melodious echoes,
with a different sound in their repercussion, but
evidently from the cries of others. The "Caxtons"
echoes back the strong shout of "Tristram Shandy;"
the historical novels, those of Scott and even James;
the history, those of Thirwall; the dramas, those of
Knowles with the poetry of Scott; the satire has
the silver ring of Pope, often his very *cæsura* in the
lines. Thus Bulwer is an imitative genius rather
than an original one. He has written because he
has had something to say, no doubt, but also
because he wished to place himself upon the same
high pedestal with the highest names in literature—
and for a time he has done it. But posterity has a
knack of taking down these plaster casts of great
ones before she puts up the alabaster statue which

shall endure.   Nevertheless, fresh plaster-of-Paris looks uncommonly well.

We have said that Bulwer can hit out with vigour, and that he ripens.   His " Horace," lately published, is a most admirable work, full, let us say, of genius in minute touches, of clever work all over.   Lastly, as we cannot in our space follow Bulwer's busy life any longer, let us thank him for his honest, hard, and, on the whole, manly work. That he has not been more so, that he has not been conducive to Christian nobleness, that his heroes are often snobs, is not his fault—it is con- genital ; and upon this natural wood, so well adapted for the Bulwerian cabinet, education has placed a very fine veneer, and art a splendid French polish.

Here, too, we add a literary curiosity—Bulwer's attack on Tennyson, and Tennyson's reply in *Punch*.   The fight was a great deal too well carried on to last.   Bulwer *loq.*, but anonymously, as the " New Timon " was published as a mystery :

> " Not mine, not mine (O Muse forbid !) the boon
> Of borrow'd notes, the mock-bird's modish tune,
> The jingling medley of purloined conceits,
> Out-babying Wordsworth and out-glittering Keats ;
> Where all the airs of patch-work pastoral chime
> To drown the ears in Tennysonian rhyme !
>   *   *   *   *   *
> Let school-miss Alfred vent her chaste delight
> On ' darling little rooms so warm and light ; '
> Chant ' I'm a-weary ' in infectious strain,
> And catch the ' blue fly singing i' the pane ; '

Tho' praised by critics and adored by Blues,
Tho' Peel with pudding plump the puling muse,
Tho' Theban taste the Saxon purse controls,
And pensions Tennyson while starves a Knowles"—

We need not more. Tennyson, who had had £200
a-year granted him, was touched to the quick, and
wrote — for once and only once in *Punch* — as
follows:

"THE NEW TIMON AND THE POET.

We know him out of Shakespeare's heart
 And those full curses which he spoke;
The *old* Timon, with his noble art,
 That strongly loathing, greatly broke.

So died the Old; here comes the New.
 Regard him: a familiar face;
I thought we knew him: What, it's you,
 The padded man that wears the stays.

Who killed the girls and thrilled the boys
 With dandy pathos when you wrote;
O Lion! you that made a noise
 And shook a mane *en papillotes*.

And once you tried the Muses too,—
 You failed, Sir; therefore now you turn;
You fall on those who are to you
 As captain is to subaltern.

But men of long-enduring hopes,
 And careless what the hour may bring,
Can pardon little would-be Popes
 And Brummels, when they try to sting.

An artist, Sir, should rest in Art,
 And waive a little of his claim;
To have a great poetic heart
 Is more than all poetic fame.

But you, Sir, you are hard to please,
    You never look but half content,
.Nor like a gentleman at ease,
    With moral breadth of temperament.

And what with spites and what with fears,
    You cannot let a body be;
It's always ringing in your ears—
    They call this man as great as me.

What profits now to understand
    The merits of a spotless shirt—
A dapper boot—a little hand—
    If half the little soul is dirt?

You talk of tinsel! Why, we see
    Old marks of rouge upon your cheeks.
You prate of Nature! *You* are he
    That spilt his life upon the cliques.

A Timon you! Nay, nay, for shame;
    It looks too arrogant a jest—
The fierce old man to take *his* name—
    You bandbox. Off, and let him rest."

Clever but wrong, as the gentleman said under
peculiar circumstances. You see these great souls
are disturbed. When one poet calls another a
school-girl, and the other retorts with the accusation
of his opponent being a rouged bandbox, the time
has come to leave off. You can say no more. But
we like these old free fights; the men are both broad
enough to forgive and to forget; their success,
immense talents, and the full appreciation that the
public has given them, are alike undeniable. May
they rest under their laurels!

MR. HARRISON AINSWORTH.

MR. HARRISON AINSWORTH.

ET us start with an opinion, fearlessly expressed as it is earnestly felt, that the existence of this writer is an event to be deplored; and the fact that he is able to assume that he is a Man of Letters who has been of service to his country, and that he has received from the hands of a Prime Minister, himself a Man of Letters, the reward of £100 a-year pension for literary services, is a disgrace to this bewildered and Philistine nation.

Mean as is the sum of £1,200 a-year which is set aside for the reward of those noble soldiers in Literature and Art who lead the van, who write for the people, who instruct the people, and help all they can with fine-hearted thoughts and words of a pure savour, it is made yet smaller by placing upon it persons who absorb a very large portion of it. Thus Lady Phipps, the wife of a Queen's servant, who saved Her Majesty hundreds of thousands, takes away a fourth; Lady Mayne, the widow of a well-paid police-officer, takes away an eighth; the widow

S

of a highly-paid President of the Royal Academy, herself earning much money, pockets a fourth; a writer of
highwaymen's romances a twelfth, and so on. If
you have speculated and built an exhibition, then
your widow may be rewarded by this Literary Civil
List. If the Queen has no other way to reward her
servants, you will be put upon this list. It is really
time that the English people should speak their mind
as to their public servants, the authors. They stand in
the stead of the prophets of old ; they form the minds
of the young ; they set the bias of the mind towards
virtue or vice, towards unholy greed, a cold lust of
selfish gain, or a generous and manly life of duty,
honesty, forbearance, and holiness.

Now, Mr. Harrison Ainsworth has not done the
latter. He is, perhaps, not so much to be blamed,
poor man, being a person of small attainments and
not a very strong intellect, as the times in which he
was born. In that yeasty and lively age, in which the
results of a long war, deeds of violence at sea and on
land, the press-gang, cheating lawyers, bad laws, a
debauched king and court, a "frowsy old Floribel,"
had produced among the people a taste for such
literature as the "Memoirs of Harriet Wilson,"
accompanied by books less vicious only in degree,
not quite as bad in intention, such as "Tom and
Jerry," "The Corinthian Club," and the like,—in
that very lively age people required a literature

that teemed with adventure and had "go" in it. Mr. Coombe, in his "Doctor Syntax," feels this, and leads his hero into innumerable scrapes, and makes him describe each scene from the playhouse to the graveyard. To judge from his lines, matters were not much better then they are now in the former. When he has seen a play Syntax exclaims:

> " 'Twas Shakspeare—but in masquerade :
> I've seen a farce, I scarce know what,
> 'Twas only fit to be forgot.
> I've seen a critic and I've heard
> The string of nonsense he preferred.
> Heaven bless me ! where has Learning fled ?
> Where has she hid her sacred head ?
> Oh ! how degraded has she grown,
> To spawn such boobies on the town ! "

The booby, John Leland, by the way, was wisely pensioned by the minister, on express condition that he would not write any more corrupting romances. Mr. Ainsworth has apparently received his money under other conditions—

> " Qualis ab incepto processerat
> Et sibi constet."

He began by writing highwaymen romances, and he has only just at present (August, 1870) concluded a story of "Claude Duval, a Tale of the Days of Charles the Second," in that widely-circulated journal, *Bow Bells*. Let us add that he writes evidently with

more decency and less open applause of robbery and
brutality for one penny, than he did when one paid
half-a-crown for his rubbish.   His Claude Duval is﹒
not the Knight of the Road after all.   The highwayman's name is merely taken as a "draw" by the
vulgar novelist.   He knows that little thieves and
incipient burglars will be taken in by the name.
He knows that in the purlieus of the New Cut, in the
wynds of Glasgow, in the slums of Manchester and
Birmingham, the name of Claude Duval is a name
of might.   He therefore takes it, but he wishes to
be virtuous as well ; he is as modest as a lady of a
certain fame and occupation is at a christening—a
great deal more modest than virtue itself.   Claude
Duval shot by the Duke of Buckingham !—(Ha, ha !
what says Dame History to *that ?*)—in single combat
in Windsor Park, is attended in his duello by a
female page dressed as a man, "with a wild shriek
that betrayed her sex "—oh, you foolish old copyist,
are not the discarded women-pages of Sir Philip
Sidney and of Shakspeare yet done with ?—but has
yet life enough left him to ride and plunge into a
morass.   Sabine, his she-page, leads him thither.

"'Not there,' rejoined Duval. 'Your father's spirit pointed
towards the lake. Take me thither—to the morass—you understand.'

She divined his terrible purpose, but did not attempt to oppose
it. She led him down the long sweeping glade, along which
they flitted like phantoms. She guided him swiftly and un-

erringly, through the thick woods encircling the lake, and brought him to the borders of the morass.

' Now leave me. Farewell for ever !' he cried.

And with a last effort he forced his horse into the fatal swamp. Sabine remained looking on in a state of stupefaction. When all was over she prepared to follow.

' Leave you! Never!' she exclaimed. 'I am yours in *life* as in *death !* ' (*sic.*)

And she plunged in after him. The morass *willingly (!)* offered them a grave in its oozy depths, and kept their secret well.

A miserable pretender afterwards appeared as Claude Duval. With him we have nothing to do. He was very deservedly hanged."

Now this is mean in the extreme. Here is this old and accomplished author, who has drawn his brilliant existence, as the sun draws exhalations from a swamp, from the *Newgate Calendar;* who has sent so many boys to prison that Government has forbidden his plays to be acted with one hand and has pensioned him with the other; and yet, in his old age, he deserts the highwaymen, and only *in the last paragraph but one* of his book, lets out the secret that the true Duval is "a miserable pretender," and was very deservedly hanged. Mean, very mean: Ainsworth is, in fact, the pretender himself.

Thirty years ago, a portly, red-faced gentleman might have been seen on the Harrow Road, humming the tune of the most popular song of the day—his own " Jolly Nose." There was a good-natured

joviality about the gentleman, a genial disposition
to feed well, sleep well, and take care of himself.
He had been a lucky, and he thought himself a
meritorious man—not at all an unusual matter.   He
was born in 1805, and is therefore of the mature age
of Lord Lytton, another author who has illustrated
the lives of thieves.   His father was a Manchester
solicitor; but his son, who was brought up to the
same profession, became, "through the allure-
ments of literature," says that "high falutin'"
biographer, Mr. Cordy Jeaffreson, "a careless
student of the law, and ere the conclusion of his
twenty-first year he presented the world (!) with
his first work of fiction, 'Sir John Chiverton.'"

Mr. Jeaffreson here makes out a great case for
his friend, whom he does not seem to care much
about, as he dismisses him in a few lines; but the
statement that he was "intended for the law,"
and that he was a student, though a careless
student, of that blessed institution, stands him in
stead.   From law to a defence of crime, indeed to
looking upon crime as a jovial and necessary (for
the lawyers) sort of occupation, is but a step.   From
"Sir John Chiverton" to "Ovingdean Grange,"
and this about Claude Duval, Ainsworth has written
some twenty-six books or romances, and taking
these at three volumes each, is author of nearly
one hundred volumes of—rubbish.   Early in his

life, the success of Dickens gave him a good opening as playing second to that author. When Dickens resigned his management of *Bentley's Miscellany*—having written therein a thieves' story, but very differently treated, by the way, and quite moral in its tenour and its results, its real abhorrence *of* not admiration *for* crime—Dickens wrote a preface to the volume containing the comic and dignified similitude of the old and new coachman. It suited literary men to be looked upon as "jarvies," or whips, and to consider Bentley as a coach. The new whip, having mounted the box, drove straight to Newgate. He there took in Jack Sheppard and Cruikshank the artist, and aided by that very vulgar but wonderful draughtsman, he made an efficient story of the burglar's or housebreaker's life. He might have done this and kept to the truth, or have pointed a moral. He did neither. He gave Jack a kind of apotheosis; he made all his villains on the side of the law, and all his rogues and slatternly strumpets, washings of the kennel and gatherings from the stews, whom he termed fair and charming women, law-breakers, but to be admired by the reader!

Bad as this bald piece of writing was, the success of Cruikshank's capital etchings, some of them equal to anything that Callot ever did, except in grace (we allude to the crowds in the space of a thumb-

nail in the hanging procession), was enormous, and
Mr. Ainsworth, who had been a publisher at one
part of his busy life, next set up *Ainsworth's Magazine*,
and in it wrote certain stilted nonsense—"The
Tower of London," "Old St. Paul's," "The Miser's
Daughter," and so forth. Of these not one could
hold the public without its illustrations. Some of
Cruikshank's best work went to these rubbishy
books, which are now bought at large prices *for the
engravings*.

Previous to this the poor scribe, whose historical
novels were a mere list of the frippery of the ward-
robe, had written another thieves' romance out of a
penny chapbook, of which he has such a great idea
that he has given the public the most touching
scene to weep over. It is the death of Dick's mare,
"Black Bess."

"Dick's eyes were blinded as with rain. His triumph, though
achieved, was forgotten ; his own safety disregarded. He stood
weeping and swearing, like one beside himself.

'And art thou gone, Bess?' cried he, in a voice of agony,
lifting up his courser's head, and kissing her lips, covered with
bloodflecked foam. 'Gone, gone ! and I have killed the best
steed that I ever crossed ! And for what?' added he, beating
his brow with his clenched hand—'for what? for what?'"

The illustrious author himself has told us how he
felt when he wrote that celebrated passage. The
feelings of Gibbon at Lausanne, after having written
the last line of his *magnum opus*, were small compared

with those of Ainsworth. After informing the public on the important point where he " achieved " this— at the Elms at Kilburn—he continues :

" Well do I remember the fever into which I was thrown during the time of composition. My pen literally *scoured* over the pages. So thoroughly did I identify myself with the flying highwayman, that once started I found it impossible to halt. Animated by kindred enthusiasm, I cleared every object in my path with as much facility as Turpin disposed of the impediments that beset his flight. In his company I mounted the hill-side, dashed through the bustling village, swept over the desolate heath, threaded the silent street, plunged into the eddying stream, and kept an onward course—without pause, without hindrance, without fatigue. With him *I shouted, sang, laughed, exulted, wept;* nor did I retire to rest till in imagination I heard the bell of York Minster toll forth the knell of poor Black Bess."

Knell of poor Black Bess! that never existed, that was never ridden to York, save in the brain of some half-starved author of a penny chapbook! And if this author had the common sense to have followed Fielding, he might, if he chose, have falsified history without making vice alluring. But such is the perverse blindness of such genius as inspires Bulwer and Ainsworth, that they represent the lazy loafer— who took to the road in fear and trembling, when he could no longer live on the wages of sin his poor female companion brought him—as a puissant knight-errant ; and the mercers, travellers, and bagmen as so many cowards, who trembled at the sight of them.

The truth is, these same "cits" sometimes frightened the highwaymen with a brass candlestick. One old beau stuck a fellow by the head on the spikes of his coach, and dragged the dirty hector into London, and cleared Hounslow Heath, by terror of this deed, for months. Once women took a highwayman prisoner; and the scoundrelly "Knights of the Road" always fled before any men equally well armed. So much for their valour!

Nor can we too often refute the foolish old saw of there being honour amongst thieves. King being arrested, and crying out for help, Turpin deliberately shot his friend, so that he could not "peach" (give information against him). "Dick," cried King, thinking that the shot was meant for the officer, "you have killed me." Nevertheless, he lived for a week, and long enough to peach about his friend's hiding-place at Hackney Marsh. Turpin then, to use the expression of this historian, "removed into Yorkshire," where he supported himself by a cunning mixture of horse stealing and horse dealing. Taken at last under his assumed name of John Palmer, found out by a returned letter, of which he had not paid the postage, he was tried, condemned, and executed. Finally, as they dress this hero on the stage, he was so shabbily dressed—no sticking-plaster boots, silver-hilted swords, gold-laced hats, or velvet coats—that he bought "a new pair of pumps and a

fustian-frock to wear at the time of his death." He
left a ring and some other articles to a "married
woman," not his wife, with whom he had been
cohabiting. He trembled and turned white when he
came to the ladder, stamped his foot with some
bravado, mounted the ladder, and there conversed
with the executioner for half-an-hour before he threw
himself off.

> " Now fitted the halter, now traversed the cart,
> And often took leave, but seemed loath to depart."

We find we have made the trifling omission of a
murder and a round dozen of brutalities in this short
sketch, but trifles are of little moment in the life of
a hero. " It is needless to add that the story of the
ride to York," says a Newgate historian, with some
contempt, " and of the wondrous deeds of the highwayman's steed, Black Bess, are like many other
tales of this fellow (!), the fabrication of *some poetical
brain !*"

When these glittering productions were dramatised,
so many young boys imitated the tinsel heroes of the
stage, that the authorities wisely forbade their repre-
sentation. Mrs. Keeley for some time acted Jack
Sheppard, and respectable women were found foolish
enough to bedizen themselves in mob caps, and
represent the "historical personages" of the trulls
and strumpets whom Ainsworth created as the
queens of the burglar's seraglio.

Well, after thirty years or so, we have seen the result. The crop of penny highwaymen books is perennial.* Jack Sheppards (spelt a little different for copyright considerations), Blueskins, Turpins, Claude Duvals, rise like foul fungi from the cheap press, and shed their poison, and die down to appear

---

* Further evidence of the pernicious effect on youthful and half-educated minds of what may be called the highwayman and burglar school of literature is furnished by a case which came the other day before the Worship-street magistrate. A boy of fourteen was charged with having stolen two sacks from his employers, and the policeman who had the conduct of the case said, that when he apprehended the prisoner he found on him (besides the stolen property) portions of certain publications called the "Boys of England," and "Tales of Highwaymen, or Life on the Roads," both referring to the achievements of notorious malefactors, which were invested with alluring colours of heroism and magnanimity. The lad was sent to prison for a fortnight, there to perform hard labour on an exhilarating diet of bread and water; but it is to be feared that, after all the trash he has read, he will regard himself as a victim to the conventional rules of society, and will make a bolder stroke for fame when he comes out. Mr. Ellison, the magistrate, called the attention of Inspector Fife to the fact that neither the name nor address of the printer is given on the publications. The publishing office is at 147, Fleet Street, but that is all the information vouchsafed. Under these circumstances the magistrate desired the inspector to speak to the Commissioners of the City Police, in order that steps may be taken to prosecute the printer, who has clearly violated the law. It were greatly to be wished that something could be done to suppress such publications, which are quite as mischievous in their way as the particular kind of books contemplated by Lord Campbell's Act are in theirs.—From a *London Paper*, May 22, 1868.

again. Copies have been taken in boys' boxes, which in the aggregate amount to thousands; chaplains of prisons have, in charges innumerable, traced the perversion of these poor boys to thieves' literature. Mr. Ainsworth and Lord Lytton have corrupted our boys by the hundred-fold. One has a peerage, the other a pension, for his services! We are rewarded for buying, they for writing this trash.

The author of Jack Sheppard may be, and possibly is, a very amiable gentleman, but he has no right to be allowed to escape scot-free from the result of his teachings. It is difficult for the candid mind to comprehend why the popular favour is extended to robbers and burglars, unless it be man envying the rich;—poor people love and admire those who rob and despoil the rich. In all children this love of the lawless seems innate. "My dear boys," said a lady of title, who was wise as well as poor, to her three children, "you will have your way to make in the world; you will have to work to achieve your fortune; now, what would you like to be?" To these young gentlemen, ranging from nine to twelve years old, and to whom law, war, and diplomacy afterwards opened their arms, but one answer suggested itself; without a pause they cried, "Freebooters, mamma!" But it is somewhat mean to take advantage of this low feeling; a great writer might have satirised, he should not have pictured the burglar in roseate hues.

Mr. Ainsworth is, we believe, as Lord Lytton is, we know, a wealthy man through this literature; but if every farthing each has received from his books, pensions and all, were a hundred-pound note, and employed in building reformatories for boy-thieves, the unhappy man could not undo the evil his perverted taste, vulgar admiration, and his fatal itch of writing to pander to the savage instincts of the thief and robber, has caused, and will yet cause, in years to come.

THOMAS CARLYLE.

THOMAS CARLYLE.

HE universal burning-up, as in hell fire, of human shams. There, readers, there is the next milestone for you in the history of mankind."

Consider well that sentence. At a time when Prince Christian is made a bencher of Lincoln's Inn; when English travellers are murdered in Greece, *because* we have been soft enough to ruin Corfu and the Ionian Islands by giving them to the Hellenes; when the value of the press, and of everything else, except money, is declining; when men dress as women, and flaunt in places of public vice for two years, with applause almost from an innocent sitting magistrate, Mr. Flowers, who would "like to liberate them without bail;" when emigration is acknowledged to be the only panacea for misery of the working-classes in the richest country in the world, which yet refuses state emigration on a proper scale; when "an old man in the Vatican" is proclaimed by most of his bishops to be Infallible,

T

"the third Incarnation of God;" when—but the reader can add many instances. "The universal burning-up of shams" has not yet commenced, and in this world probably never will.

And for forty years in London, and some fifteen years more in the country, an earnest Scotsman, Thomas Carlyle, has to the best of his power preached, Cassandra-like, against them; has added many strange German words to the language about them; has refused to bow, as he says, "before the Baals of the world, the sham captains, solemn human shams, phantasies, supreme quacks, dead sea-apes, and dull and dreary humbugs." His is not an entrancing or lively *rôle* to play, but one which is and will be always necessary, and which Carlyle has played honestly and well. He has gained for himself—and it is well for the world that he has—much love and reverence; probably no man doubts his honesty, or his directness of purpose, how much soever they may question his wisdom. Thomas Carlyle is, to a great extent, a power in this age. He has turned aside many who were frivolous and foolish; he has made his mark as an earnest, deep-thinking man; he has been classed in a book, and in innumerable reviews, as one of the three great thinkers of the age. He is one of the men whose words will live. He has fought the good battle, and, if checked and baffled, is not yet conquered; he is essentially a Protestant, and he will die protesting. Such a life has in it a something of the beautiful, compared with other lives, nay, with those of the men who have made money and could buy up Carlyle, stock, lock, and barrel—how beautiful it is!

You can see that fine old face, snowed by the winter of time, rugged and lined with channels of thought, in most photographic shops and in many albums. The earnest eyes still flash beneath the rugged brows. He wears such a beard "as youth gone out has left in ashes;" there is something scoriac about the face, as if the fires of a volcano had nearly burnt themselves out and yet reserved some force. Age has added to it, not subdued it. Compare it with earlier portraits and you will recognise the truth that, wherever wisdom dwells age steals not, but reveals true beauty. No ruin of a strong tower clothed with ivy is more fine and touching than that head. The portrait, leaning thoughtfully on the hand that has laboured so long and so well with the pen, presents the *vera effigies* of a true king of men. Here, at least, cries the gazer, is no phantasm, no sham captain, but a man.

This Man of Letters was born in 1795, of the Saxon race which settled in the Scotch Lowlands, at Ecclefechan, in Dumfriesshire, of a religious, earnest, good father, who educated his son at Annan,

and then passed him on to Edinburgh, where he
remained till he was twenty-one, and then, not liking
the priesthood of the Church maybe, he taught, for
two years, mathematics at a school in Fifeshire, and
then devoted himself to the priesthood of literature.
This was his own word, and it will at once reveal
the character of the man. "Of all priesthoods," he
wrote, "aristocracies, governing classes, at present
extant in the world, there is no class comparable
for importance to that priesthood of the writers of
books; these are the real working effective church
of a modern country. The writer of a book, is he
not a preacher?—preaching not in this parish or in
that, or on this day or on that, but to all men, in all
times and places."

With such thoughts in his head, Carlyle commenced, in 1823, writing in the *Edinburgh Encyclo-
pædia* on Montesquieu, Montaigne, Nelson, the two
Pitts; he translated Legendre's Geometry, and
Goethe's "Wilhelm Meister." Such journey-work
he ennobled; whatever he did he did well; and
truly not in that rugged way, paved with stony hard
words and German phrases, that he now uses, did he
travel on his "wander-years;" but in plain, direct
good English, pleasant to read and easy to understand. It would have indeed been difficult for one
with so remarkable a style as he now has, to obtain
admission in those days, and even now, under any

omnific editor, whose "valuable journal" delighted and delights the world. Sampson was clean shaven, and had not let his locks grow when he toiled for the Philistines. Carlyle wrote next in the *London Magazine* a life of Schiller, the magazine being upheld by Lamb, Hazlitt, John Scott, Allan Cunningham and others. "Wilhelm Meister" was published anonymously, and the young gentleman who translated it was patted on the back by various reviewers—by some, too, abused. He would be a bold man who would patronise Carlyle, however one might abuse him *now!* Goethe admired him and wrote to him; thought him worthy to have views of his cottage engraved in the German edition of his book. Carlyle lived then at Cragenputtock, with a good wife, who helped him as no other human being could, and whom he loved tenderly through life. In a letter to Goethe he gives a charming picture of his life. "Here, with no small effort," he says, "have we built and furnished a neat substantial mansion; here, in the absence of professional or other office, we live to cultivate literature with diligence in our own peculiar way. Two ponies, which carry us everywhere, and the mountain air, are the best medicine for weak nerves. This daily exercise, to which I am much devoted, is my only dissipation; this nook of ours is the loneliest in Britain, six miles removed from anyone who in any case might visit me."

A good scholar in Greek and Latin, reading any book that he much desired in any modern language, imbued with German thought and philosophy, here the philosopher dwelt in 1825, writing for the *Foreign Review* and other reviews, large and small, until 1830, when he removed to Chelsea, London, and commenced, "in his piebald style," says a writer, " Sartor Resartus," the tailor re-tailored, in *Fraser's Magazine.* "Sartor," now perhaps regarded from many points as his very best work, a supreme work in numberless ways, was of course refused by the booksellers and publishers, not without much advice to the " young man," of which advice from the publisher's taster Carlyle has given some dry specimens. Why the middle-class should be called " gigmanry " and " gigmanity," and what was the meaning of a " Baphometic fire-baptism," all-knowing editors could not make out. However, Oliver Yorke, the pseudonym for the editor of *Fraser,* found it pay, this piebald style, and readers found Herr Teufelsdröch amusing, quaint, and some even deep and wise, above the ordinary level of writing which had no style at all, piebald or otherwise.

Writing and studying for some years more, and by no means a popular writer—his popularity being always reflected, and his true fame having yet to come—Carlyle, in 1837, produced a really great work, showing us how History ought to be written.

This was the "French Revolution," a series of the most brilliant historical pictures that was ever written, given with a vivacity above measure, and a fidelity above all praise. For Carlyle does not give subjective pictures for which he has no authority.

He is not a brilliant writer after the Tom Macaulay school. For every word he utters you may swear that he has full authority; indeed, were Carlyle to note and annotate his works the probability is that we should never get through them; they would be as huge and as indigestible as the folio edition of Bayle's Dictionary, which we can't read, because the notes utterly overpower the text. From the very words of the chief witnesses of the Revolution, the reader learns what that mad time was. A more powerful picture never was drawn; we hear the clash of the sabres, the spitting of the *Dames de la Halle*, the roll of the tumbrils, the song of the Girondins, the shriek of the victims of the égorgeurs (stabbers), the fall of the guillotine, and the thud of the head in the basket of sawdust. But, oh Heavens, that this should be a sham, too; that the "green one," Robespierre, immaculate and incorruptible, and bathed in blood, should be but the victim of illusion; that all should be but an ugly dream or terrible plague-sickness, cured only by a bath of blood. Such it was in Carlyle's opinion —"An age of paper ending with a whiff of grapeshot." And yet, look you, of all wondrous peoples, working for ever, and dancing onwards and onwards to victory and slaughter, that French people from 1790 to 1815 did show themselves a people—but of a sort. God seems to have sent them a strong delusion, and they believed a lie. They set up the goddess Reason—they produced thereby Marat, Robespierre, Napoleon (First and Third), Talleyrand, and others. The student of history will do well to read Carlyle's book, and to put that living record beside some of the books by Dryasdust and Company; say by Doctor Sir Archibald Alison, and others.

After this wonderful work, which the critics did not of course understand, Carlyle produced his great monument to Cromwell—merely the man's speeches and letters without annotations, only elucidations. You, therefore, judge Cromwell by himself; you see him with his wife, his family, his servants, his army, and his God. After these letters of Cromwell the history of England by Mr. Philosophic-Deist Hume, and the pretty pictures of Sir Walter Scott, must be swept away like so much rubbish out of the corners of your brain.

We have not noticed, for reasons palpable enough, " Chartism," " Heroes and Hero-Worship," " Past and Present " (1843), and his five volumes of essays. He was not—this grim school-master—very complimentary to his beloved English country, the land of his adoption and his admiration. He told us that "England was dying of inanition, though full of wealth," and that the "happy haven to which all revolutions were driving us was to that of hero-kings and a world not unheroic." The prophecy becomes plainer and more visibly true every day. In 1850 came out Carlyle's "Latter-Day Pamphlets," and before that the Life of his friend Sterling, a sweet and touching biography, very charmingly written. In 1860-4 he published his "Life of Frederick of Prussia," in which he somewhat too much defies force; and in 1867 he contributed to *Macmillan's Magazine* a rough and somewhat violent diatribe against the times and the world as it goes, called "Shooting Niagara—and After," in which he by no means prophesies smooth things of the future of England. But if we disagree—and we by no means wholly disagree—with the philosopher of Chelsea, we must praise his style—wonderful, acute, strange enough to be attractive, and if well read, plain enough to be understood by a ploughboy, honest enough to be understood by a saint, bold enough to shame all cowards: there it is, sinewy, full of stature, all muscle and bone, without a superfluous word. But we must leave him, yet not without these few words as a specimen of Carlylese :

" But that a bad man be '*free*'—permitted to unfold himself in *his* particular way, is contrariwise the fatallest curse you could inflict on him ; curse, and nothing else, to him and all his neighbours.   Him the very Heavens call upon you to persuade, to urge, to induce, compel, into something of well-doing ; if you absolutely cannot, if he will continue in ill-doing—then for him (I cannot assure you, though you will be shocked to hear it), the one ' blessing' left is the speediest gallows you can lead him to. Speediest, that at least his ill-doing may cease *quam primum.* * * All the millenniums I ever heard of heretofore were to be preceded by a ' chaining of the Devil for a thousand years'—laying *him* up, tied neck and heels, and put beyond stirring, as a preliminary.   You, too, have been taking preliminary steps with more and more ardour for a thirty years back ; but they seem to be all in the other direction ; a cutting asunder of straps and ties wherever you might find them—with great glory and loud shouting from the multitude as strap was cut, glory, glory, another strap is gone—this, I think, has mainly been the sublime legislative industry of Parliament since it became Reform Parliament, victoriously successful, and thought sublime and beneficent—by some."

As things turn out *now*,—murders by the score, Oxonian revelling, Roman infallibility, and Government brigandage in Greece,—Carlyle speaks with reason.

HENRY W. LONGFELLOW.

HENRY W. LONGFELLOW.

THE Americans, who rightly or wrongly repudiate Aristocracy—or rather, since that word is ignorantly profaned and misused, a titled class, which is very different from the Aristoi—have an awkward habit of making their great men either judges, generals, or professors. "Professor" is a word of very modest meaning, warped from its real significance into something somewhat charlatanic. Professor Browne who cuts hair, Professor Challis who cuts out trousers scientifically, Professor Anderson who pretends to conjure and expose spirit-rapping with the agile awkwardness of a plethoric butcher, rise before one's mind as you say the word. They are humbugs, saltambanques, mere palliasses, with raddled noses and painted faces, who do their jugglery in a miserable way, poor fools!—but Professor Longfellow is a learned man, a scholar, a gentleman, and a true poet.

He does not look much like one as he walks near his home at Cambridge, U.S. He resembles a substantial English farmer.   He is more English in his look than Tennyson, quite as much so as Browning. He has a cheery red face like a farmer, white hair falling about it in long locks, and black eyebrows. Forcible lines and features adorn that face; there is more strong thought in it, and much less delicacy and womanliness in it, than one would have thought. And yet he is essentially a woman's poet.

He is easily understood, for instance, much more easily understood than even Tennyson or Swinburne. Longfellow's meaning lies on the surface.   Is this a proof that he is not a poet?   By no means.   Browning has ruined himself by his involved no-meaning. We do not want a poet who thinks in knots, and though we love Browning and rate him at a much higher value than Longfellow, we are apart from him by the space of the wide heavens in thinking his serious bewilderment a beauty.   You can read Long-fellow softly, gently, and with a calm delight; he "sweetly creeps," as the Prince of Poets says, "into your study of imagination."   You can't understand Browning unless he is wonderfully well read by a poet who *can* read, and then, with emphasis and proper inflection, you see the fine depths of the man.   Like Rembrant's pictures, his poems want a false and artificial light thrown on them.   When Mr. William Shakespeare was a young man, a scholar, not a master, he affected obscurity—for a purpose, too—

in his sonnets, but his sublimities are all daylight. *He* is no blackly dark mine, no mammoth cave with twenty-inch stalactites, but whole Alps and Himalayas, a Monte Rosa or Pilatus in the sunshine of true poetry. That poet who, like a cuttle-fish, escapes from being caught by dirtying the water, is of essentially small mind—

> " A man's best things are nearest him—
> Lie close about his feet."

And the best poetry is, like our English Prayer-book, "to be understanded of by the common people." Let us point to the admirable quotation just used, from Richard Monkton Milnes Lord Houghton—it is as good and as plain as the best Wordsworth.

Henry Wadsworth Longfellow is an earnest man and a good worker. If half of his countrymen were as earnest as he, we should have had less "Bunkum" talked, and more sound sense. He was and is well educated, and is no doubt educating himself now. Born in February, 1807, he entered Bowdoin College, New Brunswick, at the age of fourteen, graduated in honours at eighteen, and in 1825 was studying law with his father, but, offered the Professorship of Modern Languages in his college, he left home to prepare himself, by a three and a half years' travel in Europe—in France, Spain, Italy, Germany, England—and this earnest work shows itself in his

poems. *Le moyen d'y parvenir* with Henry W. Longfellow, oh Bohemian friend, who loafs in and out of
New York drinking-shops, is hard work—laying his
brains to, and achieving what he undertakes. In
1829 Longfellow returned home, and entered on his
professorship. In 1835, on the death or resignation
of Mr. G. Ticknor, Longfellow was offered the same
post at Harvard College, Cambridge, and the poet
again went abroad to cram, as it were, for his post.
He then spent more than a year in Denmark, Sweden,
Germany, and Switzerland, and in 1836 returned and
settled at Cambridge, where he has since resided,
save but for brief intervals of travel for the sake of
his health. In 1842 he was again in Europe; in
1861 his wife perished by a dreadful death, that by
fire; in 1869 Longfellow spent some time in Europe.
This is all the personal history that we shall relate.
He has been many years before the public as an
author and as a poet. In 1833 he published his
translation from the Spanish of the celebrated poem
of "Don Jorge Manrique," on the death of his father,
together with an introductory essay on Spanish
poetry; in 1835, his "Outre-Mer;" in 1839,
"Hyperion," a romance, and "Voices of the Night,"
his first collection of poems; in 1841, "Ballads and
other Poems;" in 1842, "Poems on Slavery;" in
1843, "The Spanish Student," a play; in 1845,
"The Poets and Poetry of Europe," and "The

Belfry of Bruges;" in 1847, "Evangeline;" in 1848, "Kavanagh," a tale; and in 1849, "The Sea-side and the Fire-side;" "The Golden Legend" in 1851; and "The Song of Hiawatha" in 1855; then came "Miles Standish" in 1858; "Tales of a Wayside Inn," 1863; and, some two years ago, a translation from Dante, which was received but coldly. People had been accustomed to look for something peculiar, gentle, and entirely his own, from Longfellow. His "Dante" has not been a success, and yet we want something that will render Dante in the actual *terza rima*. Our very best translation at present is that by Cary, which is decidedly Miltonic. The Messrs. Cassell have very wisely printed that with the lurid and overrated illustrations of Gustave Doré, which, by the way, are about the best illustrations that *he* has ever done, excepting the weird pictures to Balzac's "Contes Drolatiques."

No American author is so well known in England as Longfellow. Many of his verses have become household words, and many of them richly deserve to be so. Thus the last line in this extract is quoted by every young lady. It is from "Evangeline:"

"Talk not of wasted affection, affection never was wasted;
If it enrich not the heart of another, its waters, returning
Back to their springs, like the rain, shall fill them full of
    refreshment;
That which the fountain sends forth returns again to the
    fountain.

U

Patience, accomplish thy labour; accomplish thy work of
   affection!
Sorrow and silence are strong, and patient endurance is godlike."

This sweet story is founded on a tale of "British"
cruelty, by the way miserably magnified, and will
perpetuate a good deal of poetic dislike to the
English. Happily it is in a lilting hexameter, a
Greek and Latin measure which the learned Southey
was, before Longfellow, silly enough to try to bring
into use. Admirable, most admirable as it is in
Homer, sweet and excellent as it is in Virgil
and Lucretius, the hexameter does not suit our
tongue in any way. If it could have been na-
turalised, Longfellow would have done it. The
sweetest English hexameters are those in "Evangeline" where the devoted girl dies. "Still stands
the forest primeval," they commence, and end with
the picture of the two lovers lying at rest in the little
churchyard in the heart of the city :

" Daily the tides of life go ebbing and flowing beside them,
   Thousands of throbbing hearts, where theirs are at rest and
      for ever,
   Thousands of aching brains, where theirs no longer are busy,
   Thousands of toiling hands, where theirs have ceased from
      their labours,
   Thousands of weary feet, where theirs have completed their
      journey."

In the earlier portraits of Longfellow, there is a
dull melancholy imprinted on his face, and this is
to be found in his poems. It is one cause of their

popularity; it is the great proof of his own weakness. He has little of the strength of a kingly poet, little of that jovial merriment, that buoyant force of old Chapman or Daniel, let alone Shakespeare and Homer. These poets are, to use a vulgar provincialism, "all alive like a bag of fleas;" so is Burns, so is Beranger, so is Dante, even in his fiery hatred and fierce revenge. Longfellow, on the other hand, is as melancholy as a yellow-and-green sick school-miss. Even in 1840, when he was but a young man, we see this, in his "Voices of the Night," and even in the "Psalm of Life," which is so often quoted and recited, there is a condemnable return of that vile melancholy which destroys all energy:

> "Art is long and Time is fleeting,
>   And our hearts, though strong and brave,
> Still, like muffled drums, are beating
>   Funeral marches to the grave."

And this pervades the poet. Even in the earlier poems, all written before the age of nineteen, "some of which," says the writer quaintly and naïvely, "have found their way into schools, and seem to be successful," there are traces of this weak passion, and in almost his last verses we find the same fault, and we may well be angry with a poet for thus dashing his singing robes with tears. We have a great quarrel with him for his last verses in " Tales

of a Wayside Inn" (Weariness), which are yet
very beautiful.   They commence with :

> " O little feet ! that such long years
>   Must wander on through hopes and fears,"

and they end with this verse :

> " O little souls ! as pure and white
>   And crystalline as rays of light
>   Direct from heaven, their source divine ;
>   Refracted through the mist of years,
>   How red my setting sun appears,
>   How lurid looks this soul of mine ! "

This is not Christian doctrine.   Pure and white
are pretty adjectives, but a father ought to know
that there is as much possible wickedness and
actual selfishness in a child as ever there is in a
true old poet.   But this affectation—or possibly a
true humility—is also to be found in Hood, a much
healthier poet mentally, but one who suffered from
ill-health bodily.

Longfellow's translations are capital.   They are
from many languages, and they are all quaint and
good.   Look, for instance, at that capital sonnet
from Lope de Vega, " To-morrow : "

> " Lord, what am I, that, with unceasing care,
>   Thou didst seek after me,—that thou didst wait,
>   Wet with unhealthy dews," &c.,

which is worthy of all praise.   Read also, with
much gusto, many of his Danish and Swedish pieces.

That he loves the old land, and truly, is proved by many little touches; notably by his writing the very best verses, save Tennyson's, ever written about a man who in years to come will grow into a hero,—the Duke of Wellington. The poem is called, " The Warden of the Cinque Ports," and was published in the *Atlantic Monthly* shortly after the Great Duke's death. So, also, we might cite those beautiful verses on the poor dying soldier in the hospital at Scutari, kissing the shadow of Santa Filomena (Miss Nightingale) as it fell upon the wall at his bedside. The story is a poem of itself, but Longfellow, raised, as he said, to a " higher level " by the deeds in the Crimea, does not hesitate to prophecy that the light of the deed shall last

> " On England's annals, through the long
> Hereafter of her speech and song,
>   That light its rays shall cast
>   From portals of the past."

So also, to be perfectly national—and a good poet must be national—in the midst of the war with the South—when will a poet arise to sing the heroic bravery of that small unaided people ?—Longfellow prophecied the victory of the North. The Northern sloop, the *Cumberland*, was run down in Hampton Roads by an iron Southern vessel, and the men, 'tis said, went down with a cheer, whereon Long-fellow sings out :

"Ho! brave hearts that went down in the seas!
   Ye are at peace in the troubled stream.
Ho! brave land with hearts like these,
      Thy flag that was rent in twain,
      Shall be one again,
   And without a seam!"

The fellow-countrymen of America, who have not yet produced *the* national poet, are very proud, and naturally so, of this honest, manly, cleanly writer. "About Longfellow," writes an American critic, in an amusing style, "there is never any mawkish sentimentality, no versified cant, no drivelling, no diabolic gloom. His bold, broad brow catches the sunlight from the four points of heaven and disperses it, glittering and fructifying through the homesteads of his readers. Longfellow is the healthiest, the heartiest, and the most harmonious of all the American poets. True to nature, he is truest to himself. The most barren legend is made fruitful by the warmth and fervour of his intellect; but when, as in this 'Song of Hiawatha,' he adopts a tradition charged with the elements of social progress, *his genius, baring its broad pinions to the sky*, shows us only the more unmistakably how yearning it leans to man, and to man's happiness."

We have said nothing about the three best or most ambitious poems of Longfellow, one—a kind of "Faust"—the "Golden Legend," is freely and finely written. The opening is admirable, but yet it is but wine-and-water to Bailey's "Festus," to say nothing of Goethe's "Faust." The second is "Hiawatha," and the third "Miles Standish." One is to be, it is said, the epic of America, the other of New England. Neither probably will live except as curiosities. "Hiawatha" is written in smooth iambics, very easily to be imitated, and thus they run:

* * * * *

> "As unto the bow the cord is,
> So unto the man is woman;
> Though she bends him she obeys him,
> Though she draws him, yet she follows.
>
> Thus the youthful Hiawatha
> Said within himself and pondered,
> Much perplexed with various feelings,
> Listless, longing, hoping, fearing,
> Dreaming still of Minnehaha,
> Of the lovely Laughing Water
> In the land of the Dacotahs."

This, as Touchstone says, is the "right butter-woman's rank to market." One could rhyme to it a whole summer's day. Epics are not made like that. Besides, the subject of the loves of a red man and his squaw, who can be no ancestors to anybody, who were of the most cruel, brutal, and degraded of races, are hardly hero and heroine for the supreme race Caucasian. "Miles Standish" is very weak, and in hexameters, and that disposes of *that* being an epic.

But nothing will dispose of our gratitude to a sweet, good, and learned poet ; one who has honoured his country and honoured his race ; who has never written one word which, dying, he could wish to blot; whose book, like a circumambient and omnipresent fairy, has entered thousands upon thousands of American and English homes, and has never entered one without bringing with it purity and pleasure.

MR. ALGERNON C. SWINBURNE.

MR. ALGERNON C. SWINBURNE.

T is very possible Mr. Swinburne might object to being called a "man of letters." He said once publicly that he is not a literary man, and he would, rather than otherwise, cast scorn upon living by his pen. Not that such men refuse the *honorarium* given by publishers. On the contrary, we presume, purely for the good of the poor fellows who write, they demand and receive heavy rates of pay when their name is good in the market.

Mr. Swinburne, then, is a poet, but by no means pure and simple, taking those words "at the foot o' the letter;" but a poet he is of rare order—forcible, free, salt, and buoyant as the sea; full of fire, dash, feeling and expression; a poet who at one leap sat himself at the side of the crowned singers, and who divides Olympus with Tennyson, or disputes empire with Browning. For it is a thing damnable enough with Fame, that the old worn soldier of a hundred fights shall at once give place to a boy-soldier, and that the fierce flame of the hero of the day shall eclipse the constant splendours of him who has won and worn the diadem of song for years. This young, and, as we believe, almost utterly spoilt child of fortune, is the latest comer amongst letters, and has already reached to the highest form.

In appearance, as you see him, let us say at a literary dinner, in answer to some call upon him of which he does not approve, he has a young, unripe, and not very healthy look. He has ancient blood in his veins, but it has not run to form and flesh. There is no doubt as to the quality of his brain, neither is there any doubt as to that of his heart and body; one is of the finest order; of the others the less said the better. In height this poet is about five feet six; in age rising upon twenty-seven (born at Holmwood, Surrey, 1843); his hair, which is bushy and plentiful, is of a fiery red; his face has that pallor which accompanies red hair, a paleness heightened by study, passion, and the fierce rebellious spirit within. Thin, badly dressed—or badly tailored, for the "clothes he occupies," as Artemus Ward has it, seldom seem to become him—the fiery little spirit looks neither a poet nor a gentleman, and yet he is both—by birth. An Eton boy and an Oxford man—he was a Balliol student and a first-rate Grecian—the wide and correct reading of the poet 's both his college and his school. He left

Oxford without taking a degree, and in 1861 published his first poems, the "Queen-Mother" and
"Rosamond," both of which fell dead. Four years
afterwards he produced "Atalanta in Calydon," a
white quarto with a Grecian binding, which at once
took the public and the press; and it was then
remembered that the young poet was an Etonian,
Oxonian, and nephew to a baronet of ancient
descent. All these things tell in the scale. Poverty
and low birth are matters now-a-days which weigh
down many a genius—a pure diamond it may be,
but which wants the sun to make it glitter.

The sun shone on " Atalanta." The larger papers
noticed it, and to say truth it deserved all the praise
it got. It is pure Greek, as Greek in its feeling as
if Keats had written it, or as if Shelley had translated it from Œschylus. Its author must have just
risen, when he was fired with the idea, from "Orestes"
and the "Eumenides." There are, indeed, distinct
traces of the sublime Greek Trilogy in the poem,
and the mournful music is worthy the theme. The
two passions or devils which possess this little fiery
man of genius were kept pretty tightly chained
during this translation, but now and then one shows
his cloven foot. What are these devils? Incon-
tinence is one—or, if you like Teutonic best, lust—
and an arrogant rebellion against God is the other.
Mr. Swinburne would admit neither, if we believe

certain stories current in literary society. He does
not admit that there is a revelation for one matter,
and he believes that lust is a natural and excellent
law.   Now, we shall not repeat a tittle of what is
well known in literary society, and which will be
sure to be known to the world some day.   Let
gossips read what gossips write, and scavengers
collect their heaps, of which they will find enough ;
we have only to deal with the books of this really
fine poet. If he has a right—which we deny—to
publish such stuff, we have a right to criticise it.

We have said that one little devil showed himself
in " Atalanta," and this was rebellion against God.
Of course, in the Greek tragedy, veiled like a
statue of Satan covered with his wings, it looked
beautiful indeed—majestic, sorrowful, and sublime.
" Atalanta " strikes the key-note of blasphemy on the
very earliest page.   The gods give us poisonous
drink for wine, and herbs that infect our blood; but
the chorus speaks out even more plainly against
ONE God:

> " Seen above other gods of shapes of things,
>   Swift without feet and flying without wings ;
> Intolerable, not clad with death or life ;
>   Insatiable, not known of night or day :
> The Lord of love and loathing, and of strife,
>   Who gives a star and takes a sun away ;
> Who shapes the soul, and makes her a barren wife
>   To the earthly body and grievous growth of clay,

Who turns the large limbs to a little flame,
    And binds the great sea with a little sand ;
Who makes desire and slays desire with shame ;
    Who shakes the heavens as ashes in His hand ;
Who, seeing the light and shadow for the same,
    Bids day waste night as fire devours a brand :
Smites without sword, and scourges without rod :
THE SUPREME EVIL, GOD."

There can be little doubt of the spirit which dictated
this ; yet the age welcomed it and praised it, and
weak young men thought it "plucky," and spouted
it at Atheistic meetings—we beg pardon—anti-
theistic or anti-theologic is the phrase.   Not one
paper, that we remember, bore witness against it.
The *Saturday* declared that we "were listening to
one of the contemporaries of Euripides, who sought
to copy the manner of Œschylus," to a poet full
of vivid force and fulness of expression.   The *Spectator*, that the work "was a little too ingrained with
Greek awe, but still exceeding fine."   H'm.   One
God and Most High are hardly Greek!   The *Times*,
that he had a keen eye for natural scenery (that
dear old *Times!*   What had that to do with it ?)
and a copious vocabulary of rich, yet simple English!
The *Athenæum*, that "no one since Keats could touch
him"—and it might have said that Shelley could not
touch him for blasphemy.   And the matronly and
chaste *Morning Herald* introduced the poem with a
chuckling, "Assuredly this is the most complete and

304 MODERN MEN OF LETTERS.

choicest effort which has for a long time announced
that a scholar and a poet has come amongst us."

. A scholar! There's the fault. Mr. Swinburne
had prefixed two sets of Greek elegiac verse, of
very good quality as college exercises, and dedicated
to that exceedingly Greek old man and fine writer
of very plain English, Walter Savage Landor, with
whom he had sometime dwelt at Florence, and
there was little doubt that here was indeed a scholar.
But he is not only a scholar in Greek, but in French.
✗Brought up in France, he writes French with as
much ease as he does English, and his little Rondels
in that language have been very much admired.
This cross of French-Greek education, with a dash
of Landor-Italian, had been too much for a small
but very fine brain. Indeed, that brain must be
small which, after reading Job, can take the one-
sided view of God or nature, or, if he choose so to
call it, the great First Cause, that Mr. Swinburne
does. We shall shortly see whither this French-
Greek, or modern Priapeian, has brought our poet
to. We desire that our readers will think that
we have no unkindness in our criticism, but will
meditate on what we have pointed out.

For Mr. Swinburne is, as to this age, a very
fine poet; perhaps the finest that our age has produced, save one. But he has begun his fight with
the world. His intellect is subversive. He cares

not what creed, nor what system of morals he overthrows. He fights as did our old sea-dogs, yard-arm to yard-arm. "There we lay," says Commodore Trunnion, "sending shot and shell into her, hurling hand-grenades hot as hell, and throwing stink-pots into her hold." Mr. Swinburne had been long dealing out hand-grenades. In the year 1865, the house of Moxon, which used to be, until Tennyson withdrew from it, the reputed publishing house of poets, issued a certain volume of "Poems and Ballads," by A. C. Swinburne, and the press, for a wonder, discovered that a very deadly stink-pot (a fire-weapon, that with a thick fume and choking stench, almost poisoned those it slew) had been hurled into our midst. Thereon the respectable house of Moxon apologised to the public, by withdrawing the book and refusing to sell it. The placing of a work in an Index Expurgatorius was a good advertisement, and Mr. Swinburne (*Punch*, we believe, christened him Swine-born, and the epigram was received with acclamation) fitted himself with an active and enterprising publisher in the person of Mr. Hotten, and the sale went merrily on. The poet defended himself, and urged that he did not write for boys and girls, and that there was a literature far above the bread-and-butter and pinafore school,—which is very true. But, unfortunately, these poems are not written for *men*, unless

x

for those unfortunates who have been on Circe's shore, and are transformed to beasts.

The volume is a pretty volume, and contains wondrous poetry. In excellent prose Mr. Swinburne has (for he writes in the *Fortnightly*) told us of his antagonism to Christ. In this volume he not only proclaims this, but chooses to hint to the world, in most unmistakable terms, that he preferred the worship of Venus. Something yet worse is to be found in this sad book. We do not believe that any pure man or woman can realise the unutterable baseness of some of the verses, nor dare we print our exposition of them; but we will give a few specimens, and these, we need not say, are not by any means the worst. In this first musical rhapsody, the poet declares his scorn of the Saviour of the world :

" Thou hast conquered, oh, pale Galilean ; the world has grown
    grey from thy breath ;
  We have drunken of things Lethean, and fed on the fulness of
    death. * *
  Oh, lips that the live blood faints in, the leavings of racks
    and rods,
  Oh, ghastly glories of saints and limbs of gibbeted gods !
  Though all men abuse them before you in spirit, and all knees
    bend,
  I kneel not, neither adore you, *but standing look to the end.*"

In the next lines this ardent votary of Venus prophesies her triumph ; still addressing Christ :

" Though these that were gods are dead, *and thou being dead
    art a god !*

Though before thee the throned Cytherean be fallen and
    hidden her head,
Yet thy kingdom shall pass, Galilean, thy dead shall go down
    to thee dead.
Of the maiden, thy mother, men sing as a goddess with grace
    clad around;
Thou art throned where another was king; where another was
    queen she is crowned.
Yea, once we had sight of another, but now she is queen, say
    these,
Not as thine, not as thine, was our mother, a blossom of
    flowering seas,
Clothed round with the world's desire, as with raiment and
    fair as the foam,
And fleeter than kindled fire, and a goddess and mother of
    Rome !"

Reduce this to prose, and the argument is not
very strong, consisting only of the fact that Swinburne prefers the world's desire and Venus-worship
to the worship which exacts purity and submission.
We will not further insult our readers with the
parallel of the two queens of Rome—Venus and the
Blessed Virgin. The poem is itself a study, exceedingly melodious, and by an oft-repeated trick,
apt alliteration, very liquid. Let us now pass from a
senseless dislike of faith to a declaration of no faith.
The first was in an ancient guise, a " Hymn to Pro-
serpine," after the proclamation of the Christian faith
in Rome; the second is a little French song of adieu
to a certain Félise. This lady, of whom the lover
is apparently very tired, is told mockingly to pray:

" Behold ! there is no grief like this ;
   The barren blossom of thy prayer,
Thou shalt find out how sweet it is.
   Oh, fools and blind, *what seek ye there,*
     High up in the air ?
Ye must have gods—the friends of men,
. Merciful gods, compassionate,
And these shall answer you again.
   Will ye beat always at the gate,
     Ye fools of fate ?
Ye fools and blind ; for this is sure,
   That all ye shall not live but die.
Lo ! what thing have ye found endure ?
   Or *what thing* have ye *found on high,*
     Past the blind sky ?
The ghosts of words and dusty dreams,
   Old memories, faiths infirm and dead.
Ye fools ; for which among you deems
   His prayer can alter green to red,
     Or stones to bread ?"

Clearly, young Mr. Swinburne does not understand the nature of Christian prayer, and fancies that we believe in a Providence which sends down penny-loaves at our asking. But this godless and ignorant young man, who, because he can write Greek and French verse, believes his education finished, has yet something that he prays to ; and, in proving this, we shall touch but lightly upon that French-Priapeian method of his of bruising, and biting, and kissing, and sundry passionate exercitations quite Gallic or Bacchic, or Delian if you like ; but neither English nor manly. Thus hymns he to his goddess :

" Thou wert fair in the fearless old fashion,
        And thy limbs are as melodies yet,
    And move to the music of passion
        With lithe and lascivious regret.

What ailed us, oh gods, to desert you
    For creeds that refuse and restrain;
Come down and redeem us from virtue,
        Our Lady of Pain ! "

What a line—what a prayer is that! Shall we go
a step further in this passage; shall we glance
at " Hermaphroditus "? But no; to people who
comprehend, this is enough.

When the French Republic of 1870 was proclaimed
amidst so sad trials, and a situation of such unspeak-
able difficulty for the French nation, without one
omen of good import, all who loved Liberty and
advancement of the People looked grave with care,
but the Poet Swinburne lashed himself to fury, and
wrote an ode " at a sitting." We will quote the
criticism of one of the leaders of public opinion, rather
than give our own upon this very hasty production.
" The wildness, the frenzy, the incoherence of M.
Hugo's prose are even surpassed in Mr. Swinburne's
verse. It is a strain—in a double sense—of sound
and poesy : a poem which surpasses even the Swinburnian models in the tremendous vehemence of
words. We cannot describe it better than in the
bard's own phrase, as

    ' The blood of thought which travaileth
    To bring forth hope with procreant pains.'

The blood of thought labours much, but the hope is disappointed.   The produce is a deformed thing, a misshapen monster, inspiring more mirth than terror.   Strophe and antistrophe echo with portentous rumblings, but it is sound and nothing more.   Our ears are racked with groans and thunder, our eyes made red by frequent blood and fire. There is a vast amount of crying, and hissing, and biting, with the usual Swinburnian effects.   But the result is something which must be reckoned, even in the artistic part, the worst and weakest of all the productions of Mr. Swinburne's genius."

Mr. Swinburne is overborne by this age of cold proprieties at the half-life of society.   At the passion which exhales in asking for a postage-stamp, in Mr. Trollope's cold-blooded way, he is aghast and weary.   He is sick of Philistines, but he hungers not for love in the hearty, manly English fashion. Poor boy! what a career he has missed.   For, with the many glimpses of great talent that he has shown, with all his fine melody, mastery of verse, and even true genius, the books he has produced can never be read by the young—to whom a poet chiefly addresses himself.   His chief and most high works are but mocking songs of the atheist that erst might have been sung in Sodom, and lascivious hymns to Adonis that might fitly have been howled in Gomorrah.

CHARLES KINGSLEY.

CHARLES KINGSLEY.

(CANON KINGSLEY.)

IT is twenty years ago, or more, that a young man of letters—who, indeed, had not won his spurs, and was rather to be called a boy of letters—after teaching a class of working-men Mathematics and the rudiments of Latin, strolled into the coffee-room belonging to the " Institution," and looked with some interest on its walls. Heaven knows they were bare enough; Heaven knows that the rough working-men he taught were uncouth and rude, and that they only thanked him by learning quickly, and that the religious and political bookseller who had begged him to join the Institution, and to work for the benefit of the working-classes, was a humbug; but there was a glamour and an illusion, and the young fellow felt that he was doing something towards improving mankind, and making the world, in his little way, something better than he found it. This, then, was his reward, and as he looked at the white-washed walls, he felt that he was not living quite uselessly.

The Institution has broken up now, and to Latin and mathematics the working-men have unmistakably shown that they prefer the Great Vance's " Walking in the *Zoo*," " Champagne Charley," and a host of ridiculous songs. But in those days there was much stir among the people; 1848 had been and passed, but the Charter and the Five Points were still debated. The masses were seething. In France, Lacordaire preached the Gospel, and with it the benefit of the poor. The Abbé Lamennais had made a social tract of some of the words of the Saviour, under the title, we think, of " The Gospel of Freedom;" and before the spectator, upon the white-washed walls of the Institution, hung two remarkable portraits: one was that of Eugene Sue, then so well-known for his socialist novels; the other that of Charles Kingsley, M.A., author of "Alton Locke."

M. Eugene Sue, who had been in the French Navy, was a man of some forty-five years of age; unmistakably a Frenchman, although utterly different from the old Frenchman of the *haute noblesse*, and equally so from the modern production. He had a thick black beard and moustache, a high black satin stock, with a black satin waterfall over his shirt-front, short black hair, dark eyebrows, and glowing bright eyes, looking straight at the spectator, and seeming to say, "How clever I am!" The pendant, the Rev. Charles Kingsley—in the subscription of the picture he had dropped the "reverend"—was as entirely English as Eugene Sue was French. A high noble forehead, large, earnest, deep-set eyes (which the lithograph had made hollow as if with thought and work), a firm, close-shut mouth, and large and powerful jaw; here was a poet as well as a parson, a fighter as well as a writer, a leader as well as a priest. Waving black hair, now thinned by time, adorned the head, and earnest, glowing, lustrous, and true-hearted eyes shone out from beneath the forehead, and seemed to speak openly to whomsoever listened, "Come, let us work together for the good of mankind. Love me, for I love you; or if I can't convince you, then——" Such was Charles Kingsley, as good and as free-natured a soul as one would care to see. And yet the Devil was about to try him in many ways; has tried him both with adversity and prosperity, and he is still a noble-hearted man.

The young fellow turned away from the white-washed wall and solaced himself—not to be above his fustian-coated pupils—with some smoked coffee and very coarse bread and butter, for which the "institooshun," as it was called by the greasy cad of a religious bookseller who tried to make the

thing pay, and to pass off his "goody" literature
at the same time—for which, as we said, the
"institooshun" pocketed a sum that would have
afforded good viands.   But the method of the
majority of those who wanted to help the Working-
man in those days, was to get a good round sum
out of him, and to make him pay for it too.   Hence
the Institution fell to the Great Vance, to comic
singers and such obscene birds of prey, who served
out the working-man as the Harpies did the flesh
of the Pater Æneas :

> " With hideous cry
> And clattering winds, the hungry Harpies fly :
> They snatch the meat, defiling all they find,
> And parting leave a loathsome stench behind."

And even at the time these portraits hung in the
Institution, it did *not* pay.   The typical working-man,
who really wished to learn Latin and mathematics,
soon rose to be more than a working-man, and the
loafer who cared about nothing, remained a loafer.
After all these years this young author has found it
convenient for himself to believe that the typical
working-man is, like all good and great men, somewhat of a rare bird, and to acknowledge—as he
grows towards fogey-dom—that the young men of
the present day would rather play at croquet with
the girl of the period, or even dress in "drag," play
at an amateur theatre, burn statues in a college

quadrangle, or listen to the Christy Minstrels, than teach the typical working-man mechanics and the rudiments of Latin.

Mr. Charles Kingsley was at that time very fiercely assailed by Reviews. The critic-creature came out as usual very strong, and fired away blank cartridge with amazing vigour. It did not do any harm, of course, because Kingsley has long been tutor to a prince, a companion of Prince Albert, a friend of the Queen, an University Professor, and a Canon of the Anglican Church. It has even been whispered that he will be a Bishop!—and oh! please, do you hear what, according to the Reviews, he was. He was an author of revolutionary litera-ture, the inciter to ferocity, railing, and mad one-eyed excitement; he was guilty of Jacobinism and Jacquerie under the disguise of Christian Socialism; he was pupil of Albert, Ouvrier, and Louis Blanc; he believed in the visionary organisation of Labour. He is by implication in the same article found guilty of doctrines as outrageous as the maddest ravings of furious insanity—as wicked as *the most devilish spirit could by possibility have devised. Murder is openly advocated—all property is declared to be robbery, &c.* This was from a leading article in the *Times*, foisted neck and crop into the *Quarterly*, in which the Rev. F. D. Maurice and the Rev. Charles Kingsley figure as culprits at the bar. Nay, we find by a quotation

that they and (we presume) their fellows are Com-
munists to the utmost extent. (Vide *Quarterly Review*,
vol. lxxxix. p. 523, 1851.) "Community of women
follows, as an almost necessary consequence, the
community of goods;" and then follows a quotation,
whence taken it does not appear, but from " one of
these Teachers of the People." (One of twenty-one
books reviewed side by side with Kingsley's and
Maurice's.) " We do not require to introduce the
community of women ; *it has* always existed. Your
middle-class gentry are not satisfied with having the
wives and daughters of their wages-slaves at their
disposal—not to mention innumerable public pros-
titutes—but they take a particular pleasure in
seducing each other's wives. *Middle-class marriage
is, in reality, a community of wives.*"

Why do we make these painful extracts? Simply
for the instruction of young authors. Few names are
more honoured than Charles Kingsley's ; no man has
ever been more chivalrously devoted to his home ;
no lady or Queen of Beauty in the highest tourney
that ever existed—aye, even in that cloud-land of
King Arthur's Court—was ever more proud or fond
of her own true knight than she who bears his name ;
nor is there wanting that sweet after-glow of married
love, sublimed with sorrows, deepened by trials,
rooted by the lapse of years, intensified by a knowledge of general baseness, but a belief in the purity

of one, and a thousand times more beautiful because ten thousand times more rare than ring-dove cooing of the young couples whose love shines brightly in the morning, but perishes long before the noon of life. Few names are more honoured, few men so much, so worthily beloved, and yet hardly one, as we have shown, who has been so bespattered with the corroding gall of critics' ink.

Charles Kingsley was born, June 12, 1819, at Holme Vicarage, on the borders of Dartmoor, and at fourteen became pupil of the Rev. Derwent Coleridge, son of S. T. C. He afterwards studied at King's College, London; then at Cambridge, where he gained a scholarship, several prizes, and came out a first-class in classics and second in mathematics. His first cure was Eversley, and within a year-and-a-half after that, the rectory becoming vacant, it was presented to him by its patron, Sir John Cope. The Kingsleys, here let us say, are of an ancient Cheshire family, Kingsley of Kingsley. One ancestor raised a troop of horse, and the commission, signed by Ireton and Oliver Cromwell, is preserved still. A younger brother of this Republican captain went with the Pilgrim Fathers to America; and a descendant, Dr. Kingsley, was some years ago classical professor at Yale College, U.S. There was fighting blood generally in the family. General Kingsley commanded a brigade at the battle of Minden, so well known by Campbell's glorious ode. Several others have served and fought, and Kingsley has himself not only been called the Chartist parson, but the soldier-priest. Now, even when 'tis past meridian with him, he has a tall, lithe form, a broad-shouldered Norman figure, the flat cheek and strong chin of Norman blood; and he is still a capital rider, an unwearied fisherman, cunning with the angle and fly; and once he was one of the best wrestlers and foot leapers, both at the high and flat leap, known about Dartmoor. But we have to do with feats of mind, not of the body.

The old Puritan stock of piety grafted on Cole-ridgean philosophy, enlightened by such far-off touches of the great man as his son Derwent, an able pupil, caught, produced a very genuine and singular school of work-a-day Christianity—perhaps the very best known. How it has culminated, whether it has not overgrown even the breadth of Maurice and Stanley, we will not here debate, but when Kingsley began, a more noble-minded young priest seldom if ever preached. He was a devotee of the tenth or fourteenth centuries landed on the nineteenth. When he was twenty-seven he wrote his "Saint's Tragedy," a magnificent unacted drama, full of the social brotherhood that underlies all Christianity, and to which it has come before now, and will eventually come. And this "Saint's Tragedy," how

pure, how noble it is! How it made the hearts of us
youngsters beat; and let us thank God that it was
better, purer, nobler far than the poetry (?) of the
Bal Mabille and the Montagne Rouge, of the Casino
and the Alhambra, that our fervent young Mr. Swinburne gives us now. Compare Kingsley's " Elizabeth
of Hungary" with "Faustine!" Take the erotic young
Mr. Swinburne, with his biting, bruising kisses and
his prayer,

> " Come down and relieve us from virtue,
> Our Lady of Pain,"

and Kingsley's Monks' refrain,

> "A luxu et avaritia
> A carnis illectamentis
> Domine libera nos;"

and then, thank God, oh! younger brothers; for as
our outcome has been dressing " in drag " and the
girls of the period, young men with painted faces and
henna dyed eyelids, what, by the rule of contrary,
will your outcome be? With this we leave you for
the present, giving you to meditate till we finish this
article next week upon the aim of Kingsley when he
wrote " The Saints' Tragedy," and drew the picture of
Elizabeth of Hungary, thus depicted by his friend,
the Rev. F. D. Maurice: " To enter into the
meaning of Self-Sacrifice—to sympathise with one
who aims at it—not to be misled by counterfeits of it
—not to be unjust to the truth which may be mixed

Y

with those counterfeits, is a difficult task, but a necessary one for any one who takes this work in hand."

Looking back from this distance of time, we almost wonder that all lovely minds did not gather to the author of the " Saints' Tragedy " after the publication of that remarkable poem.   It contained not only poetry of a very high order, but its character and its comedy are equally good.   Its intent is also as apparent as the daylight.   But all minds, one need scarcely remind the reader, unless in gentlest satire, are by no means lovely.   The majority, perhaps, are unlovely and unloveable.   A storm of blame, mingled with faint praise, chiefly given to the weaker parts, and laid on where it was not required, followed Kingsley.   He little recked it, but seems to have abandoned poetical play-writing, leaving that to R. H. Horne, to Richard Bedingfield, John Watkins, Westland Marston, and a host of acted and unacted dramatists.   Horne had written about that time his "farthing epic," a magnificent poem, published at the price of one farthing, to show at what price the Philistine Englishmen, in the author's opinion, appraised true poetry.   Kingsley therefore left poetry, and took to studying modern matters, chiefly political, although his verse has the true ring and swing in it, and is political not only in a present but in a paulo-post-future sense, as this example will show:

" The day of the Lord is at hand, at hand !
　　Its storms roll up the sky :
The nations sleep starving on heaps of gold ;
　　All dreamers toss and sigh ;
The night is darkest before the morn ;
When the pain is sorest the child is born,
　　　　And the day of the Lord is at hand.

Gather you, gather you, angels of God—
　　Freedom, and Mercy, and Truth ;
Come ! for the Earth is grown coward and old ;
　　Come down and renew us her youth.
Wisdom, Self-Sacrifice, Daring, and Love,
Haste to the battle-field, stoop from above,
　　　　To the day of the Lord at hand."

At that time there was working in many ways a remarkable man, Bohemian *pur sang*, a *litterateur*, a newspaper writer, the originator of *Punch*, a chemist, a discoverer of the way of calcining carbon, until it became pure diamond—only without the lustre which gives the diamond value—an inventor even of patent buttons, a dreamer and a reformer—Henry Mayhew. This gentleman had, in the falling days of the *Morning Chronicle*, shed some lustre upon its pages by his articles as its commissioner among the working districts of England. Then followed "London Labour and London Poor," a series of papers gathered from working-men themselves, an undigested heap of curious and frightful matter, showing under what burden the tired-out Titan England was staggering along. The subject was one of immense interest, and awakened many. Charles Kingsley, among the rest, looked upon the business of reclaiming those poor. There were those who would work, those who could not work, and those who would not work, and heart and soul Kingsley plunged into *that* matter. He and the Rev. F. D. Maurice preached more than once on the condition of the poor, and held that it was wrong for one class to be doomed to ignorance, want, and misery, while another lived like chartered libertines in luxury, ease, and too often in vice. Kingsley had mixed much with the workers, and the result was one of the most powerful novels ever written— "Alton Locke, Tailor and Poet." It is full of character, full of Christian sympathy with, and love for, the strugglers and toilers. Of course they who could only see one side of the matter, at once branded the author as a Chartist Parson. The character of Alton Locke seems to have been based upon that of Thomas Cooper, the author of the "Purgatory of Suicides," a most remarkable poem, the product of two years of imprisonment for defending the rights of the poor, and for being the mouthpiece of much of the want and discontent of the workers of the North. Branded as a Chartist and as an atheist, he was one but not the other. Thomas Cooper, like a great-hearted man that he was, fought nobly with his political doubts and troubles, and has been for some years landed in the safe keeping of Christianity. With the same honest love for his brethren that he always had, this Christian lecturer has atoned for past errors of faith by continually lecturing and preaching in aid of truth in the very hall in the City Road where he once taught infidelity.

By the side of Alton Locke, tailor and poet, there move in the novel various life-like characters, one of the best of which is Sandy Mackaye, newspaper editor, lecturer, Chartist spouter, and general exciter, but of a noble nature, and one who wishes well to his fellows. Strong in his conviction, Sandie—who in our opinion has a great touch of Carlyle in him, to whom, indeed, we fancy Kingsley was somewhat indebted, as far as a painter is indebted to a lay-figure—bursts out and tells Alton Locke to "Sing awa'; get yoursel' in child wi' pretty fancies and gran' words, like the rest o' the poets, and gang to hell for it." "Why?" asks Alton Locke. The old editor lifts up his fine head, and, pointing to a miserable court, tells him that a merely pretty poet is but "a flunkey and a humbug, wasting God's gifts and kenning it, for the charms o' vanity o' self-indulgence." Then pointing again to the alley, he cries: "Look! there's not a soul in that yard but's either beggar, drunkard, thief, or worse. Write aboot that! Say how ye saw the mooth o' hell, and twa pillars thereof at the entry—the pawnbroker's-

shop o' one side and the gin-palace at the other—
twa monstrous deevils, eating up men and women
and bairns, body an' soul. Look at the jaws o' the
monsters." "What jaws, Mr. Mackaye?" "The
faulding doors o' the gin-shop, goose. Are na they
a mair damnable man-devouring idol than any red-
hot statue o' Moloch, or wicked God-Magog, wherein
they auld Britons burnt their prisoners? Look at
thae bare-footed, bare-backed hizzies, with their
arms roun' the men's necks, and their mouths full
o' vitriol and beastly words! Look at that Irish
woman pourin' gin down the babbie's throat! Look
at that raff o' a boy gaun out o' the pawnshop, where
he's been pledging the handkerchief he stole in the
morning, into the gin-shop to buy beer poisoned wi'
grains o' paradise, coculus indicus, and saut, and a'
damnable, maddening, thirst-breeding, lust-breeding
drugs! Look at that girl that went in wi' a shawl
on her back and cam' out wi'out ane! Drunkards
frae the breast!—harlots frae the cradle!—damned
before they are born! John Calvin had an inkling o'
the truth there, I'm a'most driven to think, wi' his
reprobation deevil's doctrines." "Well—but—Mr.
Mackaye, I know nothing about these poor creatures."
"Then ye ought. What do ye ken about the Pacific?
Which is maist your business? You a poet!"

This, the reader will think, is strong language,
but it is not a whit too strong. It awakened many a

large-hearted man, and the world is the better for its having been written. It is not dead yet. The *Quarterly Review* had, of course, an immense deal to find fault with in this Chartist Socialist. His temper, it said, was almost ludicrous, as if any one could write in a fine sweet temper, with such want, misery, and wretchedness about him. "Whatsoever of real honesty, charity, good sense, and good feeling the story evolves, is (with almost, if not quite, a single exception) among the rich—all the contrary qualities are among the poor; and every page is full of the merits of the poor, and the follies and crimes of the rich."* Exactly so, Mr. Reviewer, because Kingsley had a purpose to serve, and because, as Sandy Mackaye says, the circumstances of many of the poor make them "damned before they were born." It is precisely against *that* system that Kingsley wrote.

It was not alone with writing that he was contented. He established, with the aid of others, a Tailors' Labour Agency, or Working Tailors' Association, and other associations in other trades followed, all having some measure of success. Next came "Yeast," a novel in three volumes, full of the wrongs of the agricultural poor, and containing—for Charles Kingsley is a lyrist of no mean order, and when the fit is on him, writes songs that live—a fine

---

* *Quarterly Review*, vol. lxxxix.

wild lyric which set the blood in the veins of the Tories, and especially the Editor of the *Quarterly*, in a ferment. But why bark and shut up the teeth? Such a song Kingsley had heard, no doubt, but he put order and fire into it. The song is sung by a gipsy boy, "at a revel of discontented labourers."

> "I seed a vire o' Monday night—
>   A vire both great and high ;
> But I wool not tell you where, my boys,
>   Nor I wool not tell you why.
> The varmer he came screeching out,
>   To save un's new brood mare :
> Says I, you and your stock may roast,
>   For aught us poor chaps care.
>   *Chorus*—Here's a curse on varmer's all
>   That toil and grind ye poor,
>   To reap the fruit of all their work,
>   In —— for evermore—r—r !"

This is "direct and offensive," said the reviewers ; but "we have a more recent, more direct, and more offensive adoption and exposition of these detestable doctrinations." Mr. Drew, minister of St. John's, Fitzroy Square, London, invited Kingsley to take part in some evening lectures in June and July, 1851. On the 22nd of June, Kingsley preached the sermon, and after it was over Mr. Drew stood up in his reading-desk, and said to his congregation, that he "believed the doctrine of a great part of the discourse was untrue." Mr. Drew was perhaps right in freeing his soul from what he thought was

error ; but Professor Maurice, through whose inter-
vention Kingsley had preached, states that Mr.
Drew especially invited Mr. Kingsley because he
had read and admired his works. And what was it
that was so offensive in the sermon ? One sentence,
full of "subversive doctrine," the censor of Kingsley's
ethics gives us. Prepare yourselves for a dreadful
outburst ! " I assert that the business for which
God sends a Christian priest in a Christian nation is
to *preach and practice* liberty, equality, and brotherhood, in the fullest, deepest, widest, simplest meaning of those three great words." There was much
more to the same effect. Kingsley had dared to say
that the accumulation of capital out of the needs of
the poor was contrary to God's wish ; that He would
cry out, " Woe unto you who to make *few* rich make
many poor. Woe unto you that oust the masses
from the soil their fathers possessed of old ;" and he
had even said that " the history of the Church in
every age is full of the sins of the clergy against the
people." All this is fearfully subversive, but nineteen
years have not gone by since, and Montalembert—
staunch son of Rome though he was—has borne his
dying testimony about *one* such ; and the Parliament
of England has given to the Irish masses an alien-
able right to the soil whereon they live, if only they
pay that which God, Nature, and man alike demand
—the rent of labour.

Since that time Kingsley's fortune has always marched onwards, if but slowly. He has never been a rich man, but always one held in honour. He has been made a chaplain to the Queen, a tutor to the Prince of Wales, a canon of Chester. In 1859 he was appointed Professor of Modern History in the University of Cambridge. He wrote other works: "Phæton," "Alexandria," "Glaucus," "Hypatia;" a novel, "Westward Ho:" A finer, nobler story for boys does not exist.

After this came miscellanies, studies, and review articles chiefly; a fairy story, "The Water Babies," which is praised as a poetic *chef d'œuvre;* "The Celt, the Roman, the Dane," lectures on history; "The Hermits," "Hereward the Wake," and "Letters from the Tropics." But our space has run out. We have not even room to sum up the character of this most excellent writer, who has done so much good in presenting manly and true thoughts, which, although they seem now latent enough in the hearts of the young, will, we know most assuredly, spring up and bear fruit a hundred-fold, when we, and he, and his sons, and sons' sons, are resting and awaiting the Judgment-day.

RALPH WALDO EMERSON.

RALPH WALDO EMERSON.

MONG the Curiosities of Literature, a profession beset with so many thorns and so much trouble (stones and stumbling-blocks to the weaklings and trials to the strong), there should be preserved a late curt answer from Mr. Carlyle to an inquiring spirit. "Sir," wrote the inquirer, "people say you are a Pantheist; is it true?" "Sir," answered the philosopher, "I am neither a Pan-theist nor a Pot-theist.—Yours, T. CARLYLE."

It is impossible to write of Emerson without recalling Carlyle; it is difficult to think critically of his writings without remembering that to him also the grave charge of Pantheism has been laid, and if one were a special pleader it would not be difficult to establish that charge. Indeed, both to Carlyle and Emerson, but to the latter especially, the charge preferred against Socrates might well be laid. They do "corrupt and lead aside the youth of this city." But Emerson does it in a

much wider and efficient way than Carlyle, because
he is a much less man, much less of a Christian,
much less in heart, in feeling, and in deep earnestness. We pray any one who reads this to believe
that not one word is written that is not written in
true love and honesty, and without cant. Emerson
never pretends to be a Christian in the accepted
sense, while his faith in the precepts of the *Man*
Jesus are about as strong as is his belief in
Zoroaster or Confucius (Koonfootze). The most
ardent admirer of Emerson will find that we
appreciate him as much as he does. But we love
not that mind which is destructive and critical
rather than consoling and edifying. To edify,
Mrs. Brownjohn, is *to build up*. As regards Faith,
Emerson has done his best to fill all young men
with a vast unutterable longing, an admiration for
the great, a windy, wide, and dispersed ambition,
a love of nature and a curious pantheistic reverence
for something—what it is, it is not known. He is
an admirable purveyor for the Papacy and creeds
that restrain, for these unutterable longings never
get realised, these wide and windy thoughts die
out like sudden gusts, these negative faiths leave
the heart empty and comfortless, and then the
reader becomes the *habitans in sicco*, and, after
wandering about for some time, betakes him to a
" concrete creed," a firm footing, and the seven

devils of superstition, so that his last state is worse than his first.

The biography of Emerson will just show us what the man is and how he is. He is an American of the old school, an honour to his country, one of the greatest men of his age. Wide and windy as he is in faith, he appears firm set to the wandering stars of America; he has plenty of culture, wide reading, scholarship, research, cleverness. He has little tenderness, no pathos, and yet much poetry of a sort—and that a subtle and good sort. Here *in petto* is what he is and what he has done.

He is a sharp, thin, thoughful man, *aigre*, clever-looking, with high but not very ample forehead. He is nearing his seventieth year, having been born in 1803; is an ultra-Unitarian—if so much (or so little) in Christian creed. He graduated at Harvard in 1821; was ordained minister of the Second Unitarian Church at Boston, a high seat of wide views of Faith, and having after some time embraced peculiar, and we presume even wider, notions, abandoned his pulpit, and settled in the peacefully-named village of Concord, to betake himself to the study of man and of Nature.

Being an American he soon began to "orate;" had he been a Britisher he would have lectured. In 1837 he delivered an oration called "Man Thinking," before the Phi-Beta-Kappa Society of Boston, and

in 1838 published " Literary Ethics : an Oration."
Mr. Emerson took the world by surprise.   His
talk embraced innumerable subjects; was ambitious,
daring, grandiose.   It was especially suited to
young men and a young country.   He said that
he did not pretend to argue, he announced ; he
did not teach, he exhibited.   Similarly, he did
not lecture to persuade, he " orated."   Bear this
in mind, and you have the key to the Emersonian
popularity. In 1839 Mr. Emerson published " Nature :
an Essay ; " in 1840 he commenced *The Dial*, a
magazine of Literature, History, and Philosophy,
in which all three were very wild, and utterly
unlike anything that would be published in Germany, France, or England.   The conditions of
literature are so different in new America to what
they are in old Europe.   Here our writers in
some degree subordinate themselves to public
opinion ; there they subordinate a raw and untaught public opinion to themselves.   They are,
therefore, the more free and daring, while European
thought is the more solid, compressed, and
enduring.

Emerson now began pouring out his bottles of
mental champagne very quickly.   In 1841 he gave
us " The Method of Nature," " Man the Reformer,"
three lectures, and the first series· of his Essays.
In 1844 the second series, " New England Re-

formers," "The Young American," and a lecture on the West Indian Emancipation. In 1845-9 he delivered lectures on Swedenborg, Napoleon, and others, afterwards published as "Representative Men." In 1852, working with Mr. Ellery Channing, he , published the "Memoirs of the Countess D'Ossoli" (Margaret Fuller). After a visit to England he published, in 1856, a work called "English Traits," in 1860 another, a very little but very sweet book, called "The Conduct of Life," and early in the spring of 1870, "Society and Solitude," his last, and by far the slightest and worst work he has written.

Now, in all these books there is a certain amount of honest work and thought, if there be also a good deal of gilt gingerbread and flash jewellery. Let us speak of the faults first. Let us take two or three sentences hap-hazard from his last book, which, weak as it is, is very entrancing for a boy or a young man to read. " 'Tis sweet to talk of kings," say the old satirists, and when Emerson familiarly gossips of "Paul, Plato, the Zendavesta, Vishnu, Brahma, Socrates, Jesus, and such teachers of men," we half believe that we know something of such · good company. But just sit down after reading an essay by Emerson, and ask, What have I got out of it? That is the test. Hear him, for instance, on Art:

z

" Herein is the explanation of the analogies which exist in all the Arts. They are the reappearance of one mind working in many materials to temporary ends. Raphael paints wisdom ; Handel sings it ; Phidias carves it ; Shakespeare writes it ; Wren builds it ; Columbus sails it ; Luther preaches it ; Washington arms it ; Watt mechanises it. Painting was called ' silent poetry,' and poetry, ' speaking painting.' The laws of each Art are convertible into the laws of every other."

Now, in addition to this last truism being a lame expansion of Horace,—*De Arte Poetica :*

" Pictoribus atque poetis
Quidlibet audendi semper fuit œqua potestas "

we find in the first the simple Pantheism of the last few verses in the Laureate's last volume, and, indeed, he has compressed the whole into those curious rhymes, " Flower in the Crannied Wall," wherein he is so bold as to say " plucking it out of the crannies " that, if he only knew how the flower " growed," as Topsy has it, he (Mr. Tennyson) " would know what God is and man is." In the very much " lower Pantheism," as our sages would call it, of Pope, God not only " paints and mechanises, arms, sails, and preaches," acting through all things, as indeed He does, but He is in all things worshipped ; He is " Jehovah, Jove, our Lord," all in one. Perhaps one of the missions of the Saviour was to beat down that folly, into which those who reject Him are sure to fall. Beyond these two matters, and a glib enumeration of names, there is nothing. Here, again, is a peculiarly Emersonian sentence upon the "Bibles of the World,"—one Bible, by the way, to him, as good as another:

> " I mean the Bibles of the world, or the sacred books of each nation, which express for each *the supreme result of their experience.* After the Hebrew and Greek Scriptures, which constitute the sacred books of Christendom, there are the Desatir of the Persians and the Zoroastrian Oracles ; the Vedas and Laws of Menu ; the Upanishads ; the Vishnu Purana ; the Bhagvat Geeta of the Hindoos ; the books of the Buddhists; the Chinese Classics, and others of four books, containing the wisdom of Confucius and Mencius. Also such other books as have acquired a semi-canonical authority in the world. Such are the Hermes Trismegistus, pretending to be the Egyptian remains ; the Sentences of Epictetus ; of Marcus Antoninus ; the Vishnu Sarma of the Hindoos ; the Gulistan of Saadi ; the Imitation of Christ of Thomas à Kempis ; and the Thoughts of Pascal."

This braggadocio sentence cannot fail to remind the reader of the merry old gentleman who takes in the vicar of Wakefield with his flood of learning, comprised in one sentence, which he is always repeating. " The cosmogony or Creation of the World has puzzled philosophers of all ages. What a medley of opinions have they not broached upon the Creation of the World ! Sanconiathon, Manetho, Berosus, and Ocellus Lucanus have all attempted it." We are almost, indeed, inclined to interrupt Mr. Emerson, and ask him, "Is not your name Ephraim Jenkinson, with the simple Dr. Primrose when awakened from his dream ?" We are

not learned enough to pronounce on the Chinese
Classics, nor on the Desatir of the Persians, but we
know enough of the Bhagvat Geeta, the Talmud,
and the philosophy of Confucius (by far the best),
to assure the reader that these sacred books are
wild and nonsensical fairy tales, dogmatic nonsense,
mere Eastern drivel, and clotted follies, entangled
with wild fancies and prurient stories, which no
sane man dare compare with the clear reason and
power of the New Testament.

Look again at the wordy sentence. The *Imitatione
Christi* and the *Pensées* of Pascal are put last. Why,
there are more sound high thoughts, sublime resolves,
and God-taught endeavour, in one section of either
of these books than in all the far-Eastern nonsense
ever raked together! Epictetus or Marcus Antoninus
would beat the lot!

But put him on his own ground, not upsetting his
mind with windy ideas from big books with which
he is not fully acquainted, and Emerson is a first-
class writer. No man would do better as an editor
of a Quarterly Review, or a contributor thereto.
His two most valuable books are " English Traits,"
a most generous, thoughtful, and valuable estimate
of the English people and nation, beyond all praise
for its honest truth, its acute perception, its interesting and thorough style, its fearless speaking—fearless
in blame and in praise; and the " The Conduct of

Life." In the last we meet Mr. Emerson as a poet, wild, novel, suggestive; but he has written other poems besides these heads of chapters. As rhyme and melody are to be distinguished from poetry properly so called, so Emerson, it must be remembered, writes poetry with melody or rhyme. His lines are not exactly verse, and yet they are poetry. Generally this poetry is in short verse—as uneasy as a macadamised road new done, and much resembling a translation from the Anglo-Saxon, or a passage from Tusser's "Hundred Points of Husbandry." Here, however, is a sonnet:

"RHODORA.

"In May, when the sea-winds pierced our solitudes,
  I found the fresh Rhodora in the woods,
  Spreading its leafless blooms in a damp nook,
  To please the desert and the sluggish brook.
  The purple petals, fallen in the pool,
  Made the black water with their beauty gay ;
  Here might the red-bird come his plumes to cool,
  And court the flower that cheapens his array.

"Rhodora ! if the sages ask thee why
  This charm is wasted on the earth and sky,
  Tell them, dear, that if eyes were made for seeing,
  Then beauty is its own excuse for being :
  Why thou wert there, O rival of the rose !
  I never thought to ask, I never knew ;
  But in my simple ignorance suppose
  The self-same power that brought me there, brought you."

In this you find a parallel thought to that of

Tennyson's very insufficient "Flower in the Crannied Wall"—but how much truer, greater, and better!

We conclude with an astute passage from "English Traits:"

"England is the best of actual nations. It is no ideal framework,—it is an old pile built in different ages, with repairs, additions, and makeshifts; but you see the poor best you have got. London is the epitome of our times, and the Rome of to-day. Broad-fronted, broad-bottomed Teutons, they stand in solid phalanx foursquare to the points of the compass: they constitute the modern world, they have earned their vantage-ground, and held it through ages of adverse possession. They are well-marked and differing from other leading races. England is tender-hearted. Rome was not. England is not so public in its bias; private life is its place of honour. Truth in private life, untruth in public, marks these home-loving men. Their political conduct is not decided by general views, but by internal intrigues and personal and family interest. They cannot readily see beyond England."

Emerson is not the best of actual essayists; neither the most tender, nor the most true, the most powerful, nor the wisest. But he looks the wisest and most knowing of all; he is and will be always a great favourite with the young; he does not speak to your heart, but he does to your head. The effect of reading his works, until you are *quite* behind the scenes and know something, is that which a college lecturer has upon a freshman; and yet, after all, of himself Emerson says little; and what he does say stimulates, but it does not nourish.

MR. T. W. ROBERTSON.

MR. T. W. ROBERTSON.

SIGNOR MAZZINI, who, in the years to come, when the mists of contemporary prejudice and falsehood shall have cleared away, will be considered a very great man, writes to his friend Edward Quinet a letter which takes an extremely desponding view of present times. The view is, in a great measure, a true one, but it is one which is natural to all old men, but especially so to one who, like Mazzini, has seen the cherished hopes of his youth disappointed, who has believed, and nobly believed, in humanity, but has found at last that his faith was but a dream resulting from his own nobleness. Thus Brutus, when dying on the field of battle, found virtue but a shade, and Mazzini wearies of this generation, which he says, truly enough, is "a mere instrument, having no faith, but only opinions; which abjures God, Immortality, Love, and a belief in an intelligent and providential law; receives laws as regulations, forms without substance, means without an end, while justice is regarded as Utopian, and worship is reserved for success; an age growing in intelligence but not in purpose." Upon this the *Spectator* remarks, " His view of this age is too desponding, but is confirmed in great part by every teacher, religious and secular, around us; " and it is with this in our mind that we would begin an essay on, or a review of, Mr. T. W. Robertson and his comedies. For dramatic work is like none other literature—it reflects the age, or the wishes of the age. An author like Bacon, or Milton, or Gibbon, or Hobbes of Malmesbury, might and can afford to wait, but a man like Shakespeare, or Ben Jonson, or Beaumont and Fletcher cannot. In a modified sense, also, Dr. Johnson's couplet is quite true :

> " The Drama's laws the Drama's patrons give,
> And they who live to please, must please to live."

There is no approval so delightful as a full house ; no criticism so damning as a beggarly account of empty boxes. Hence the decline of the Drama, and hence the merit of the courageous endeavour of Mr. Robertson to render one English theatre at least worthy of the name, and to present a comedy which reflected the manners of the age, and justly satirised the follies of the day. This, too, at a time when almost all the plays that we have are stolen or taken from the French, without leave often, frequently with the consent of the authors ;

dramas which cannot possibly picture English manners, which have almost all of them a stain of original sin so deep that it cannot always be washed away by any amount of English cleansing powder, and which if washed away leaves the adaptation weak, colourless, and worthless.

Mr. Thomas William Robertson is one of those few dramatic authors who have been originally actors. The great name of Shakespeare heads the list ; those of Carrick, Tobin, Colley Cibber, Buckstone, and a few others have to be included ; but it follows that either the author is a bad actor, or, if a good actor, he is a poor and weak author. The one *rôle* must subordinate the other. Colley Cibber succeeded in both if we take his "Careless Husband" as a specimen, but in general the actor-author is a mistake. Dramatic literature has a despotic Muse who will not be conciliated with a merely partial courtship. Shakespeare taught one actor how to read his Ghost in " Hamlet," and himself made but a lame representative of old Adam in " As You Like it." Mr. Robertson, we believe, never achieved distinction as an actor, and indeed was, we have been told, little better than a second-rate walking gentleman at second-rate theatres. But he gained therefrom an immense knowledge of stage business and effect, and that chief part of knowledge, to know what to say and to say no more. He

never overloads his parts ; he writes with excessive
neatness, and taking the measure of his audience,
never treats it—whatever may be its component
parts—to any deep reflections, poetical rhapsodies,
long lengths of verse or measured prose, or pathos
of any depth. What he means is always transparent, and hence his jokes never miss fire. He
has been seconded by such good actors and actresses
that, although by no means acute, they seem to
be so, for while his plays really display their own
merit more than any other writings that we know
of, and in a very clever way too, they have the
singular merit of persuading the actors that they
are profoundly clever. When a man or a woman
has to say for a hundred consecutive nights a piece
of flat English to which the situation gives point,
and finds that the sympathetic audience always
grins, giggles, or applauds the platitude, he or she,
insensibly at least, becomes persuaded that the
words contain a deep meaning, a recondite wit,
which escapes or is above the ordinary perception.
Hence the author has a sort of doubly-reflected
fame. The merit which was at first denied him is
forced upon the actor's mind, and by him, by extra
point, upon the audience.

Born in June, 1839, at Newark-on-Trent, Notting-
hamshire, Mr. Robertson came before the footlights
by nature, for his father was a theatrical manager

very well known in what some facetious persons and the theatrical profession generally will call "the Provinces." It is one of the virtues of the " profession " that it will persist in clothing small and miserable matters with large names. Notoriety is called "fame," a struggle for existence "unbounded success," a sparse audience "a crowded house," and a small English county, not much bigger than a Russian or American farm, one of the " Provinces." By thus carefully disguising the size of matters, these wise people keep up a constant illusion, and live happily though surrounded with squalor, degradation, and misery. Nothing is more deceptive, as indeed it should be so, than the theatre, and so thoroughly powerful is it in this way, that those who have once taken to it never waken from the dream. Did they do so they would be miserable, and like the man in Horace cry out,

> "———— O, by Apollo, friends !
> Me thou hast killed,—not served."

We may be sure that Mr. Robertson "took very kindly" to the stage, but of that we have little to say. He lived "more or less from his birth to 1860 as an actor," to quote a theatrical authority, but in 1860 he abandoned the stage for the career of literature. His first original production was a piece at the Olympic called " A Night's Adventure," in 1851. In 1861 he had written a farce called "The

Cantab," at the Strand; in 1864, "David Garrick," a play, from the French, at the Haymarket; in 1865, "Society," first acted at Liverpool in May, was in November produced at the Prince of Wales's Theatre; and in the same year he wrote the libretto of an opera, "Constance." In 1866, his comedy of "Ours" was produced at the same London theatre, having been previously tried in Liverpool. In 1867, he wrote "Shadow Tree Shaft" for the Princess's, "A Rapid Thaw" for the St. James's, and "Caste" at the Prince of Wales's, and wrote an entertainment for German Reed, called "A Dream of Venice," and his comedy "For Love" was produced at the Holborn. His succeeding and very successful plays at the Prince of Wales's Theatre were "Play," "School," which ran for 381 nights, and his last and least, "M.P." His intermediate and unsuccessful pieces were "Dreams" at the Gaiety, the "Nightingale" at the Adelphi, and a translation called a "Breach of Promise" at the Globe. Mr. Robertson has spent some time in Germany, and has married a lady born in that country, and has evidently studied with much advantage the French stage, from which he has adopted more than one incident. "School," his most poetical and successful play, was adapted, rather than translated, from the German play, "The Aschenbrödel," but so skilfully has it been done that no trace of the original remains. An angry attack upon this unacknowledged adaptation in the *Times*, from a correspondent, was followed by an acute parallel of the two plays by Mr. John Oxenford; but Mr. Robertson himself very discreetly kept silence. It must be acknowledged that "School" is so very skilfully adapted that there is no proof of its German origin to be found in the piece itself. With the curious exception of having a male teacher, Mr. Krux, as an instructor of girls, which might be well accounted for if we suppose that the doctor kept a boys' and his wife a ladies' school, there are very few inconsistencies. The examination of a number of school-girls for the delectation of an old beau and two young men, is unnatural and ridiculous in its untruth; but the play as a whole is so charming that we wisely follow Horace's rule, and forgive all its faults.

Let us, however, finish the "historical account" of our author. He has not flown at very high game in literature, but it is due to him to say that he very rightly, in one sense, despises the pompous assumption of the larger magazines and reviews. *London Society* is perhaps the most advanced magazine that he has contributed to; but previously to his great success as a dramatic writer, he worked very hard as a journalist; he contributed to *Fun;* edited, with Mr. Hingston, the lecture of Artemus

Ward ; contributed to the " Savage Club Papers,"
and wrote more than one truthful and pathetic
story in the Christmas numbers of various magazines.

It is, however, especially as a dramatist that
Mr. Robertson must be viewed, and, curiously, as a
successful dramatist at *one* theatre.   Never was the
policy of getting a good working company, and of
keeping it together, more thoroughly proved to be
the right one.   At the Prince of Wales's Theatre,
under the management of Mrs. Bancroft, and with
the London company managed by Mr. Frederick
Younge, there is absolutely nothing to be desired.
So well do the actors and actresses enter into the
parts played, that each one seems to have been
born for the character.   Mrs. Bancroft (Marie
Wilton), her husband, and Mr. Hare, act so well
that all trace of acting disappears.   The style is
simply that of the drawing-room ; the theatre is so
small and yet so elegant that it *looks* like a drawing-
room ; the actors and actresses like ladies and
gentlemen indulging in very pointed conversation.
And, wondrous to relate, when we repeat that very
pointed conversation the next day, it is dull and
pointless ; yet so well is it given by the company,
so thoroughly is every cue taken up, that what is
actually dull enough to be real conversation, becomes
burnished and glows with theatric polish on the
stage.   And this fact will account for the failure

of all, or nearly all, of Mr. Robertson's pieces when produced at any other theatre but that in Tottenham Street. Look, for instance, at the fate of "A Rapid Thaw," "Shadow Tree Shaft," "For Love," "Dreams," "A Breach of Promise," and the "Nightingale," produced at other theatres, compared with that of "Society," "Ours," "Caste," "Play," "School," and "M.P.," produced by Miss Marie Wilton. The suggestion which carries with it an accusation of dishonesty, namely, that the author keeps all his best pieces for his favourite theatre, is untrue. "Dreams," for instance, played at Marie Wilton's theatre would have run as long as "School." The fact is, that one company in London knows how to appreciate and to play Mr. Robertson's works, and the others do not; and this is proved by the actual dulness of the dialogue in reading, which on the stage appears so brilliant.

Happily for his reputation, our playwright has published few plays. We can therefore only quote from "Society" and from "M.P.," the first from a printed copy, the second from our own notes.

Maud.—To give up all his fortune, to ruin his bright prospects, to keep unsullied the honour of his brother's name was an act—
Lady Ptarmigan.—Of a noodle! And now he hasn't a penny but what he gets by scribbling—a pretty pass for a man of family to come to. You are my niece, and it is my solemn duty to get you married if I can. Don't thwart me, and I will. Leave sentiment to servant wenches who sweetheart policemen,

it's unworthy of a lady. I've a man in my eye—I mean a rich one—young Chodd.

Maud (with repugnance). —Such a common-place person.

Lady P.—With a very uncommon-place purse. He will have eighteen thousand a-year. I have desired him to pay you court. and I desire you to receive it.

Maud.—He is so vulgar.

Lady P.—He is so rich. When he is your husband, put him in a back study, and don't show him.

Maud.—But I detest him.

Lady P.—What on earth has that to do with it? You wouldn't love a man before you were married to him, would you? Where are your principles? Ask my lord how I treated him before our marriage (*hitting Lord P. with her fan*). Ferdinand!

Lord P. (awaking)—My love!

Lady P.—Do keep awake.

Lord P.—'Pon my word you were making such a noise I thought I was in the House of Commons. (*With fond regret.*) I used to be allowed to sleep so comfortably there.

Lady P.—Are you not of opinion that a match between Mr. Chodd and Maud would be most desirable?

Lord P. (looking at Lady P.)—Am I not of opinion—my opinion—what is my opinion?

Lady P. (hitting him with her fan)—Yes, of course.

Comparison between this and the dialogue of Congreve or of Sheridan, or of Goldsmith, Vanbrugh, or Wycherley, would not hold for a moment, yet as given by Miss Wilton, Mrs. Buckingham White, and Mr. Hare, it bristled with point, and sparkled like cut glass under the lime-light—that is, it looked very much like diamonds. Again, take the following *morceaux* from " M.P." each of which brought down a torrent of applause on the first night, and ask

whether the wit is very exhilarating? Talbot
Piers is accepted and also beloved by Cecilia
Dunscombe, and urges the force of the marriage-
vow of the woman to "honour and obey" the
man. "Oh," says Cecilia, archly, "that's a mere
form," at which the audience laughed heartily.
Chudleigh Dunscombe (a very young fellow) gives
vent to the Platonic sentence, "Nature could not
put bad thoughts into so beautiful a *skin*," and is
rewarded by a round of applause for so transparent
an untruth; and Isaac Skoome, a low-born manufacturer, who has made money, brags that "he
worked hard, and Providence has done its duty,"
i.e., had enriched him, upon which the house is in
ecstacies! But not more so than when Dunscombe
(acted by Mr. Hare) calls him "a ready-made man,"
instead of "a self-made man," or Chudleigh Dunscombe tells him to "take away his *metallic* hand."
Metallic is a favourite epithet of Robertson, and is
used once or twice in "Society" and in "Play." It
must again be insisted on that these "points," being
well placed and led up to, are very effective—on the
stage.

To conclude, Mr. Robertson is the dramatist of
the age, and reflects the artificial manners of society.
He has no depth, little pathos, small humour; but
he knows his business and his audience, his time,
stage, and actors thoroughly. Well mounted, his

pieces have a freshness, a cleverness, and a charm
which belongs to a fine piece of art *a la* Watteau,
or in Dresden or Sevres china. "School" has even
more; it has the effect of the prettiest little idyll on
the stage, but we must not compare its idyllic force
with that of "As You Like It," but rather with
that of one of those old English operas, "Love in
a Village; or, the Mountain Sylph," now too
seldom acted. Robertson has not high art nor
high feeling, but he very successfully assumes a
tone of high-breeding and well-bred cynicism. His
pieces are not highly moral, but they are not immoral, and are quite up to the morality of the age.
He has been accused of sneering at everything:
this he does not do, he only sneers at what he and
society does not believe in. He is exceedingly
artificial, but then so are the times; he appreciates
Tennyson, whom he quotes; he is at any rate on
the side of virtue and of manliness so far as that
is consistent with kid gloves and an evening dress.
He dares to satirise what is weak and foolish in
John Stuart Mill, and to give a wholesome opinion
of the silly burlesques which are vitiating the taste
of society.

M. EDMOND ABOUT.

M. EDMOND ABOUT.

HERE are two men* whose names are more frequently cited by our chief writers — either in the *Spectator*, the *Saturday*, or the *Times*—than those of any others, and whose views are eagerly looked for, translated, quoted, and put forward, by such conductors of papers—and their

---

* For the purpose of compactness, we have treated here the MM. Erckmann-Chatrain as one author, as, in fact, they are as to the effect they have on the public. The following, from a weekly review, will explain the dualism :—" As some curiosity is expressed about the personality of the two men, who alternately count as one man under two names, and two men under one name, and who bid fair to be accepted as the Siamese Twins of literature, we quote the details given in this paper. According to Herr Julian Schmidt, the partnership of Erckmann-Chatrian consists of M. Emile Erckmann, born at Pfalzburg in 1822, and M. Alexandre Chatrian, born near the same town in 1826. Erckmann came to Paris in 1842 to study law, but made little way with it ; M. Chatrian was first employed in a Belgian glass manufactory, then set up as a teacher at Pfalzburg, and came to Paris in 1852. It was then the two became friends, and engaged jointly in literature, which M. Erckmann had already tried alone, but unsuccessfully."—*Athenæum*, Sept. 10th, 1870.

names are *not* legion—as are sufficiently educated and advanced to have any opinion upon the matter. For, in this war, opinion has curiously varied, and has not always been based upon principle. But of this hereafter.

These two men are not men of war, but of peace; not generals, but writers; and · their names are Erckmann-Chatrain, author of " Le Blocus " (" The Blockade ")—who has described the country now desolated by war—and Edmond About, the once chief penman of the Emperor, and the famous correspondent of *Le Soir*.

M. About is the more famous of the two. M. Chatrain, it is true, is recalled by the scenes brought so vividly before our eyes by the newspaper histories of each morning, and the grand courage and enduring pluck that he pictures are now again brought into use at Phalsburg and Strasbourg. But Edmond About is a war chronicler and correspondent. He is, or has been, with the armies; was reported dead; and had to fly, with his wife and children, from the comfortable quarters assigned to him. Like the pious Æneas, he has " been a great part of what he has seen ; " has travelled to the forefront of action ; speaks like one having authority ; and is versatile enough to translate and render to our eyes every shade of grief, terror, elation, which moves his excellent but chameleon-like nation. Nor is there

anything better, or more incisive, or more peculiar
and epigrammatic in the whole range of literature
than these queer letters of Edmond About. They
are just as "spicy" and *goguenard* in their way as
are those of Mr. George Sala—one of the very best
English correspondents who ever drew pen in any
foreign "row;" but they are more solid, reflective,
luminous—have more of the scholar and the gentleman in them, to use an old phrase. As for M.
About's little eccentricities in abusing the Germans,
they are not only natural—being shared in by all
his countrymen, and therefore to be excused—but
they are, from his pen, although more incisive, a
thousand times less coarse and vulgar than you
see in the French prints every day. Whatever
may happen—and it is yet possible for France,
by a gigantic effort, to shake off the grip of the
armed thousands who hold her down—France has
been so deceived and cajoled that she is under
the influence of a strong delusion, and believes
a lie!

"Why did you make war so readily, M. le Duc?"
asked a member of the Jockey Club of the Duke of
Gramont, the other day.

"I believed we were ready. I went to the Minister
of War, and I asked him, 'Are you ready? Can we
move at once?' 'Ready!' he answered; 'pah!
ready *twice over!*' If I had not believed that, I would

never have entered on a war which I might have
avoided in a dozen ways."

It is quite lawful, moreover, for those who are
beaten to scold. This also should be remembered in
About's favour, if two or three harsh words now and
then escape him.

M. Edmond François Valentin About is about
forty-two years old, having been born at Dieuze on
the 14th of February, 1828. His patron saint of the
day of his *fête* is the good Bishop Valentine, and
this will account for one of his Christian names. He
was educated at the Charlemagne Lyceum, and was
early distinguished. When he was twenty he won
the prize of honour, and three years afterwards he
passed to the French School at Athens. He here
made himself thoroughly acquainted with Greece as
it is; knew it to be a nest of rogues and robbers;
knew it, also, to his cost—as during his archæological
studies he had often to fly from some Alkibiades or
Peisistratos, who was looking at him over a ruin
and assisting his vision by glancing along the barrel
of a gun. The result of these studies—political,
social, and archæological—was published in 1855 as
" La Grèce Contemporaine." Of course, the diplo-
matic people of England and France received the
work with disdain. About had told the plain truth:
therefore he was not believed by diplomatists. He
then tried to tell the truth with a laughing face,

and imagined that his next work, carried out on that Horatian maxim, would awaken Europe. This wonderfully true and witty work was called " Le Roi des Montagnes," and is simply the history of a Greek brigand, acting in connivance with Greek troops and a Greek minister. M. Hadji-Starros, Mary Anne, Mrs. Simons, with the French, German, and Greek characters, are drawn to the life. And it is not too much to say that this book, published in 1857, anticipated—though hardly in its full horrors —the whole of the terrible Greek massacre of English gentlemen and an Italian nobleman in 1870. Had the lessons of that book been attended to, the companions of Lord Muncaster would have been alive. M. About—although no · English writer has yet pointed out the fact—may claim the honour of being a prophet. In his last chapter—it only consists of a line or so—the author again " resumes his conversa-. tion," and says, seriously, " Athénien, mon bel ami, les histoires les plus vraies ne sont pas celles qui sont arrivées." But all that the Greeks replied to that warning was to swear that About was untrue, and that their fine country was slandered. They absolutely persuaded England to give them Corfu and the Ionian Islands ; and proceeded, amidst the lamentations of the inhabitants, to ruin and undo the security and civilisation of years.

In style, About, in this book. showed himself a

master. His is simply the best style in the world—
that is, of the French. It is based upon that clear,
clean method of Voltaire, in the "Candide" and his
other romances. We are not talking, if you please,
of the morality of Voltaire, but of his marvellous
style. Full, without overflowing; clear, without
being bare; deep, without obscurity, it unites the
incisiveness of Swift—and marvellous prose is his—
the grace of Addison, and the wit of Congreve.

Such a writer, living in Paris and not in London
—where Philistine publishers never originate a work,
and chiefly live on ideas furnished by the neglected
and hack author—such a writer in Paris was at once
sought for, and had plenty to do. In 1855 he published, in the *Revue des deux Mondes,* a curious but
very beautiful work, "Tolla;" in 1856, "Les
Mariages de Paris," which was a great success; and
in 1857, "Germaine," a very beautiful, miserably
sad story of a *mariage de Paris*—that is, of the
legitimate and honourable sale of the heroine by
way of marriage.

About is a moralist in a high sense; and his books
are as moral as the scalpel which removes proud
flesh is beneficial. It was about this time that our
author seems to have entered into some sort of pact
with Louis Napoleon to assist him with his pen. It
would be well if monarchs would, like Frederick,
condescend to put themselves on an equality with

the Voltaire of the day. The result of this "pact"
—which we by no means affirm, but which has been
often hinted at—was that M. About seems to have
given a grace to several French State papers; and
that in 1859 he published " La Question Romaine,"
which laid bare the rottenness of that capital in a
manner that must have made Archbishop Manning,
and Sir George Bowyer, and other ultramontanes,
mad. " Pardon me," he says in his preface, "certain
vivacities of style, which I had not time to correct;
and plunge boldly into the heart of the book. You
will find something there. I fight fairly, and in good
faith. I do not pretend to have judged the foes of
Italy without passion; but I have calumniated none
of them. If I have sought a publisher in Brussels,
while I had an excellent one in Paris, it is not
because I feel any alarm on the score of the regulations of our press or the severity of our tribunals.
But as the Pope has a long arm, which might reach
me in France, I have gone a little out of the way
to tell him the plain truths contained in these
pages."

In commencing this work he referred to a case
then occupying the public mind—the abduction of a
Jewish child against the wishes of its parents. One
cannot help being at once struck with the extraordinary force of the following antitheses, even when
translated :—

"The Roman Catholic Church, which I sincerely respect, consists of one hundred and thirty-nine millions of individuals —*without counting little Mortara !*

It is governed by seventy cardinals, princes of the Roman Church—*in memory of twelve poor Apostles !*

The Cardinal Bishop of Rome, who is also called Vicar of Jesus Christ, Holy, Most Holy Father, or Pope, is invested with boundless authority over the minds of these hundred and thirty-nine millions."

The author then traces, with a stinging satire and crushing effect, the history of the Popes.

With the exception of one or two slight works, Edmond About has been silent until the opening of this war; when, with Thiers, Jules Favre, and others, he raised his voice energetically against it. M. Thiers has since explained that he did so because France was unprepared, not because the war was unjust. And certainly About may have done the same ; for, after warning France, he seems to have been borne away with the enthusiastic shouts of "*A Berlin!*" and, perhaps against his better judgment, accepted the post—said to be accredited by the Government—of correspondent of *Le Soir*. To one who, if he be not an academician, has the style and more than merit of one, such an appointment seemed *infra dignitatem;* but the public rejoiced that he had accepted the post, and learned from About the follies of the campaign, the unreadiness, the ignorance of the officers, the folly of the leaders, the brag and emptiness of the whole.

After Saarbrück, About's style changed, and he attacked the Emperor violently. He mourned, like a true Frenchman, over the slaughter of his friends, and of that army of which he was so proud; and, even while making the best of it, his pen wept tears of good French ink as he described the rout of the army of the Rhine. After Weissembourg he was lost for more than a week; his wife and children fled to Paris; and he, sick and weary of slaughter, was silent; and not only Paris, but all Europe feared that he was among the killed—as, indeed, more than one patriotic correspondent had fallen in the *mêlée*. But it was not so. After being for some time lost, About made his way to Paris, and began a series of most brilliant, most sarcastic, and bitter attacks on the empire, the Government, England, and all neutral powers, and on the French people. We can pardon his anger against us for the grief these bitter truths must cost him:

"The report of yesterday's sitting, and that storm in the Chamber, carried me back 417 years. I asked myself whether we had not become, to some extent, Byzantines. In 1453, while Mahomet II. was besieging Constantinople, the Greeks of the Lower Empire were divided upon questions of theology, just as the Parisians of the present day are divided upon political questions. They quarrelled among themselves with such bitterness, that they forgot the presence of the enemy, and allowed him to take the city. The Turk entered, and reconciled them all by means of the stick. The same fortune might fall to our lot if the nation did not show itself possessed of more good sense and more enlightened patriotism than the two parties in the Chamber. The Right and the Left are incessantly accusing each other of having caused these public disasters. The Government party insists that Alsace and Lorraine would not have been invaded if the Opposition had not haggled about subsidies and annual contingents : ' You have so railed against standing armies, that you have disarmed the country.' The Opposition retorts the incapacity of courtier generals ; the squandering of the funds intended for supplying war material ; the mistrust on the part of personal government, which would never allow the people to be armed, and which still refuses them muskets even when the enemy is at our gates. ' You are afraid of the nation. You would rather sacrifice France than lose your own power.' How sad is all this ! Each of these stormy sittings is worth 50,000 men to the Prussians who are marching upon us. Cannot these quarrels be deferred until the country has been delivered? France should wash her dirty linen at the proper time and place, but she should wait until we are again *en famille.*'

Then, again, he glances back to what the Empire has been—how it has spoiled and humiliated *La belle France*—and he extracts this bitter consolation :

" Well, all is perhaps for the best. If the supporters of the personal power had been acquainted with the first elements of the military art ; if Marshal Lebœuf had had a plan ; if we had been ready ; if we had had 500,000 effective troops instead of 200,000 ; if the millions destined for armament had not for years been wasted or turned to other uses, we should beat the Prussians, and free the Rhine Provinces. We should take Saarbrück and Sarrelouis, Mayence, and Coblentz ; we should light tapers in the cathedrals of Trèves and of Cologne ; the Prince Imperial might collect enough spent balls to *form a chaplet for his godfather, the gentle Pius IX.*—AND AFTER ?"

And, after having soundly abused England, he thus makes the *amende honorable* in these words :

" Our neighbours on the other side of the Channel shower me with reproaches, and I ought to thank them. Nothing is more sweet to the heart of a true Frenchman than this English revolt against an unfounded accusation. More than a hundred letters, in less than a week, have repeated to me, in every form of expression—' You deceive yourself. You are unjust. . . . . The citizens of Great Britain have only sympathy for the French nation. The officers of the fleet and of the army never forget that they found friends as well as comrades in your sailors and soldiers. The intellectual classes consider your country as the fortress of European civilisation. We should never be consoled if we saw France destroyed, or even seriously weakened. We suffer and hope with you.' Such is the substance of the letters which are addressed to me from all parts of England and Scotland. The kindly communications which I have received are signed by honourable, by aristocratic names, as well as by ladies. There are poems, there are articles which the writers wish me to publish, and which I would gladly print if the limits of my space permitted. I can only thank these innumerable correspondents, and say to them, ' Vivent la France et l'Angleterre, united for the peace and prosperity of the world. You have rendered me quite happy in showing me my error !'"

We have not extracted in this article any of the epigrams, surprises, points, and brilliant sayings of the author, save a few from "La Question Romaine," because the war itself absorbs all our interest; but we hope we have fairly introduced one of the most honest and brilliant writers of the day—one who is a true patriot, and shares with the same eagerness the sorrows as well as the glory of his great nation. To some of us it may seem that the Government of France has been deservedly punished; to some, that French vain-glory has received a proper and a

wholesome check. Yet they who think thus may
sympathise with a brave people in its misfortune;
and pray that sounder counsels and wiser governors
may raise *La belle France* out of her distress, and
place her on that true pinnacle of greatness, wherein
her glory, arising from herself and her children, will
not be sought by the humiliation or subordination of
another. And, indeed, M. About is typical of France.
He has done so much that is good, that he need not,
even in the agony of suspense and the humiliation of
defeat, drive his excellent style into hysterics to
attract attention.

UNWIN BROTHERS, PRINTERS, 24, BUCKLERSBURY, LONDON.

A Selection of Works

FROM

HODDER & STOUGHTON'S CATALOGUE.

MODERN MEN OF LETTERS HON-ESTLY CRITICISED. By J. HAIN FRISWELL, author of "Essays on English Writers," &c., &c. Crown 8vo. 7s. 6d.

FIRST PRINCIPLES OF ECCLESIAS-TICAL TRUTH. Essays on the Church and Society. By J. BALDWIN BROWN, B.A. 8vo. 10s. 6d.

By the same Author,

THE DIVINE MYSTERIES: the Divine Treatment of Sin, and the Divine Mystery of Peace. New Edition. Crown 8vo. 7s. 6d.

DR. PRESSENSE'S HISTORY OF CHRISTIANITY.

I. *JESUS CHRIST: His Times, Life, and Work.* Cheap Edition, large crown 8vo. cloth, 9s.

II. *THE EARLY YEARS OF CHRIS-TIANITY.* A Sequel to "Jesus Christ : His Times, Life, and Work." 8vo. cloth, 12s.

III. *THE MARTYRS AND APOLO-GISTS.* By E. DE PRESSENSE, D.D. Being the Second Volume of the "Early Years of Christianity." 8vo. [*Nearly ready.*

THE LIFE AND TIMES OF THE
REV. JOHN WESLEY, M.A., Founder of the Methodists. By the Rev. LUKE TYERMAN. Vol. I., 8vo. 12s. To be completed in 3 vols., 8vo. price 12s. each.

THE WORLD OF ANECDOTE: an
Accumulation of Facts, Incidents, and Illustrations, Historical and Biographical, from Books and Times, Recent and Remote. By E. PAXTON HOOD. Crown 8vo. 10s. 6d.

THE WORLD OF MORAL AND RE-
LIGIOUS ANECDOTE. Illustrations and Incidents gathered from Words, Thoughts, and Deeds, in the Lives of Men, Women, and Books. By E. PAXTON HOOD. Crown 8vo. 10s. 6d.

CHRISTIAN WORK ON THE BATTLE-
FIELD: Being Incidents of the Labours of the United States' Christian Commission. With an Historical Essay on the Influence of Christianity in alleviating the Horrors of War. Eight full-page Illustrations. Crown 8vo. 6s.

A SELECTION OF COMMON SAYINGS,
WORDS, AND CUSTOMS: their Origin and History. By HENRY JAMES LOARING, author of "Signs—their Antiquity and Derivation," &c., &c. Crown 8vo. 3s. 6d. cloth.

THE INTERIOR OF THE EARTH.
By H. P. MALET, E.I.C.S., author of "New Pages of Natural History," &c. Crown 8vo. 4s. 6d. cloth.

MODEL WOMEN. By the Rev. WILLIAM
ANDERSON, author of "Self-made Men." Crown 8vo. 5s. cloth, gilt edges.

PERSONAL RECOLLECTIONS OF
ENGLISH ENGINEERS, and of the Introduction of the Railway System in the United Kingdom. By a CIVIL ENGINEER, author of "The Trinity of Italy." 8vo., 12s.

PICTORIAL SCENES FROM THE

PILGRIM'S PROGRESS. Drawn by CLAUDE REIGNIER CONDER. Chromo-lithographed by VINCENT BROOKS, DAY & SON. Imperial 4to. elegantly bound, 15s.

THE COMING OF THE BRIDEGROOM.

Advent Sermons. By the Very Rev. HENRY ALFORD, D.D., Dean of Canterbury. Imperial 32mo. 1s. 6d.

THE STATE OF THE BLESSED

DEAD. Advent Sermons. By the same author. Third Thousand. Imperial 32mo. 1s. 6d.

ONE THOUSAND GEMS FROM REV.

HENRY WARD BEECHER. Edited and compiled by Rev. G. D. EVANS. Crown 8vo. with Portrait, 5s.

ECCLESIA : Church Problems considered in

a Series of Essays. Edited by HENRY ROBERT REYNOLDS, D.D. Second Thousand. 8vo. 14s. cloth.

DR. STOUGHTON'S ECCLESIASTICAL HISTORY OF ENGLAND.

I. THE CHURCH OF THE CIVIL

WARS, AND THE CHURCH OF THE COMMON-WEALTH. By JOHN STOUGHTON, D.D. Being the First and Second Volumes of "The Ecclesiastical History of England." 2 vols. 8vo. 28s.

II. THE CHURCH OF THE RESTORA-

TION. Forming the Third and Fourth Volumes of "The Ecclesiastical History of England." 2 vols. 8vo. 25s.

DR. HAGENBACH'S CHURCH HISTORY.

THE HISTORY OF THE CHURCH IN

THE EIGHTEENTH AND NINETEENTH CEN-TURIES. By K. R. HAGENBACH, D.D., Professor of Theology in the University of Basle, author of "German Rationalism." In 2 vols., 8vo. 24s. cloth.

CHRISTUS CONSOLATOR; or, The Pulpit in Relation to Social Life. By ALEXANDER MACLEOD, D.D. Crown 8vo. 5s.

THE LAND OF THE SUN: Sketches of Travel. With Memoranda, Historical and Geographical, of places of interest in the East, visited during many years' service in Indian Waters. By Lieut. C. R. LOW (late H.M. Indian Navy), author of " Tales of Old Ocean," &c. Crown 8vo. 5s.

THE EARLY YEARS OF ALEXANDER SMITH, POET AND ESSAYIST. Chiefly Reminiscences of Ten Years' Companionship. By the Rev. T. BRISBANE. Fcap. 8vo. 4s. 6d. cloth.

IPHIGENE. A Poem. By ALEXANDER LAUDER. Handsomely bound. 4s. cloth.

THE FAMILY: Its Duties, Joys, and Sorrows. By Count A. DE GASPARIN. Crown 8vo. 7s. 6d. cloth.

THE EDUCATION OF THE HEART: Woman's Best Work. By Mrs. ELLIS, author of " The Women of England," &c. Fcap. 8vo. 3s. 6d. cloth.

THE KING'S DAUGHTERS: Words on Work to Educated Women. By ANNIE HARWOOD. Fcap. 8vo. 2s. 6d. cloth extra.

MASTERPIECES OF PULPIT ELOQUENCE, Ancient and Modern, with Historical Sketches of Preaching in the Different Countries represented, and Biographical and Critical Notices of the several Preachers and their Discourses. By HENRY C. FISH, D.D. In 2 vols., 8vo. 21s. cloth.

SECULAR ANNOTATIONS ON
SCRIPTURE TEXTS. By the Rev. FRANCIS JACOX.
Crown 8vo. 6s.

AD CLERUM: Advices to a Young Preacher.
By JOSEPH PARKER, D.D. Crown 8vo. 5s.

ECCE DEUS: Essays on the Life and
Doctrine of Jesus Christ. By the same Author. Fourth
Edition. Crown 8vo. 5s.

SPRINGDALE ABBEY: Extracts from
the Diaries and Letters of an English Preacher. Edited
by JOSEPH PARKER, D.D. 8vo. 7s. 6d. cloth.

INCIDENTS IN THE LIFE OF
EDWARD WRIGHT. Including Reference to his Work
among the Thieves of London. By EDWARD LEACH,
Author of " Sketches of Christian Work among the Lowly."
Crown 8vo. 5s., with Portrait.

FIJI AND THE FIJIANS. By THOMAS
WILLIAMS, and *MISSIONARY LABOURS AMONG*
THE CANNIBALS. Extended, with Notices of Recent
Events. By JAMES CALVERT. Edited by GEORGE
STRINGER ROWE. Cheap and Revised Edition, in One
Volume, 608 pages. Illustrated. Crown 8vo. 6s.

DR. TODD'S VISIT TO CALIFORNIA.

THE SUNSET LAND. By JOHN TODD,
D.D., Author of "The Student's Manual." Small crown
8vo. 5s., cloth.

LAMPS, PITCHERS, AND TRUM-
PETS : Lectures on the Vocation of the Preacher. Illus-
trated by Anecdotes—Biographical, Historical, and Eluci-
datory—of every order of Pulpit Eloquence, from the Great
Preachers of all Ages. By E. PAXTON HOOD. Second
Thousand. 10s. 6d. cloth.

TALES FOR FAMILY READING.

THE BAIRNS; or, Janet's Love and Service. By the Author of "Christie Redfern's Troubles," &c. Second Thousand. Crown 8vo. 5s.

TALES OF OLD OCEAN. By Lieut. C. R. Low. Illustrated. Second Edition. Fcap. 8vo. 5s. cloth.

THE BEGGARS; or, the Founders of the Dutch Republic. A Tale. By J. B. DE LIEFDE. Second Edition, crown 8vo. 5s., cloth elegant.

WALTER'S ESCAPE; or, The Capture of Breda. By the same Author. Twelve Illustrations, Fcap. 8vo. 3s. 6d.

MADELEINE'S TRIAL, and other Stories. By Madame DE PRESSENSE. Translated by ANNIE HARWOOD. Four Illustrations. Fcap. 8vo. 3s. 6d.

SERMONS FROM THE STUDIO. Stories Illustrative of Art and Religion. By MARIE SIBREE. Crown 8vo., handsomely bound, price 7s. 6d., gilt edges.

VESTINA'S MARTYRDOM. A Story of the Catacombs. By EMMA RAYMOND PITMAN. In crown 8vo. 7s. 6d. cloth.

CONSTANCE AYLMER. A Story of the Seventeenth Century. Crown 8vo. 6s. cloth.

PRIEST AND NUN. A Story of Convent Life. By the Author of "Almost a Nun," &c., &c. Crown 8vo. 7s. 6d. cloth.

LONDON : HODDER & STOUGHTON, 27, PATERNOSTER ROW.

THE CHURCH OF THE RESTORATION. By JOHN STOUGHTON, D.D. In 2 vols., 25s. cloth.

"An author who has brought to the execution of his work, not only unusual capacity and knowledge, but also a spirit of strict impartiality."—*Illustrated London News.*

"Without exception, Dr. Stoughton's is the most candid and equitable history of the ecclesiastical controversies involved in the period he reviews which has ever been written : it must also, we think, be admitted to be the most accurate, penetrating, and comprehensive."—*London Quarterly Review.*

"His book is largely the fruit of independent research, which he has prosecuted both among public and private records to which he has had free access, and is entitled to take high position as the most complete, honest, and impartial history of the ecclesiastical movements of the time which we possess."—*Literary World.*

BY THE SAME AUTHOR.

THE ECCLESIASTICAL HISTORY OF ENGLAND, from the Opening of the Long Parliament to the Death of Oliver Cromwell. 2 vols. 8vo, 28s. cloth.

VOL. I. THE CHURCH OF THE CIVIL WARS.
VOL. II. THE CHURCH OF THE COMMONWEALTH.

"A markedly fair, charitable, large minded, and honestly-written history."—*Guardian.*

"Speaking of the book as a literary work, and a history which was wanted upon the most important period of the ecclesiastical career of the country, it is one which will win for its author a permanent place in the increasing rank of Church historians, and will repay a careful perusal."—*Gentleman's Magazine.*

ECCLESIA : Church Problems considered in a Series of Essays. Edited by HENRY ROBERT REYNOLDS, D.D. Second Thousand. 8vo. 14s. cloth.

CONTENTS.

1. Primitive Ecclesia : Its Authoritative Principles and its Modern Representations. By JOHN STOUGHTON, D.D.
2. The Idea of the Church regarded in its Historical Development. By J. R. THOMSON, M.A.
3. The "Religious Life" and Christian Society. By J. BALDWIN BROWN, B.A.
4. The Relation of the Church to the State. By E. R. CONDER, M.A.
5. The Forgiveness and Absolution of Sins. By the EDITOR.
6. The Doctrine of the Real Presence and the Lord's Supper. By R. W. DALE, M.A.
7. The Worship of the Church. By HENRY ALLON.
8. The Congregationalism of the Future. By J. G. ROGERS, B.A.
9. Modern Missions and their Results. By JOSEPH MULLENS, D.D.

"A breadth of thought and charitableness of feeling is here displayed which will surprise those readers who have adopted conventional ideas with regard to Nonconformity and its professors. The present volume will go far towards the correction of such ideas."—*Athenæum.*

"The essays before us are, for the most part, written with such ability, good sense, and good feeling, that they cannot fail to contribute something to the settlement of the 'problems' which they discuss. We may say generally that we have read it through with great pleasure, that it reflects the greatest credit on the communion which it represents, and that while we differ from many of its conclusions, we have noted no indications of a defective or narrow study on the part of its writers of the topics which they discuss."—*Spectator.*

NEW VOLUME OF SERMONS.

LIFE PROBLEMS ANSWERED IN CHRIST. Six Sermons. By LEIGH MANN. With Preface by Rev. A. MACLAREN, B.A. Just Published, crown 8vo, 4s. 6d.

CONTENTS :

Christ and Suffering—Christ and Death—Christ and Faith—Christ and the Law—Christ the Cup of Blessing—Christ and Destiny.

"The work of a mind and heart singularly tender and strong, pure and true, touched with an imaginative beauty and penetration by loyal attachment to our dear Lord."—FROM MR. MACLAREN'S PREFACE.

"In freshness, in spiritual penetration, in devout feeling, in spiritual and assimilating power, Mr. Mann's sermons will bear comparison with any that we have seen of late years."—*British Quarterly Review.*

"A short collection of sermons, in which Christ stands out as the great example in all the various trials and events of life. They are written with much force and beauty, and with true spiritual insight."—*Christian Work.*

"Is a series of six exceedingly earnest and well-composed sermons."—*Daily Telegraph.*

"Mr. Maclaren's commendation of these sermons is well deserved."—*European Mail.*

BY REV. T. BINNEY.

Now Ready.   Fourth Edition.   With NEW PREFACE.

1. *THE PRACTICAL POWER OF FAITH.* An Exposition of part of the Eleventh Chapter of Hebrews. Crown 8vo, 5s. cloth.

2. *MONEY: A Popular Exposition in Rough Notes.* With Remarks on Stewardship and Systematic Beneficence. Third Edition. Crown 8vo, 5s. cloth.

3. *MICAH THE PRIEST-MAKER.* A Handbook on Ritualism. Second Edition, enlarged. Post 8vo, 5s. cloth.

DR. LILLIE ON PETER.

LECTURES ON THE FIRST & SECOND EPISTLES OF PETER. By JOHN LILLIE, D.D., Author of "Lectures on the Epistles of St. Paul to the Thessalonians," &c. With a Preface by PHILIP SCHAFF, D.D. In 8vo, price 12s. cloth.

"In treatment there is an endeavour to combine the advantages of the exegetical commentary with the popular discourse. The style is plain and unadorned, but clear and forcible ; the doctrine is sound, the lesson practical, and the spirit high-toned and devotional."—*Pulpit Analyst.*

"We very heartily commend this exposition to Biblical students. It is a valuable contribution to the exegesis of the New Testament, enriched with all the lights of modern scholarship."—*English Independent.*

"Hitherto the exposition of Leighton on the First Epistle of St. Peter has held an unchallenged place ; but Dr. Lillie's is, in our estimation, far before it, though in some respects the two can scarcely be compared. It is a noble volume, got up in a style which well befits the subject. Preachers will find it singularly full and suggestive."—*Methodist Recorder.*

WORKS BY DR. PRESSENSÉ.

1. *THE EARLY YEARS OF CHRISTIANITY.* A Sequel to "Jesus Christ: His Times, Life, and Work." 8vo, 12s. cloth.

"To a writer of Pressensé's powers, it was comparatively easy to give a graphic narrative of those portions of the history which bear upon the lives of the Apostles. To throw a popular charm around such themes as the various types of doctrine in the Apostolic Church, the origin of the New Testament Scriptures, and all the questions which modern criticism has raised regarding their age and character, was evidently a more difficult undertaking. It is here, however, that his success has been most complete. The lofty and animated eloquence which he has always at command, and a certain happy faculty of finding, even in doctrinal discussions, some picturesque trait, some feature with life and colour, have enabled him to overcome the difficulties which stand in the way of a popular history of the Christian life and literature of the first century."—*Contemporary Review.*

"English students will be grateful for this handsome English rendering of Dr. Pressensé's valuable work. It hardly reads like a translation at all. We need hardly speak of the merits which distinguish M. de Pressensé as a philosophic and thoughtful historian. No one who has not yet read it but will find his account in doing so."—*Literary Churchman.*

2. *JESUS CHRIST: His Times, Life, and Work.* Third and Cheaper Edition. Crown 8vo, 9s. cloth.

"M. de Pressensé is not only brilliant and epigrammatic, but his sentences flow on from page to page with a sustained eloquence which never wearies the reader. The Life of Christ is more dramatically unfolded in this volume than in any other work with which we are acquainted."—*Spectator.*

"The successive scenes and teachings of our Lord's life are told with a scholarly accuracy and a glowing and devout eloquence, which are well presented to the English reader in Miss Harwood's admirable translation."—*British Quarterly Review.*

3. *THE MYSTERY OF SUFFERING, AND OTHER DISCOURSES.* New Edition. Crown 8vo, 3s. 6d. cloth.

"In these sermons we recognise the same intellectual power, the same exquisite felicity of diction, the same sustained and dignified eloquence, and the same persuasive invigorating Christian thought which are conspicuous in that work—('Jesus Christ: His Times, &c.')"—*British and Foreign Evangelical Review.*

4. *THE LAND OF THE GOSPEL: Notes of a Journey in the East.* In crown 8vo, 5s. cloth.

"He gives us his first and freshest impressions as entered in his journal upon the spot; and these will be found full of interest, especially to every thoughtful reader of the New Testament."—*Evangelical Christendom.*

"Brilliant life-like sketches of persons, places, and events."—*British Quarterly Review.*

5. *THE CHURCH AND THE FRENCH REVOLUTION.* A History of the Relations of Church and State from 1789 to 1802. In crown 8vo, 9s. cloth.

"M. de Pressensé is well known and deservedly respected as one of the leading divines of the Evangelical section of the French Protestant Church. He is a learned theologian, and a man of cultivated and liberal mind. In the present monograph he comes before us as the historian of a period which he rightly judges to have a more than local and temporary interest in the fortunes of the national Church of France. And, on the whole, he has done his work not only ably, but impartially. . . . . We are not aware that any previous writer has treated the subject from the purely ecclesiastical point of view."—*Saturday Review.*

J. BALDWIN BROWN, B.A.

THE DIVINE MYSTERIES; the Divine Treatment of Sin,
and the Divine Mystery of Peace. New Edition. Crown 8vo, 7s. 6d. cloth.

"This is a second edition of two deeply interesting volumes, which are now embodied in one. This was a wise proceeding, and will provoke many to a second perusal of some of the strongest, sweetest words of one of the noblest preachers of our generation."—*British Quarterly Review.*

MISREAD PASSAGES OF SCRIPTURE. New Edition.
Crown 8vo, 3s. 6d. cloth.

"In this volume, which is the production of an earnest and vigorous mind, the author impugns, for the most part, with a force which carries conviction to the mind, the accuracy of some generally received interpretations of Scripture. He has carefully studied the subjects handled, and he expatiates upon them with no common eloquence, freshness, and originality."—*British and Foreign Evangelical Review.*

IDOLATRIES, OLD AND NEW: Their Cause and Cure.
Crown 8vo, 5s. cloth.

THE DIVINE LIFE IN MAN. Second Edition. 7s. 6d.
cloth.

THE DOCTRINE OF THE DIVINE FATHERHOOD
IN RELATION TO THE ATONEMENT. 1s. 6d. cloth.

REV. CHARLES STANFORD.

"One of the sincerest, manliest, and clearest writers we have."—*Christian Work.*
"Mr. Stanford has an order of mind, and has acquired habits of study eminently adapting him to be a teacher of wise and thoughtful men."—*Evangelical Magazine.*

SYMBOLS OF CHRIST. Second Edition. 3s. 6d. Small
crown 8vo, cloth.

CENTRAL TRUTHS. Third Edition. Small crown 8vo,
price 3s. 6d. cloth.

POWER IN WEAKNESS: Memorials of the Rev. William
Rhodes. New Edition. 3s. 6d. cloth.

INSTRUMENTAL STRENGTH; Thoughts for Students and
Pastors. Crown 8vo, price 1s. cloth.

JOSEPH ALLEINE: His Companions and Times. Second
Thousand. Crown 8vo, 4s. 6d.

DR. HOFFMANN ON THE NEW TESTAMENT PROPHECIES.

THE PROPHECIES OF OUR LORD AND HIS
APOSTLES. A Series of Discourses delivered in the Cathedral Church
of Berlin. By W. HOFFMANN, D.D., Chaplain-in-Ordinary to the King
of Prussia. Crown 8vo, 7s. 6d. cloth.

"These discourses are worthy of the highest commendation. They partake more of the form of the homily than of the doctrinal or expository discourse. They are characterized by extreme simplicity of style, and abound in rich suggestive reflections, penetrative thoughts, and a fine analysis of human feelings and motives."—*Contemporary Review.*

"Dr. Hoffmann is an eminent German divine who has made the prophecies of the New Testament a special study, and gives us in these discourses, originally preached in the Cathedral of Berlin, the results of a considerable amount of thoughtful research."—*English Independent.*

DR. HAGENBACH'S CHURCH HISTORY.

THE HISTORY OF THE CHURCH IN THE EIGHTEENTH AND NINETEENTH CENTURIES. By K. R. HAGENBACH, D.D., Professor of Theology in the University of Basle, Author of "German Rationalism." Translated by JOHN F. HURST, D.D. In 2 vols., 8vo, 24s. cloth.

"Hagenbach is a genial and graceful writer. Over the simplest and driest details he throws a grace and a charm which is more akin to poetry than to prose. He is thoroughly Evangelical in his views, and very successfully combats the errors and fallacies of the Neologian school of his country."—*Rock.*

"The name of Dr. Hagenbach is favourably known among us as a divine of high talent and learning. The translation of this work has been well executed by Dr. Hurst, and the volumes deserve a place in every well-furnished library."—*Edinburgh Daily Review.*

"The study of this history will be found easy and pleasant work. It is adapted not only for the professional student, but for the general reader, who will find in these volumes some of the ripest thoughts of the most learned students of modern Church history that our age has produced."—*Methodist Recorder.*

"The history of Dr. Hagenbach is worthy of his great learning and his pictorial and vivid style. The work before us is extremely interesting, readable, and instructive."—*British Quarterly Review.*

"The author of this excellent and voluminous work is one of the most genial, attractive, and fruitful theologians on the Continent. The work is most comprehensive in its embrace, most catholic in its spirit, most graphic in its description, and most suggestive and elevating in its reflections. We scarcely need recommend it. Every student of sacred history and theological science will feel it to be a necessary article for his library."—*Homilist.*

GREAT PREACHERS.

MASTERPIECES OF PULPIT ELOQUENCE, Ancient and Modern, with Historical Sketches of Preaching in the Different Countries represented, and Biographical and Critical Notices of the several Preachers and their Discourses. By HENRY C. FISH, D.D. In 2 vols., 8vo, cloth, 21s.

"This work is unique both in design and arrangement, and supplies a want which has been long felt. We have here not only a history of preaching in all ages and in all parts of the world wherever the pulpit has been felt as a power, but we have brought within the reach of all the great masterpieces of pulpit eloquence—the best discourses of all countries and times, hitherto locked up in foreign languages, or procured with much difficulty and expense. There are able historical sketches of the Greek and Latin, the English, the German, the Irish, the French, the Scottish, the American, and the Welsh pulpits, with numerous discourses as specimens of each."—*Pulpit Analyst.*

FROM THE PREFACE.—"The design of the work may be stated in a few words. It is, first, to render available to the lover of sacred things the great 'masterpieces of pulpit eloquence,' and the best discourses of all countries and times, hitherto either locked up in foreign languages, or procured with much difficulty and expense. Secondly, to furnish a history of preaching in all parts of the world where the Christian religion has prevailed, from its introduction into each respective country down to the present time, with a view of the pulpit as it now stands. Thirdly, to bring again upon the stage the great and good of other days; keeping alive and promoting their acquaintance and allowing them to speak to the living, which is done by giving sketches of their lives, and by reproducing their choicest discourses."

"The historical sketches of the Greek, Latin, English, German, and Irish Pulpits, French, Scottish, and American Pulpits are critical as well as historical, and abound in facts and thoughts of extreme value to those who study the eloquence of the pulpit. The selections chosen to illustrate the different styles of the different pulpits are characteristic and fair; and many of them are extremely fine specimens of eloquence. It is a work which no clergyman anxious to speak his best for God's glory to his people should be without."—*Rock.*

"To ministers and students of divinity these volumes will have a peculiar value. The natural interest which such must feel as to the different styles of pulpit address may be here fully gratified. Many a fruitful hint and suggestion may be gathered from the sermons here given, not a few of which have a historical value from the influence they have had at the time of their delivery and subsequently. And what is more than this, high views of the sacred calling, and ambition to follow the steps of those in past ages who have magnified it, cannot but be fostered by their perusal."—*Edinburgh Daily Review.*

JOSEPH PARKER, D.D.

I.

Now ready, handsomely bound in cloth, red burnished edges, price 6s.

THE CITY TEMPLE:

SERMONS PREACHED IN THE POULTRY CHAPEL, 1869-1870.

"There is something very refreshing about these sermons. As a rule, pulpit discourses do not form very pleasant or attractive reading, but Dr. Parker is one of the few men who really know how to preach. He puts thought into all that he says, and, notwithstanding all his unquestioned ability, it is doubtful if he ever insults his hearers by coming before them without having previously prepared his remarks with all the care of which he is capable. These sermons bear ample traces of the study bestowed upon them. In the terse, epigrammatic sentences of which they are mainly built up, grand ideas are put forth, the general style showing that while the preacher in no wise underrates the importance of the message he has to deliver, that on the contrary, he is powerfully impressed with the responsibilities attaching to his office, he at the same time quite understands that if the hearts of those addressed by him are to be got at, their ears must in the first place be secured. Some of the lectures, more especially those delivered on Thursday mornings, are cast in an altogether different mould from that which usually gives shape to pulpit discourses, being rather allegories or parables illustrating in each case some great central truth. This style could not be adopted with safety by many persons, but with Dr. Parker there is no need to fear lest the idea to be conveyed should be lost in the wrappings wherewith it is surrounded, and, indeed, these sketches are, as a whole, singularly effective, from whatever point they are regarded. We are glad to see that the 'City Temple' has now become firmly established, and trust the accomplished orator, whose utterances are here given for the benefit of a larger congregation than any human voice can reach, will be spared to send forth many such volumes as the one before us."—*City Press.*

All the Numbers (1 to 45) can be had, price One Penny each; and Cases for Binding, price 1s. each.

II.

A HOMILETIC ANALYSIS OF THE GOSPEL AC-CORDING TO ST. MATTHEW. With an Introductory Essay on the Life of Jesus Christ, considered as an appeal to the imagination. In 8vo, price 7s. 6d. cloth.

"This is the only English work which deserves to be ranked along with Lange's 'Bibelwerk' for value in affording really useful hints to ministers and preachers. The thoughtful and original essay with which this volume is introduced opens or points out a new and interesting mode in which the truth of the Evangelical history can be defended."—*Evangelical Christendom.*

III.

SPRINGDALE ABBEY: Extracts from the Diaries and Letters of an English Preacher. 8vo, 7s. 6d. cloth.

" An interesting and amusing volume."—*Pall Mall Gazette.*
" Full of new and enlivening thought."—*Churchman.*
" It is unquestionably able and interesting."—*Nonconformist.*

IV.

ECCE DEUS: Essays on the Life and Doctrine of Jesus Christ. Fourth Edition. Crown 8vo, 5s.

" A very able book. The thought is fresh and suggestive, often rich and beautiful; the style is vigorous and epigrammatic."—*British Quarterly Review.*
" A brilliant and masterly argument for the proper divinity of our Lord."—*London Quarterly Review.*
" A remarkable and very instructive discussion of many points in that vast subject which no human exposition will ever exhaust, and in which every really thoughtful and religious student is sure to find something to repay his own labour, and make it useful to others. There is much which is really beautiful and noble in the general view which 'Ecce Deus' presents of Christian ethics."—*Contemporary Review.*

CHRISTIAN WORK ON THE BATTLE-FIELD: Being
Incidents of the Labours of the United States' Christian Commission.
With an Historical Essay on the Influence of Christianity in alleviating
the Horrors of War. Eight full-page Illustrations. Crown 8vo, 6s.

"The account given of the origin, the labours, the trials, and the successes of the United
States' Christian Commission during the late Civil War, would be at any time interesting
and touching, but is just now especially attractive. It will secure, and deserves to secure, a
great number of attentive readers."—*Echo.*

MEN OF FAITH; or, Sketches from the Book of Judges. By
the Rev. LUKE H. WISEMAN, M.A., Author of "Christ in the Wilderness." Crown 8vo, 5s. cloth.

CONTENTS.

1. The Period of the Judges.—2. Barak and Deborah.—3. Gideon.
4. Jephthah.—5. Samson.

"Mr. Wiseman has shown remarkable power of combining accuracy of detail with vividness
of effect. Careful and minute study of the sacred text, unobtrusive but watchful labour in
detecting and exhibiting the graphic touches of the original writer which our translation has
not fully caught, picturesque delineation of the scenes recorded, keen appreciation of men and
character, reverent recognition of God's working in and by the heroes of the history and
the people they delivered from heathen domination, are amongst the leading characteristics
of this delightful book, which is as profitable as it is interesting."—*London Quarterly
Review.*

"This is an admirable work. The author deals with a portion of Hebrew history of great
interest, though, we fear, not much studied; and he traces it with great skill and power. He
writes in a style of pure, dignified English, and his language not seldom rises into passages of
true eloquence. The practical remarks, interleaved with the sketches of the history, are
worthy of all praise."—*Edinburgh Daily Review.*

MISSIONARY LABOURS AMONG THE CANNIBALS.
By Rev. JAMES CALVERT. To which is prefixed an Account of the
Islands and Inhabitants of Fiji, Rev. by THOMAS WILLIAMS. Edited
by GEORGE STRINGER ROWE. Cheap and Revised Edition, in one
volume, 608 pp., illustrated, price 6s.

". . . No romance has so many exciting crises, wild scenes, hair-breadth escapes, and
horrors. No history, even of the Church, contains such a straightforward and convincing
account of a moral transformation—of rapid and steady victories gained by the labours of
gentle men and heroic women over unutterable ferocity."—*London Review.*

"Exceedingly interesting, both as furnishing the history of a strange people, and giving a
minute account of their evangelization. The engravings which accompany the work are
numerous and really illustrative."—*Clerical Journal.*

"The book is complete and well written. The additions Mr. Rowe has made, as far as we
can trace them, seem judicious."—*Contemporary Review.*

"It is not often that we have presented to us volumes so rich as those now before us are, in
observation, in glimpses of wild life, and in descriptions of men, whose disposition and habits
are all we can picture a savage's to be."—*North British Review.*

"The volume is as interesting as a romance, and in the results it records is not unworthy to
be regarded as a continuation of the Book of Acts."—*Freeman.*

"The execution of the volumes is very thorough. They contain an astonishing mass of
small facts compressed skilfully together, and when we close them, we feel as if we understood
the Fijians as well as civilized men can ever understand savages with whom they have never
come into actual contact."—*Saturday Review.*

REV. R. W. DALE, M.A.

THE EPISTLE TO THE HEBREWS: A Popular Exposition. Second and Cheaper Edition. Crown 8vo, 6s. cloth.

DISCOURSES DELIVERED ON SPECIAL OCCASIONS. In crown 8vo, 6s. cloth.

" In Mr. Dale's ' Discourses on Special Occasions ' we have some of the finest specimens of modern preaching."—*Contemporary Review.*

" It is long since we read sermons more full of stimulating thought, of catholic sympathies, of manly and noble eloquence."—*British Quarterly Review.*

REV. E. PAXTON HOOD.

I.

Just published, a New Edition of

DARK SAYINGS ON A HARP, and other Sermons on some of the Dark Questions of Human Life. In crown 8vo, 6s. cloth.

" Christians who have found out that there are some mysterious questions to be answered, some terrible things in righteousness, some dark sayings upon the harp to be listened to, and who are longing for light, and divine promise, and perfect rest, will read it with interest and gratitude. His dark sayings very often sparkle with light."—*British Quarterly Review.*

" There is a remarkable originality throughout the volume, and great freshness and brilliancy of thought."—*Evangelical Magazine.*

II.

LAMPS, PITCHERS, AND TRUMPETS: Lectures on the Vocation of the Preacher. Illustrated by Anecdotes—Biographical, Historical, and Elucidatory—of every order of Pulpit Eloquence, from the Great Preachers of all Ages. Second Thousand. 10s. 6d. cloth.

" All who know the fertility of our author's pen, the extraordinary affluence of his literary resources, the rare abundance of his illustrative anecdotes, the vigour and *abandon* of his style, will also know that it would be difficult in a brief notice like this to do justice to a work of such compass and multifarious aim."—*British Quarterly Review*

" Containing much interesting matter, carefully collected and well put together."—*Blackwood's Magazine.*

III.

THE WORLD OF ANECDOTE: An Accumulation of Facts, Incidents, and Illustrations—Historical and Biographical—from Books and Times, Recent and Remote. Second Thousand. Large crown 8vo, 10s. 6d. cloth, 700 pp.

SUMMARY OF CONTENTS.

Ways and Means of Doing Good—Romantic Transformations of Human Life—Great Events from Trifles—Dogs, and the Animal World—Crime and Cruelty—Silence and some of its Votaries—Illustrations of Adventure—Ghosts, Dreams, and the Supernatural—Anecdotes of Life and Character—Humour and the Humorous Side of Life—Things Clerical, and Pulpit Celebrities—Cooks and Cookery—Varieties of Womanhood—Instances of Human Folly—Lawyers and some of their Words and Ways—Death and Dying.

" Full of wit and wisdom. So much taste and judgment have been exercised in the selection of the extracts, which, being of a varied and absorbing character, are grouped artistically around well-defined subjects of thought and study, that Mr. Paxton Hood has made his book as entertaining and instructive as any novel."—*Standard.*

" A complete repertory of wise and smart anecdote."—*Nonconformist.*

" The humorous, the pathetic, the romantic, the instructive, have all a place, and the classification, along with the copious index, makes the volume the more useful for reference by those who desire to have convenient access to picturesque illustrations of subjects on which they have to speak or write."—*Edinburgh Daily Review.*

THE PULPIT ANALYST.

DESIGNED FOR PREACHERS, STUDENTS, AND TEACHERS.

Vols. I. to IV., price 7s. 6d. each, handsomely bound in cloth.

Vol. I.—*Summary of Contents.*

A HOMILETIC ANALYSIS OF THE GOSPEL ACCORDING TO MATTHEW. Chaps. I. to XII. By JOSEPH PARKER, D.D.

THE PULPIT. Discourses by various Clergymen and Ministers.

NOTES UPON DIVINE REVELATION AS RELATED TO HUMAN CONSCIOUSNESS. By the EDITOR.

SEVENTY SUGGESTIVE OUTLINES OF SERMONS.

THE GOSPEL OF ST. JOHN. Chaps. I. to X. With an Interlinear Translation. By T. D. HALL, M.A.

THE ILLUSTRATOR. Preachers and Preaching.

REVIEWS OF CURRENT LITERATURE, &c., &c.

Vol. II.—*Summary of Contents.*

A HOMILETIC ANALYSIS OF THE GOSPEL ACCORDING TO MATTHEW. CHAPS. XIII. to XXVI. By JOSEPH PARKER, D.D.

SOCRATIC SERMONS ON FAITH AND REVELATION. By the EDITOR.

THE GOSPEL OF ST. JOHN, with an Interlinear Translation by T. D. HALL, M.A. Conclusion.

THE PULPIT. Discourses by various Clergymen and Ministers.

SIXTY SUGGESTIVE OUTLINES OF SERMONS.

ELEMENTARY RULES OF GREEK SYNTAX.

REMOTER STARS IN THE SKY OF THE CHURCH. Biographical Sketches by the Rev. GEORGE GILFILLAN, Author of "The Gallery of Literary Portraits," &c.

ILLUSTRATIVE EXTRACTS FROM ANCIENT AND MODERN SOURCES.

REVIEWS OF CURRENT LITERATURE, &c., &c.

Vol. III.—*Summary of Contents.*

DISCOURSES by Revs. R. VAUGHAN, D.D., J. C. JACKSON, J. STOUGHTON, D.D., EDWIN JOHNSON, B.A., Professor R. FLINT, MAURICE J. EVANS, B.A., H. ALLON, and WM. BELL, M.A.

MISREAD PASSAGES OF SCRIPTURE. By the Rev. J. BALDWIN BROWN, B.A.

THE FOREIGN PULPIT: Discourses by J. J. VAN OOSTERZEE, D.D., PASTEUR BERSIER, E. DE PRESSENSÉ, PASTEUR VERNY, ALEXANDRE VINET.

FIFTY SUGGESTIVE OUTLINES OF SERMONS.

ROUGH NOTES FOR EXTEMPORE PREACHING.

GERMS OF SERMONS.

THE TRANSLATOR:—New Translation of St. Mark's Gospel, with Notes. By Prof. J. H. GODWIN.

PREACHER'S DIRECTORY:—Permanent Preaching for a Permanent Pastorate. Method in Sermons.

REVIEWS OF BOOKS, MISCELLANEA, &c., &c.

Vol. IV.—*Summary of Contents.*

THE STATE OF THE BLESSED DEAD. Advent Sermons by HENRY ALFORD, D.D.

AD CLERUM; ADVICES TO A YOUNG PREACHER. By JOSEPH PARKER, D.D., Author of "Ecce Deus," &c.

THE EPISTLES TO THE CORINTHIANS. With the Unemphatic Words indicated as a Guide to the best method of Public Reading. By ARTHUR J. BELL.

NOTES ON THE INCIDENTS OF OUR LORD'S LIFE. By the EDITOR.

A NEW TRANSLATION OF ST. MARK'S GOSPEL. Conclusion. By Prof. J. GODWIN. With Notes.

HOMILETICAL NOTES ON SCRIPTURE TEXTS.

THE FOREIGN PULPIT. Discourses by Eminent Continental Preachers.

STRAY SIDE LIGHTS ON SCRIPTURE TEXTS.

ILLUSTRATIONS OF SCRIPTURE TEXTS.

SUGGESTIVE OUTLINES OF SERMONS.

REVIEW OF CURRENT LITERATURE, EXTRACTS, &c.

THE DAILY PRAYER-BOOK, for the Use of Families, with additional Prayers for Special Occasions. Edited by JOHN STOUGHTON, D.D. Crown 8vo, 5s. cloth ; or morocco antique, 10s. 6d.

LIST OF CONTRIBUTORS.

Rev. HENRY ALLON.
Rev. THOMAS BINNEY.
Rev. R. W. DALE, M.A.
Rev. J. C. HARRISON.
Rev. W. PULSFORD, D.D.

Rev. J. STOUGHTON, D.D.
Rev. ROBT. VAUGHAN, D.D., the late.
Rev. JOSIAH VINEY.
Rev. EDWARD WHITE.

"An admirable Daily Prayer Book. It breathes the spirit of true devotion."—*New York Observer.*

"The prayers glow with holy feeling, and are beautifully expressive of our deepest wants and highest aspirations. There is no preaching in them, but a rich and sweet and elevating fellowship with God. The collection of prayers is judicious, wise in conception, and tender in execution."—*British Quarterly Review.*

THE GOSPEL ACCORDING TO ST. MARK. A New Translation, with Critical Notes and Doctrinal Lessons. By JOHN H. GODWIN, Author of "A New Translation of St. Matthew's Gospel," &c. Crown 8vo, 4s. 6d. cloth, red edges.

"The translation is in vigorous English of our own day. The notes contain much valuable research and many excellent suggestions. The book is a real addition to our critico-theological literature."—*Christian Work.*

REMARKABLE FACTS : Illustrative and Confirmatory of Different Portions of Holy Scripture. By the late Rev. J. LEIFCHILD, D.D., with a Preface by his Son. New and cheaper Edition, crown 8vo., 3s. 6d. cloth.

"The narratives are admirably told, and many of them of the most singular character. A more impressive book, or a weightier testimony to the truth of Bible principles, it would be difficult to find."—*Christian Work.*

"Preachers who like anecdotes should buy this book. The narratives are valuable because they are authentic."—*Pulpit Analyst.*

CREDO. Crown 8vo, 5s. cloth.

CONTENTS.

A SUPERNATURAL BOOK.
SUPERNATURAL BEINGS.

SUPERNATURAL LIFE.
SUPERNATURAL DESTINY.

"The book is clearly original, thoughtful, and readable. The writer is thoroughly in earnest, and really writes because he has something to say. The aim of his little volume is to defend the broad grand truths of Christianity against the attacks of all enemies, especially that school which makes it their express business to doubt, to pull down, and to destroy."—*Standard.*

THE STATE OF THE BLESSED DEAD. Advent Sermons. By the Very Rev. HENRY ALFORD, D.D., Dean of Canterbury. Third Thousand. Square 16mo, 1s. 6d. cloth.

"Characterized by clearness and vigour of thought. The Dean has carefully traced from Scripture his account of the intermediate state, and he gives also a view of the condition after the resurrection which is comprehensive and satisfying."—*Christian Work.*

THE THEOLOGY OF THE NEW TESTAMENT: A
Handbook for Bible Students. By the Rev. J. J. VAN OOSTERZEE. Translated by the Rev. M. J. EVANS, B.A. Crown 8vo, 6s. cloth.

THE SON OF MAN: Discourses on the Humanity of Jesus
Christ. Delivered at Paris and Geneva. With an Address on the Teaching of Jesus Christ. By FRANK COULIN, D.D. In fcap. 8vo, 5s. cloth.

"He who wrote this book must have gazed upon the face of Jesus Christ till in it he gained knowledge of the glory of God. M. Coulin has not only the faculty of the seer, but he can reveal what he has seen. His cultured heart has traced the lines of grace and beauty in that inimitable image of truth, of goodness, and of love."—*London Quarterly Review.*

"The life of Christ is illustrated as that of perfect humanity, and in a singularly fresh, interesting, and instructive manner."—*Daily Review.*

THE IMPROVEMENT OF TIME: An Essay, with other
Literary Remains. By JOHN FOSTER, Author of "Essays on Decision of Character," &c. Edited by J. E. RYLAND, M.A. Crown 8vo, 6s. cloth.

"The reader will find in it all the characteristics of the author's mind, great power of observation, strong originality of thought, with more ease and freedom of style than is always met with in his later writings. The fragments of sermons are many of them deeply interesting, and the same may be said of the letters."—*British Quarterly Review.*

THOUGHTS IN THEOLOGY. By JOHN SHEPPARD, Author
of "Thoughts on Devotion," "An Autumn Dream," &c. Second Edition. Fcap. 8vo, 4s. 6d. cloth.

CHOSEN WORDS FROM CHRISTIAN WRITERS ON
RELIGION: Its Evidences, Trials, Privileges, Obligations. Edited by the Author of "Thoughts on Devotion," &c. &c. In fcap. 8vo, price 4s. 6d. cloth, red edges.

"The selection appears to be a good one."—*Guardian.*

"They are intended for men of mature age and busy lives, to whom they well serve as useful aids to reflection."—*Evangelical Christendom.*

THE MELODY OF THE TWENTY-THIRD PSALM.
By ANNA WARNER. Square 16mo, 2s. cloth.

"A most comforting little gift-book at this or any other season, especially to the afflicted or distressed."—*Record.*

"Marked by true Christian feeling, and deep thought."—*City Press.*

THE SONG OF CHRIST'S FLOCK IN THE TWENTY-
THIRD PSALM. Third Edition. Crown 8vo, 3s. 6d. cloth.

"Mr. Stoughton's volume may be earnestly and warmly reccommended. Its chaste piety will make it deservedly acceptable to a large class of readers. Looked at with the purpose of the writer, we know of no recent volume of religious meditation which is likely to be more profitably read or pleasantly remembered."—*Daily News.*

REV. WILLIAM TAYLOR, CALIFORNIA.

1. *THE ELECTION OF GRACE.* In small crown 8vo, price 3s. cloth.

2. *CALIFORNIA LIFE ILLUSTRATED.* New Edition, with 16 Illustrations. Crown 8vo, 4s.

3. *CHRISTIAN ADVENTURES IN SOUTH AFRICA.* With Portrait and 15 Illustrations. Crown 8vo, 6s. 6d.

ANECDOTES OF THE WESLEYS : Illustrative of their Character and Personal History. By the Rev. J. B. WAKELEY. Second Edition, crown 8vo, 3s. 6d. cloth.

"There is not one page of the book without interest. Samuel Wesley, sen., Susannah Wesley, Charles Wesley, and Samuel Wesley, jun , are all brought before us in sprightly form ; but John Wesley fittingly receives the largest attention."—*Watchman.*

"The whole family were remarkable during several generations for wit, intelligence, and accomplishments ; and Mr. Wakeley's collection is interesting, not merely because it relates to men so distinguished as the Wesleys, but for the intrinsic wit and vivacity of the anecdotes themselves."—*European Mail.*

THE LIFE OF THE REV. DANIEL JAMES DRAPER, Representative of the Australasian Conference, who was lost in the "London," Jan. 11, 1866. With Chapters on the Aborigines and Education in Victoria, and Historical Notices of Wesleyan Methodism in Australia. By the Rev. JOHN C. SYMONS. Crown 8vo, 5s. cloth. With Portrait.

"This volume is well worth reading. It is a faithful history of a man of very considerable gifts, who consecrated himself perseveringly and sagaciously to the service of his Master, as indeed the present condition of Wesleyan Methodism in the Australian Colonies is manifestly the fruit of his wise and loving exertions."—*Presbyterian.*

THE STUDENT'S HAND-BOOK OF CHRISTIAN THEOLOGY. By Rev. BENJAMIN FIELD. Second Edition. Edited, with a Biographical Sketch, by the Rev. JOHN C. SYMONS. Crown 8vo, 5s. cloth.

"Scholarly, well arranged, and carefully executed."—*Sword and Trowel.*

"To students it will be found invaluable ; its arrangement is clear, and matter carefully selected."—*Rock.*

"The present issue has an additional chapter, and the last corrections of the truly excellent and amiable author; also a very interesting biographical sketch of Mr. Field, by the editor, the Rev. John C. Symons."—*Watchman.*

IPHIGENE. A Poem. By ALEXANDER LAUDER. Handsomely bound. 4s. cloth.

"The whole conception of the poem is very vivid, and much of the detail is manipulated with exquisite grace."—*Literary World.*

"In a poem which appears to us of great merit, Mr. Lauder celebrates, under the name of Iphigene, the most tragic story of Jephthah's daughter. He introduces us into the scenes of ancient life in Palestine with much power. His pictures are complete and graphic, and his rhythm generally effective and musical."—*Christian Work.*

HELPS TO FAITH AND A HOLY LIFE. By Rev. J. P. BARNETT. Crown 8vo, 4s. 6d. cloth.

THE EDUCATION OF THE HEART: Woman's Best Work. By Mrs. ELLIS, Author of "The Women of England," &c. Fcap. 8vo, 3s. 6d. cloth.

"To show the comprehensive character of the book, we may state that it includes Female Education—Women on Education—Preparation for Life—Good Faith—Good Principle—Early Training—Love and Hate—Truth and Fiction—Moral and Physical Courage—Law and Order —and the Mother. With all these subjects, Mrs. Ellis deals with her usual power and attractiveness."—*Christian Work.*

THE KING'S DAUGHTERS: Words on Work to Educated Women. By ANNIE HARWOOD. Fcap. 8vo, 2s. 6d. cloth extra.

"Full of quiet womanly observation, good sense, and feeling, and therefore well worth reading. It contains very much that is worthy of careful thought at the hands of all those who are practically interested in the great work of woman's education."—*Standard.*

THE FAMILY: Its Duties, Joys, and Sorrows. By COUNT A. DE GASPARIN. Crown 8vo, 7s. 6d. cloth.

"The advice is sensible, the style pleasing: it is the result of sustained thought and careful observation, and as it is a handsome volume, would be an appropriate present to a newly-married pair."—*Guardian.*

BIBLE-CLASS STUDIES ON SOME OF THE WORDS OF THE LORD JESUS. By JESSIE COOMBS. Small Crown 8vo, 3s. 6d. cloth.

THOUGHTS FOR THE INNER LIFE. By the same Author. Crown 8vo, 5s. cloth.

WHOLESOME WORDS; or, Choice Passages from Old Authors. Selected and Arranged by J. E. RYLAND, M.A. Fcap. 8vo, 1s. 6d. cloth.

"The compiler has shown admirable judgment in the selection of passages. As a collection of seed-thoughts and spirit-gleams for the scattered moments of leisure in busy lives, there could be nothing more delightful or, scarcely, more precious."—*Nonconformist.*

COUNCILS, ANCIENT AND MODERN. From the Apostolical Council of Jerusalem to the Œcumenical Council of Nicæa, and to the last Papal Council in the Vatican. By W. H. RULE, D.D., Author of "The History of the Inquisition." 18mo, 1s. 6d. cloth.

THE HERITAGE OF PEACE; or, Christ our Life. By T. S. CHILDS, D.D. Square 16mo, 2s. cloth.

"A very clear and logical appeal on behalf of Christ to all reasonable men. It is irresistible as an argument, and admirable as an appeal."—*Rock.*

ANCIENT HYMNS AND POEMS; chiefly from St. Ephraem of Syria, Prudentius, Pope Gregory the First, and St. Bernard. Translated and imitated by the Rev. T. G. CRIPPEN. Fcap. 8vo, price 2s. cloth, red edges.

"Mr. Crippen has selected some of the most beautiful poetical effusions of the early and mediæval Church."—*Clerical Journal.*

HODDER & STOUGHTON'S PRESENTATION BOOKS.

Price Seven Shillings and Sixpence.

PRIEST AND NUN: A Story of Convent Life. By the Author
of "Almost a Nun," &c. Nine Illustrations. Second Thousand. Crown
8vo, cloth.

VESTINA'S MARTYRDOM: A Story of the Catacombs. By
EMMA RAYMOND PITMAN. Crown 8vo, cloth elegant.

*SERMONS FROM THE STUDIO: Stories Illustrative of Art
and Religion.* By MARIE SIBREE. Crown 8vo, cloth elegant, gilt edges.

*COBBIN'S CHILD'S COMMENTATOR ON THE
HOLY SCRIPTURES.* Twelve Coloured Illustrations and many
Woodcuts. Square 16mo, embossed cloth, gilt edges.

Price Five Shillings.

THE BAIRNS; or, Janet's Love and Service. By the Author
of "Christie Redfern's Troubles," &c. Second Thousand.

TALES OF OLD OCEAN. By Lieut. C. R. Low. Illustrated. Second Edition. Fcap. 8vo, cloth.

THE BEGGARS; or, the Founders of the Dutch Republic.
A Tale. By J. B. DE LIEFDE. Second Edition, crown 8vo, cloth elegant.

*GEOGRAPHICAL FUN: Being Humorous Outlines of Various
Countries.* Printed in Colours by VINCENT BROOKS, DAY & SON. 4to,
cloth elegant.

OLD MERRY'S ANNUAL FOR 1866, 1867, 1868, 1869.
Profusely Illustrated. Square 16mo, bevelled cloth elegant, gilt edges.

OLD MERRY'S ANNUAL FOR 1870.

Price Three Shillings and Sixpence.

OLIVER WYNDHAM: A Tale of the Great Plague. By the
Author of "Naomi; or, the Last Days of Jerusalem," &c. Frontispiece.
New and Cheaper Edition. Fcap. 8vo, cloth elegant.

THE FRANCONIA STORIES—Stuyvesant, Caroline, Agnes.
By JACOB ABBOTT. In one volume. Fcap. 8vo, cloth.

THE WEAVER BOY WHO BECAME A MISSIONARY.
Being the Story of Dr. Livingstone's Life and Labours. By H. G.
ADAMS, Author of "Our Feathered Families," &c. Portrait and Illus-
trations. Second Edition. Fcap. 8vo, cloth elegant.

LOST IN PARIS, AND OTHER STORIES. By EDWIN
HODDER. Illustrations. Square 16mo, cloth elegant.

WALTER'S ESCAPE; or, the Capture of Breda. By J. B.
DE LIEFDE, Author of "The Beggars." Twelve Illustrations. Fcap. 8vo.

Three and Sixpenny Books—CONTINUED.

MADELEINE'S TRIAL, and OTHER STORIES. By
Madame DE PRESSENSÉ. Fcap. 8vo. Four Illustrations.

BIBLE LORE; or, Brief Studies on Subjects relating to the Holy
Scriptures. By Rev. J. COMPER GRAY, Author of "Topics for
Teachers." Fcap. 8vo.

BEACONS AND PATTERNS: a Book for Young Men. By
the Rev. W. LANDELS, D.D. Fcap. 8vo.

TOSSED ON THE WAVES: A Story of Young Life. By
EDWIN HODDER. Frontispiece. New Edition. Square fcap. 8vo.

THE STORY OF JESUS IN VERSE. By EDWIN HODDER.
Ten Full-page Illustrations. Square 16mo.

WITH THE TIDE; or, a Life's Voyage. By SIDNEY DARYL.
Illustrations. Square 16mo.

STORIES FROM GERMANY. Translated by ANNIE HAR-
WOOD. Illustrations. Square 16mo.

SILVER LAKE; or, Lost in the Snow. By R. M. BALLANTYNE.
Illustrations. Square 16mo.

Price Half-a-Crown.

ADRIFT IN A BOAT. By W. H. G. KINGSTON. Illustrated.
Square 16mo.

OLD MERRY'S TRAVELS ON THE CONTINENT.
Profusely Illustrated. Second Edition. Fcap. 8vo.

RECONCILED; or, the Story of Hawthorn Hall. By EDWIN
HODDER. Illustrated. Square 16mo.

PITS AND FURNACES; or, Life in the Black Country. By
Mrs. ALFRED PAYNE, Author of "Village Science." Square 16mo.

BENAIAH: A Tale of the Captivity. By the Author of
"Naomi; or, the Last Days of Jerusalem," &c. New Edition.

TOLD IN THE TWILIGHT. Short Stories for Long Even-
ings. By SIDNEY DARYL. Illustrations. Second Edition. Sq. 16mo.

QUEER DISCOURSES ON QUEER PROVERBS. By
OLD MERRY. Illustrations. Square 16mo.

FIRESIDE CHATS WITH THE YOUNGSTERS. By
OLD MERRY. New and Cheaper Edition. Frontispiece. Sq. 16mo.

WASHED ASHORE; or, the Tower of Stormount Bay. By
W. H. G. KINGSTON. New Edition. Illustrations. Square 16mo.

BUSY HANDS AND PATIENT HEARTS. By GUSTAV
NIERITZ. Translated by ANNIE HARWOOD. Illustrations. New Editions. Square 16mo.

THE CONTRIBUTIONS OF Q.Q. By JANE TAYLOR.
Thirteenth Edition. Fcap. 8vo.

THE BUTTERFLY'S GOSPEL, and OTHER STORIES.
By FREDRIKA BREMER. Illustrations. Square 16mo.

Price Eighteen-pence.

THE YOUNG MAN SETTING OUT IN LIFE. By Rev. W. GUEST, F.G.S. Cheap Edition. Fcap. 8vo, cloth.

THE JUNIOR CLERK: A Tale of City Life. By EDWIN HODDER. With a Preface by EDWYN SHIPTON, Secretary of the "Young Men's Christian Association." Third Edition. Fcap. 8vo, neat boards.

HYMNS FOR INFANT MINDS. By ANN and JANE TAYLOR. Frontispiece. New and improved Edition (the Forty-seventh). 18mo, cloth elegant.

CHILDHOOD IN INDIA: A Narrative for the Young. Founded on Facts. By the Wife of an Indian Officer. Illustrations. 18mo, cloth extra.

Hodder & Stoughton's Shilling Presentation Series.

THE ROMAN PAINTER AND HIS MODEL. By MARIE SIBREE.

THE DYING SAVIOUR AND THE GIPSY GIRL. By MARIE SIBREE.

AFFLICTION; or, the Refiner Watching the Crucible. By Rev. CHARLES STANFORD, Author of "Central Truths."

THE SECRET DISCIPLE ENCOURAGED TO AVOW HIS MASTER. By the late Rev. J. WATSON, of Hackney.

AROUND THE CROSS. By NEHEMIAH ADAMS, D.D.

MEDITATIONS ON THE LORD'S SUPPER. By NEHEMIAH ADAMS, D.D.

Hodder & Stoughton's Little Books on Great Subjects.

In neat Wrapper, 2d. each, or 12s. per 100, assorted.

PERSONAL RELIGION: A Letter to some Young Friends. By JANE TAYLOR.

WHERE SHALL I BE ONE HUNDRED YEARS HENCE? By Rev. J. METCALFE WHITE, B.A.

SANDY FOUNDATIONS. By Rev. J. METCALFE WHITE, B.A.

SHIPWRECKS. By Rev. J. METCALFE WHITE, B.A.

SECRET PRAYER. By Rev. CHARLES STANFORD, Author of "Central Truths," &c.

FRIENDSHIP WITH GOD. By Rev. CHARLES STANFORD.

LONDON: HODDER & STOUGHTON, 27, PATERNOSTER ROW.

Pardon & Son, Printers,] [*Paternoster Row, London.*